2795

D0435491

7/1/88

Diagnostic Marketing

Diagnostic Marketing
Finding and Fixing
Critical Problems

C. Davis Fogg

100716
JAN 7 1988
L'ÉCOLE DES HAUTES ÉTUDES
COMMERCIALES

ADDISON-WESLEY PUBLISHING COMPANY, INC.
Reading, Massachusetts • Menlo Park, California • Don Mills, Ontario
Wokingham, England • Amsterdam • Sydney • Singapore • Tokyo • Mexico City • Bogotá
Santiago • San Juan

Library of Congress Cataloging in Publication Data

Fogg, C. Davis.
    Diagnostic marketing.

    Includes index.
1. Marketing.   I. Title.
HF5415.F563   1985   658.8   84–16743
ISBN 0–201–11506–9

Copyright © 1985 by Addison-Wesley Publishing Company, Inc.

All rights reserved. No part of this publication may be reproduced, stored in a retrieval system, or transmitted, in any form or by any means, electronic, mechanical, photocopying, recording, or otherwise, without the prior written permission of the publisher. Printed in the United States of America. Published simultaneously in Canada.

Cover design by Marshall Henrichs.
Text design by Diana Eames Esterly.
Set in 10 point Clearface by Compset, Inc., Beverly, MA.

ISBN 0–201–11506–9

ABCDEFGHIJ–AL–865

Acknowledgments

I owe much to the many people, organizations, and business situations that gave me the experiences that made this book possible:

First, and foremost, to the Corning Glass Works, an open and supportive organization that gives its people plenty of leeway to try new ideas and to learn from experience. To Tom MacAvoy, Corning's Vice-Chairman, who has not only been a good friend over the years but has given and continues to give me and my career great support. Second, to Dick Hanselman, Chairman and CEO of Genesco, an absolutely first-rate executive from whom I learned a great deal and who strongly encouraged me to tackle this project. Both Tom and Dick were exceptionally generous in letting me adapt material and experiences developed and gained as an employee or consultant to their companies.

My grateful appreciation to those who undertook the immense burden of reviewing my manuscript: Bill Brandt, Impact Planning Corporation, New York; Bill Dragon, General Manager of the Johnston & Murphy Shoe Company; Warren Keegan, Warren J. Keegan Associates, Rye, New York; Mike Kormos of Kormos and Associates, Nashville, Tennessee; Allan Shocker, Owen Graduate School of Management, Vanderbilt University; Dave Wilson, College of Business Administration, The Pennsylvania State University; and Jerry Wind, the Wharton School of Business, University of Pennsylvania.

To Jo Smith and Julie Bryan, who had the staggering task of interpreting my illegible handwriting and turning it into a readable manuscript, and to Tobie Sullivan, who so effectively helped me edit the manuscript, shorten it, and clarify it as only a professional writer can do.

Finally, I thank my dedicated Addison-Wesley editors, Genoa Shepley and Scott Shershow, who patiently piloted me through the publishing process.

Contents

Preface

This book was written for the seasoned, young, or soon-to-be marketing practitioner. I had four specific audiences in mind:

First, marketing managers from top to bottom — VPs of marketing down to assistant product managers — who are charged with getting results, daily, through marketing;

Second, MBA students who need a dose of reality to supplement their texts and cases: material to illustrate the things that they actually have to *do* to be successful marketing managers, beyond the theory and the limited, mostly "grand strategy" experiences that can be gained from a few cases;

Third, the young, growing general manager in a marketing-oriented business (shouldn't they all be?) who needs practical tools to improve results through marketing;

Finally, those presidents and general managers who have significant marketing problems or whose companies have just "discovered" professional marketing as a way to profitability and want to learn more about how it's done.

The book illustrates diagnostic marketing by applying its principles to eight of the toughest marketing problems and opportunities I have faced in planning, executing, and controlling the marketing function:

PLANNING

>   Redefining a business
>
>   Developing implementable, market-driven, strategic plans
>
>   Establishing effective marketing plans

EXECUTING

>   Fixing and repositioning sick product lines
>
>   Revitalizing new product programs
>
>   Repricing a product line to achieve penetration and profit objectives
>
>   Solving the many "small" marketing problems that, collectively, cost big money

CONTROLLING

>   Controlling the marketing function; flagging potential problems in time to take corrective action

The diagnostic approach to each problem in the real world as presented in this book is simple.

First, you should look for and try to identify the *symptoms* of marketing problems with high potential impact on your business. Look inside your organization and outside in the marketplace. Look objectively with proven organization development and diagnostic and market research techniques. Look informally yourself.

Second, *diagnose* what's really wrong with your organization. Go beyond the superficial problems and focus on the tough, often camouflaged heart of the matter.

Third, quickly develop intelligent, simple *fixes* to the problems that realistically can be executed by your organization.

I emphasize three keys to success in diagnosing and solving marketing problems. The first is to listen to your people and customers — frequently. They'll tell you what your problems are and, most of the time, how to fix them.

Next, realize that most solutions that work are simple and basic. They can be understood easily by those who must execute them; the logic behind them is crystal clear, practical, and, at "the gut level," right.

The last and most important key is to make sure you're absolutely convinced that the solutions to problems *can* and *will* be implemented by your organization. Any solution to a problem has to be carried out by people; and people have varying capacities that must be taken into account in prescribing solutions to problems. If there is a secondary purpose to the book, then, it is to insure that your people have the skills required and the desire to achieve your goals — or that you are willing to train or change them so they can.

This book should be read in its entirety so that you are familiar with all the potential problems that can hurt you, as well as their symptoms. Forewarned is forearmed. Each chapter, however, stands alone, and can be read as needed when facing the problems covered by that chapter. Most chapters have appendices which include detailed analytical techniques and examples that support the chapter's major points.

For each problem presented I discuss its symptoms, explain how to diagnose what's wrong in your particular situation, and present fixes to the problem that should work. I also note the all important "soft," unquantifiable, practical keys to success, pitfalls to avoid (I've fallen into enough to know), and management philosophies that can help guide the day-to-day decision making that leads to top-notch performance.

The problems presented here are fundamental ones that businesses have faced for decades. So why write about subjects that, by now, should be hackneyed, overdone, and second nature to anyone who has a marketing title? Simple. It has been my experience that the fundamentals of marketing are either not being practiced at all or are being executed poorly in many companies today, from Fortune 500 companies down to the smallest. Moreover, an increasing number of enlightened "small" corporations with annual sales of $20–60 million are *consciously planning* their transitions from entrepreneurial management to professional general and marketing management. They are seeking practical guidance on planning and managing their business and marketing direction. In addition, precious few are teaching — in school or on the job — the fundamentals of marketing. It's sink or swim, learn by yourself or fail. Furthermore, when marketing is taught, the focus is either on theory or "here's what you do," instead of on the *process* of problem solving.

Most importantly, to my knowledge, no one has ever summarized symptoms of key marketing problems — how to diagnose the real problems underlying them and develop and effectively implement solutions to these problems.

While my emphasis is on the process of solving problems, this is also a prescriptive book. Here's what you do, here's what you look for, here are ways of fixing the problems. Caution. The specific fixes that have worked for me may or may not work for you, your business, or your organization precisely as they're presented here. So, pay attention to the *processes* that I recommend to arrive at effective fixes and the basic principles that have led to success. The processes *do* work. If my fixes work and fit, fine. If they don't, the process will lead you to the ones that are right for your situation.

There are no citations, references, or footnotes in this book — or, at least, precious few. I did no scholarly or library research. Everything in this book is taken from 20 years of experience — the processes, the advice, the examples, the fixes.

Introduction

WHAT IS DIAGNOSTIC MARKETING?

Diagnostic marketing is a systematic *process* for quickly identifying and fixing critical marketing problems. It focuses on recognizing the *symptoms* of key problems; diagnosing their *cause* using proven analytical techniques; and developing *solutions* to problems through testing research and analytical methods, organizational creativity, and knowledge of historically successful solutions.

Conversely, traditional marketing decision making often hastily diagnoses "obvious" problems by making seat-of-the-pants judgments and implementing familiar, expedient or "common-wisdom" solutions without seeking a better way.

Run-of-the-mill problems (if there are such things) can sometimes be solved by traditional methods. Critical problems require *diagnostic marketing* techniques to develop effective, profitable solutions with a competitive edge.

Diagnostic Marketing

Part I

BUSINESS DEFINITION OUT OF DATE

Chapter 1

Redefining Your Business

The Problem

Ignoring changes in the marketplace until competition redefines your business for you — to their advantage. Failing to address the question, "What business do I really want to be in?" and therefore becoming something less than you could have been.

THE CHAPTER

This chapter addresses:

- Why business definition is crucial to future success;
- How definitions become outdated, and the subsequent consequences;
- Determining whether your business definition is adequate;
- A process for updating it; and
- Methods to help insure that it remains timely.

WHAT IS BUSINESS DEFINITION?

A business definition describes the business that you're in or want to be in, and is sometimes called your mission or charter.

Businesses are defined by their "strategic mix," which includes:

Purpose, or the general consumer/customer needs to be met or problems

1

solved; for example, the working woman's need for high-quality, high price, professionally appropriate personal accessories;

Target market to be served, such as upscale professional women, 20–49 years old, earning in excess of $30,000 per year in the top 30 U.S. cities;

Important subsegments to be addressed, such as professional women whose jobs or workplaces require "formal" attire and behavior and/or professional women in less structured workplaces, where wide latitude is given to individual dress;

Products and services to meet these needs, such as various clothing types (suits, dresses, coordinates, slacks, blouses), shoes, jewelry, and leather accessories, and personal shopping and advisory services;

Technologies to produce the products and services at competitive cost, such as computerized pattern generation and styling and laser cloth cutting; and

Distribution channels needed to reach the market, such as company-owned stores dedicated to company merchandise.

Why Is It Important?

Precise and timely business definition is the single most important key to success. It guides day-to-day business decisions. It is the first and most important element in a strategic plan. It influences the decisions that will determine the company's future businesses. Along with the development and execution of strategic plans, the business definition is one of the three factors that determine the level of your success, as measured by market share and sales volume, and the quality of your success, which includes profitability and corporate image.

What's a Good Definition?

A good business definition precisely defines the technical and market boundaries within which the business will be developed and run. The limits must be narrow enough to give crisp direction, but broad enough to allow plenty of room for creativity, growth (if that's strategically appropriate), and accomplishment.

Table 1-1 illustrates a good and a bad business definition. Note that the good definition is very specific about the target market and the needs to be met, yet broad enough to accommodate various ways to meet these needs. The good definition is feasible. It takes into account your ability to develop a profitable business and effectively compete in the future in your target business and markets. It would be senseless, for example, for Black and Decker's small appliance division to include video games in its business definition, however tightly defined, unless it had formidable competitive advantages to bring to bear on that market.

The "bad" definition is vague and unchallenging. It says, in essence, that the company will manufacture cameras and film and process pictures — hardly an

Table 1-1.   Good and Bad Business Definitions

Good

Purpose of Business: Meet the needs of private individuals to conveniently take and quickly obtain inexpensive, high-quality, color or black-and-white still and moving pictures. Methods include using permanent or reusable recording and reproduction.

Target Market: Individuals 15–65, with household incomes in excess of $14,000 per year; technically unsophisticated buyer (point-and-shoot variety); wants pictures of ordinary life events — family, travel, friends, special events, milestone events.

Important Subsegments: (a) purchasers of equipment and services for own use; (b) purchasers of gifts.

Products and Services currently include conventional cameras, films, film and print processing services, and videocassette cameras, recorders, players, and tapes.

Technologies Available: Optical, photographic, electronic, and magnetic information and image recording, processing, output and display.

Distribution: Currently, independent photographic stores, retail photographic chains, mass merchandisers, discount chains, catalog houses, video and appliance outlets. Captive and independent photoprocessing facilities.

Bad

Purpose of the Business: Provide high-quality, easy-to-use camera–film combinations and photoprocessing chemistry and services, color and black-and-white, for the unsophisticated amateur and family photographer.

---

inspiring charter in this electro-optical, magnetic–digital age, and one likely to ruin a business if literally executed.

Why Must Definitions Change?

Inevitable changes in consumer values and needs, available technologies, and competitive products, strategies, and services will affect your business and its definition. For example, the invention of the integrated circuit and digital electronic displays revolutionized the watch and calculator businesses, which had been based upon mechanical, not electronic, technology. Some firms quickly included the new technologies in their strategic mix. In the early 1970s, Seiko understood the consumer's desire for high-technology, high-quality, moderately priced, tastefully designed watches. They introduced analog and digital electronic movements and displays, and now dominate the worldwide midprice, high-quality watch market.

Texas Instruments used its expertise in electronic circuits and displays to move into the low-price electronic watch and calculator markets. Despite this timely and intelligent strategic move, product and marketing programs were poorly conceived and executed. Potentially high sales and profits were not achieved.

On the other hand, Timex, which dominated the low-price watch market in the United States, chose to ignore both the new technologies and a shift in consumer taste to more sophisticated esthetic design, thereby losing much of its market to Casio and other modern, low-cost manufacturers. As an expensive last-ditch effort to save the company, Timex hired new management and moved heavily into electronic watch technologies. It completely redesigned its outdated product line and embarked on a heavy high-tech advertising campaign in an attempt to regain lost market share and credibility.

TYPES OF REDEFINITION

There are two types of business redefinitions: revolutionary and evolutionary.

The revolutionary redefinition is usually prompted by a single obvious event, such as the invention of the practical commercial airplane, the invention of television, the deregulation of air traffic routes, the partial deregulation of telephone communications, or the invention of the computer. Necessarily, revolutionary redefinitions are often based as much on guts and management intuition as on careful market research.

Evolutionary redefinitions, faced by the vast majority of companies, involve detecting and capitalizing on changes in known markets and familiar technologies. A firm may redefine itself by exploiting an evolutionary internal invention or product extension outside the bounds of the existing business.

A good example occurred in the late 1960s when Sony, TEAC, and Nakamichi introduced high-fidelity home tape recording to the mass market by developing and marketing high-quality cassette recording and playback equipment. This transition from cumbersome, expensive reel-to-reel equipment and tape was based on:

> The development of the small, inexpensive, easy-to-handle tape cassette (originally intended for low-quality voice-grade recording);
>
> The invention of the Dolby™ tape noise-reduction system (originally applied to professional recording equipment); and
>
> The formulation of recording tapes that could produce high fidelity from a small, narrow tape that moved through the recorder at low speed, thereby allowing long recording times on limited tape lengths.

Cassette decks drastically expanded, if not created, the market for amateur tape recorders by meeting the consumers' need for low-cost, compact, high-quality equipment for transcribing records and recording music from FM broadcasts. Most mass-market manufacturers of high-fidelity equipment felt obliged to include tape decks in their business plans and product lines, and virtually killed the limited amateur market for reel-to-reel recorders.

CONSEQUENCES OF NOT CHANGING DEFINITION

The consequences of ignoring significant changes in the market include:

- Poor future profitability and profit volume;
- Loss of market share;
- A shrinking available target market;
- Large expenditures to regain lost position;
- Large potential gains relinquished permanently; and
- Business failure.

When the optical industry failed to define its sunglass and spectacle-frame business as a fashion industry, European and other imports captured 60 percent of the market.

The automotive industry did not respond to consumer demands for stylish, responsive, high-quality, fuel-efficient cars. Result? Loss of 30 percent of the market.

The television and high-fidelity industries, pioneered in the United States, ignored the low cost of foreign manufacture and the trend toward small solid-state electronic sets. Because American manufacturers assumed that foreign firms would not deliver a quality product and that the public would buy American, the U.S. industry now is dominated by the Japanese, and technical leadership has shifted abroad.

The structure of these industries — dominant suppliers, products offered, cost structure, and, in some instances, major distribution channels — changed permanently. In each case, market share losses stemmed from burying the corporate head in the sand and not anticipating or recognizing market and competitive changes and *doing* something about them.

Why People Let It Happen

There are four basic reasons why individuals and companies cope ineffectively with the definition of their businesses: inertia; lack of skill; internal problems; and ingrown industries.

1. *Inertia* is a powerful force acting to maintain the status quo. Many managers don't want to acknowledge change for a variety of reasons. Sometimes they're "old line" and persist in seeing things as they used to be, or take the easy way out by maintaining a support system of friends, contacts and business colleagues who think as they do. It's often easy to concentrate on the day-to-day, manage in traditional ways, and focus on "traditional" businesses and markets. For such managers, change sometimes is threatening and can appear too tough to handle. They fail to recognize the significance of major competitive changes ("Things will get back to normal — they'll learn the correct way of doing things"), and don't

get out into the field to look at and *listen to* the market, the customer, the sales-force, and industry leaders and gurus.

2.   *Lack of Skill:* Some managers don't know how to detect and assess changes in the market or how to react because they haven't been trained to think strate-gically. They think domestic, not international, in terms of *product,* not of *target market* and *competition.* Such managers don't know what questions to ask, of whom, or when.

3.   *Internal Problems* such as power struggles, management turnover, or cur-rent financial difficulty draw attention from the outside world and the long term.

4.   *Ingrown Industries:* Many ingrown, slow-moving industries feed on and be-lieve in their own wisdom. They fail to see that both the industry and individual companies can be threatened. They are extremely susceptible to attack by aggres-sive people outside the industry who see their businesses more objectively and opportunistically.

Well-managed companies *can* be surprised by or will move slowly in response to events — an invention, a creative competitive move — but they usually can turn changes to their advantage.

IBM, for example, a late entrant in the personal computer market, quickly achieved high penetration of the market through intelligent product and software development, an incisive retail strategy (despite no retail experience), and the strength of the corporate name. IBM's reputation for quality and service, along with the priceless assurance that, unlike some small entrepreneurial companies, it would always be around to service its products, constituted an overwhelming competitive advantage.

Significantly, IBM changed its mission to include personal computers but did not insist on its traditional use of internal resources. Instead, IBM bought critical integrated circuits, and some hardware, software, and product assembly from other companies and ensured quick market entry through independent re-tail chains. Once the mission was clear, the strategy was dictated by the rapidly growing market and fierce competition for market share by dozens of competitors.

A TYPICAL CHANGE

Table 1-2 presents a hypothetical change in business definition for a manufacturer of housewares. The change is in response to market changes detected, defined and evaluated by methods described in the following sections.

Note that the analysis contains the following:

I.   Prior Definition: a summary of the original business definition.

II.   Significant Trends: quantitative and qualitative data showing a shift away

Table 1-2.   Hypothetical Business Definition Analysis/Change

I. Prior Definition

Purpose in Life:	To supply the needs, nation-wide, of $20,000 plus income private households for top-quality, durable, easy to clean, branded cookware and food-preparation accessories
Market Need:	Durable, mid-America-style stovetop; easy clean, freezer-to-oven ovenware
Products:	Complete bake, stovetop line and accessories. Medium-high price points — $20 retail, contemporary through traditional styling
Technologies:	Proprietary laminated metal and ceramic
Distribution:	High-quality department stores, hardware, and general merchandise outlets
Competitive Advantages:	Brand name, superior cleanability, quality, design leadership

II. Significant Baseline Information Trends

	Percent of Units $20 and Up Cookware by Channel			Company Sales $MM			Qualitative Inputs
Year	1	2	3	1	2	3	
Department Stores	55	53	48	45	46	41	Trade, salesman, marketing department say competitors selling to discounters have helped industry volume, hurt our market share as we are not in discount channels
Hardware	20	18	17	15	12	11	
General Merchandise	10	12	13	5	6	7	
Discount	5	8	14	0	0	0	
Specialty	10	9	8	5	4	4	
Total	100	100	100	70	68	63	

Conclusion: $ sales, market share being lost to discount chains

III. Probe Results

Method	Conclusion
Consumer Focus Groups	Will buy more through discount outlets; discounters won't hurt brand image
Interviews with Discounters	Want brand. Would increase company business by 20–25% (units), net of losses in other channels. Retail price cuts = 20%. Lower price line needed

Table 1-2.   Continued

Method	Conclusion
Interviews at Department Stores	Will keep substantial portion of business. Discounters inevitable. Brands too important to drop. Price cuts 5–10%
Interviews at Hardware Stores	Will ultimately drop products. Product volume insufficient. Discounters will sell
Interviews of General Merchandise	No effect except on resale price. Price down 5–10%

IV. Definition Change

Distribution: Add quality discount chains

Product: Drop price-point minimum to $12 to pick up lower-income families

Target Audience: Drop household income to $15,000 to conform with discount chain profile

V. Impact

Detailed forecasts show that volume will grow in excess of 10% per year in units. Profit before tax will increase by 8% per year accounting for dilution caused by lowered average selling price.

from traditional outlets (department and hardware stores) and toward other channels (general merchandise and discount stores).

III.   Probe Results: findings from a variety of market research studies projecting the impact of new discount outlets on the business's sales, pricing, products, customers, and trade channels.

IV.   Definition Change: recommendation to include discount outlets and change product policy and the target audience accordingly.

V.   Impact: summary of a separate, detailed financial analysis projecting probable sales and profit changes resulting from the change in business definition.

FINDING OUT IF YOU HAVE A PROBLEM

There are obvious numerical and qualitative signs that a redefinition of your business may be in order.

Numbers: Steady erosion of sales, profits, and market share signal serious problems that could result from an improper business definition and the lack of appropriate subsequent strategic action.

By the time market and financial performance suffer, it's often too late to exploit changes in the market. Retaining what you have or making modest gains are the best that can be expected.

Qualitative Signs: Qualitative early-warning signs indicating the need for business redefinition include:

- *Complaints* by the salesforce, representatives, customers, and distributors about products and distribution that you don't have and worrisome competitive moves, however small. Because these people are in direct touch with the market and often compensated by commission in direct proportion to marketing success, they are acutely sensitive to changes that could threaten their future income.

- *Technological leaders,* companies or individuals, that maintain that your product or production methods may be outmoded.

- *Competition* which is offering, experimenting with, or test marketing something that you aren't.

- *Trade gossip* in the financial and publishing community questioning your business and your company's future.

- *Product categories* that you could be in but aren't developing.

- *A competitive advertising* thrust that's different from yours.

- *Patent* activity on a competitor's part signaling product or cost changes.

- *New distribution* channels in which you don't participate.

- *New companies* entering and succeeding in your market.

- *Forward thinkers,* the young, in-touch managers in your company who grumble about their future — and leave.

Some of these signs, of course, could result from using inappropriate strategies to pursue a well-defined business, or from poor execution of sound strategies. The quick personal probe detailed below should determine within two weeks whether the problem is one of definition, strategy, or execution.

The Quick Personal Probe: First, ask top management for a written statement of the business's mission, charter, or definition. You're in trouble if there isn't one. You're in double trouble if it's changed every year.

Second, ask key management members what they think the definition is and should be. If it differs from the "official" version, you have problems.

Third, run a three–five year history of key numbers, particularly sales, profits and market share. If there's deterioration, find out why.

Fourth, quickly touch base with knowledgeable key customers, salespeople, technical and business leaders to see if your business definition makes sense, if any current changes threaten it, if there are any of the negative qualitative signs mentioned above, and, if so, whether the problem is one of definition, strategy or execution.

A quick probe, stacking up your business definition with what's happening in the real world, is only a two-week venture for a skilled marketing manager.

FIXING THE PROBLEM

There are two ways to redefine a business: seat-of-the-pants judgment or factually based analysis.

Seat-of-the-Pants Judgment: Unfortunately, most business redefinitions are done hastily during a crisis or at strategic planning time. The resulting definition is often based on collective internal wisdom, popular internal sentiment, readily available and often shallow research, and superficial discussion. And though the mission statement may be crisp, well-written, and credible in an annual report, it's likely to lead the company astray if it's untested against market facts.

A "seat-of-the-pants" definition may be a good starting point, but one shouldn't stop there.

Factual Analysis involves three steps (see Figure 1-1):

1. Defining where you are;
2. Evaluating select market and competitive changes, how they affect you, and how you can take advantage of them;
3. Redefining the business.

The first two steps require accurate market and competitive information.

Defining Where You Are: The objective of this step is to define the current market and your place in it, and to identify any substantial changes or overlooked opportunities that require further study and focused research.

You will need "baseline" information to accomplish this objective. The specific information varies from industry to industry but should include market and competitive dimensions critical to success in your business. Typical data usually include quantitative market segmentation of appropriate end customers; product, service, price, distribution methods, and other competitive dimensions; your and your key competitors' shares and strategies; market segment size and growth trends; and recent qualitative inputs on market trends and competitive activity. Several years' history is helpful in establishing trends and pinpointing major changes.

If up-to-date baseline information is not available, you'll need one-shot, "catch-up" surveys that focus not only on "where is the industry and where are we in it?" but also on what key trends will affect you and how you can capitalize on them. Survey techniques are described later in this chapter and its appendices.

One-shot surveys providing large quantities of "catch-up" information that should have been collected in the past are difficult and extremely expensive to accomplish in a short period of time. Six to 12 months of work and an expenditure of $200,000–$500,000 are not unusual for large firms. Such sums often inhibit people from effectively laying the groundwork for their company's future.

For example, the new general manager of a major manufacturer of electronic components commissioned a series of studies of the future of electronic equip-

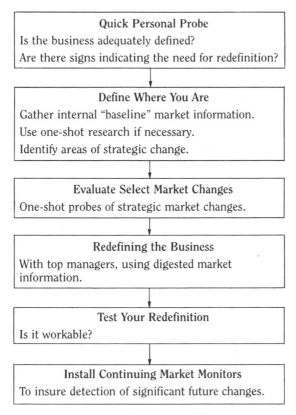

Figure 1-1.   Steps in Defining or Redefining Your Business

ment. The studies, which took a year and a half to complete, used internal personnel and outside consultants, and cost in excess of $300,000, indicated that the company's markets would stagnate and that ten specific avenues of growth requiring in-depth study were available. The company redefined its business and successfully developed and executed a new strategic plan.

Note, however, that many managers, particularly in small firms, successfully develop a business definition with far less data or on an ad hoc, "What do we know about the market?" basis. They may take greater risks by relying on minimal research, but they *do* define the business and act on the definition.

Evaluating Select Market Changes: The purpose of this step is to conduct focused research on the important identified changes, forecast the opportunities or threats that the changes present, and to propose changes in the business definition and subsequent strategies to cope with the change.

Typical focused one-shot studies include probes of emerging growth markets, products, channels of distribution, or technologies; changing consumer attitudes;

competitors' technical and marketing strengths and weaknesses; and market acceptance of recent competitive actions.

Studies of key changes usually are quickly and relatively inexpensively accomplished. For example, a shoe manufacturer that recognized the rapid growth in the number of managerial women commissioned studies to determine how they dressed, what shoe styles they considered appropriate, where and how they shopped, whose shoes they purchased, the strength of the competition, and perceived unmet needs. The study, which took six months and cost about $60,000, resulted in a redefinition of the manufacturer's business and a successful new venture.

Redefining the Business: This is the responsibility of top management, usually the CEO or general manager, with the support of key marketing, sales, planning, manufacturing, and financial subordinates. It normally is accomplished as part of the strategic planning process. Leadership and staff support usually come from the marketing department or a professional planning staff, which gathers information, interprets it, and presents recommendations at the end of each phase, including a draft business definition for testing.

Interactive planning meetings, described in Chapter 3, are the best means of achieving a realistic business definition.

TESTING YOUR BUSINESS DEFINITION

If you can answer "yes" to each of the questions posed in Table 1-3, then you have realistically defined your business, can build appropriate objectives and strategies, know where you're going, and can probably succeed under smart management.

CONTINUING MARKET MONITORS

Continuing monitors or surveys of market and competitive activity should be installed to detect changes requiring business redefinition and alteration of the strategic plan. This is the least expensive and most effective method of accumulating baseline information that can prevent competition from getting the jump on you.

Information from monitors should be reviewed quarterly or whenever there is a strong indication that fundamental market changes are taking place. The types of monitors available and their use are discussed in the next section.

SURVEY AND ANALYTICAL TECHNIQUES

The uses of major survey techniques in establishing business definition are summarized in Table 1-4 and detailed in Appendix I-1.

Table 1-3.   Testing Your Business Definition

Element	Key Questions
Target Market	*Is it real?* Are the dimensions (age, income, etc.) based on fact, not guess?
	Is it big enough? Is its size and future growth sufficient to be of interest?
	Can you own it? Are you strong enough, is competition weak enough, or are you early enough to be a major factor in this market?
Market Needs	*Do you know them?* Are they based on fact?
Products and Services	*Can you potentially provide them?* Better than anyone else? At a competitive (or better) cost?
Technologies	*Do you know which ones are important?* Materials, information handling, manufacturing.
Distribution	*Is it right?* Can you distribute your product/services the way that the market wants to buy? Can you get an advantage?
Competitive Advantages	*Do you have them?* Have you identified your competitors and defined what advantages you need to succeed?
	Significant? Has the market judged them to be significant?
	Sustainable? Can you potentially sustain them against competition?
Basic Business	*Will changes help or at least not hurt your basic business?* Have you accounted for negative effects of your definition changes?

One-shot Surveys

One-shot surveys for obtaining catch-up information or focusing on identified change use many of the following sources: *Internal data* derived from probes of management and professional employees' opinions, along with market surveys and financial data, are useful in determining the current business definition, and

Table 1-4. Which Strategic Research Techniques Give What Answers

If You Want to Find Out	Consider
Now	
1. About your target market — what it is, should be, your place in it now, its needs	Focus groups, trade probes, purchase panels, limited surveys, quantitative surveys
2. Where your market is going in the short term	Focus groups, trade probes, purchase panels, quantitative surveys
3. What competitors are doing/planning to do; your current/potential competitive advantage	Trade probes, interviews of suppliers, ex-employees of competitors
Future	
4. Where your target market is going in the long term	Lifestyle studies, Delphi studies, interviews of industry experts
5. What your target market could be, what it needs, when, and how to reach it	Lifestyle studies, Delphi studies, interviews of experts
6. What technologies can help or hurt you	Delphi studies, interviews of suppliers and experts
Will It Work?	
7. Does a new business definition make sense?	Focus groups, limited field surveys, quantitative field surveys
8. What is blocking you internally?	Internal probes
9. Can you get a competitive advantage?	Trade probes, interviews of suppliers, ex-employees of competitors, analysis of competitors' condition, public published, technical and other business literature

what people feel it should be, as well as helping you ascertain the inside consensus on important market changes that should be addressed. (See Appendix I-2 for questions to be used during internal probes.) *External data,* such as published statistics and studies, usually provide useful background but little depth or good strategic insight. *Limited surveys* of the consumer, trade and suppliers are usually sufficient to identify and confirm major issues to be addressed, gather sufficient information to resolve these issues, and successfully redefine the company's business. *Extensive surveys* are required only when issues are complex, call for extensive interviews to obtain valid information, or are highly technical and involve sophisticated projections.

When to Quit: Start data collection, analysis, and surveys with the simplest and cheapest methods such as internal data probes and limited market surveys. A simple business operating in a short time-frame with low technical complexity, a low rate of technical change, and reasonable accumulated internal information usually can redefine its business with a minimum of effort. Internal and external data with carefully focused limited surveys should suffice.

A complicated or highly technical business that expects to experience significant change over a long period of time will require significant information and, probably, extensive surveys.

How Much Survey Work To Do: The rules of thumb are:

Do as little as possible — it's expensive, so ask only critical questions for which you don't have answers.

Test for management consensus on a redefinition at the end of each survey step.

Test whether the redefinition satisfies the test questions in Table 1-3.

Stop as soon as management agrees that the definition is workable and that effective strategies can be developed and implemented under its umbrella.

Continuing Monitors

The goals of ongoing monitors, or market surveys, are to flag events that signal a structural change in your markets and to give you time to act effectively. Techniques for continuing monitors and when they should be considered are summarized in Appendix I-3. There are two types of monitors: annual surveys that provide information for the annual plan and periodic in-depth studies that probe slow-moving, long-term trends.

The following annual monitors should be considered:

Purchase panels of consumers are inexpensive and excellent for spotting shifts in products or brands purchased, where they shop, and style, price, and geographic purchase patterns. Extrapolated nationally, panels can usually yield estimates of the magnitude of shifts.

Focus group updates, which periodically probe consumer attitudes and planned purchasing behavior, are excellent tools for identifying emerging consumer-product distribution segments for in-depth exploration.

Trade probes are individual interviews or panel discussions with members of the trade (distributors or retailers). These are good for spotting short-term trends and changes in competitive activity.

Supplier probes determine competitors' plans, market direction, and upcoming technologies and materials that will influence it. Suppliers' views are often medium- to long-range because of the time required to develop and produce new materials or components.

Retained experts may include style or design professionals who forecast style, color, texture, and design, and technological experts who consider the implications of technology 5–20 years ahead.

Internal probes of key managers, as a regular part of the planning process, elicit their observation of changes affecting the company's fundamental business. Examples of internal probes appear in Appendix I-3.

Periodic surveys worth considering include:

Life style / demographic / social trend studies that forecast fundamental changes in consumer values and living, shopping, and purchasing habits.

Technological studies probing the future of a technology and the commercial products and services that might result.

Competitive studies to identify short- and long-term competitors, their strengths and weaknesses (product, distribution, financial, organization, etc.), their probable future business definition and strategies, and the effect on your plans.

Competitive personnel who have left the employ of competitors frequently can be hired as consultants or as permanent employees. A valuable source of competitive and market information, they often see the world differently than does your management. Be extremely careful not to request proprietary information or breach prior employment agreements so that neither you nor the ex-employee are sued and your business conduct remains ethical.

WHAT SHOULD YOU DO? HOW OFTEN?

Strategic and market research is expensive. There is no magic formula to tell you what and how much you should do. List the key changes you need to track, such as new competitive products, changing distribution patterns, or price-point shifts, and select the least expensive technique that will yield that information.

Table 1-5 indicates an ideal research mix for a large consumer or industrial products firm with the money and staff to fund research. Small firms, which should monitor the same critical factors and address the same issues in redefining their businesses, must rely more on informal experts and internal knowledge and use limited inexpensive research where absolutely essential; consequently, their decisions will be more risky. Small firms, however, often can recruit inexpensive local consultants to conduct their research without hiring permanent staff or paying the Fortune 500 price. They also can act more quickly upon detected market changes than their larger, more cumbersome, competitors.

KEYS TO SUCCESS

There are seven keys to success in maintaining an up-to-date definition of your business.

Table 1-5. Continuing Monitors Recommended for Large Consumer and Industrial Firms

	Consumer	Industrial
Annual		
Purchase Panels	X	
Focus Group Updates	X	
Trade Probes	X	X
Supplier Probes	X	X
Retained Experts	X	X
Internal Probes	X	X
Review of Available Internal/External Studies	X	X
Periodic		
Lifestyle/Demographic Studies	X	
Technological Studies		X
Competitive Studies	X	X

1. *Install market monitors* and continue them through thick and thin. Don't cut them to gain short-term profits — they could save your life in the long term.

2. *Appoint one person or department responsible* for managing the monitoring process and reporting significant events. Market research or planning departments usually handle this function.

3. *Incorporate monitoring into operations.* The job description for the CEO or general manager should include "watching the monitors." Critical information should be discussed at quarterly business reviews, during the strategic planning process, or when signals demand quick action.

4. *Act* when signals mandate action, even if it's only to gather additional information to confirm an early trend.

5. *Know when to act.* Carefully separate the few key trends from the mass of data. Develop concepts of how your business should change in response to these trends. Test the concepts through research, calculate the financial impact of proposed changes, and then decide how to act.

6. *Don't overspend.* It's tempting to gather lots of data as a security blanket. Specify exactly what you want and tailor research methods to obtain it at minimum cost.

7. *Keep independent counsel.* Cultivate personal advisors, inside and outside of your company, who are thoughtful and articulate and have good insights and judgment. They're often *not* the powerful people constantly in the spotlight.

BASIC PRINCIPLES

Redefining the business is widely considered simple. In fact it's the toughest job in the world to those who have to do it and live with the consequences of what they've done. Remember, inside opinions on future change are generally inaccurate and should be avoided while objective research that signals significant change will be rejected or rationalized half the time. Some people cannot make the conceptual jump from documented change to its impact on the business; others don't like the work involved in changing.

Hard-core holdouts who downplay research will become believers when they see that it helps improve their business and earnings. Chopping research at the drop of a hat is an easy way to boost profits now — and do in the business later. Any threat to a proprietary product or position will be dismissed as ridiculous, and everybody will parrot the popular wisdom espoused by the top dog until the threat becomes fact. Good CEOs, of course, have sense enough to distinguish between hypothesis and truth.

Part II

SICK STRATEGIC PLANNING

Chapter 2

Diagnosing Your Specific Problems

The Problem

Without a strategic plan that's right and controlled, you're drifting aimlessly, going wherever competition takes you — maybe on the rocks.

THE CHAPTER

The purpose of this chapter is to help you find out what's right or wrong with your strategic planning. It defines the strategic plan, addresses the symptoms and causes of poor strategic planning, and presents examples of a company that planned its future well and succeeded — and a company that failed. It explains how to audit your business to see if your strategic planning and its execution are good, bad, or indifferent.

WHAT IS A STRATEGY?

A strategy is the means of achieving your stated goals while thwarting competition and meeting defined market needs.

WHAT IS A STRATEGIC PLAN?

It's the playbook that tells you what to do and when to *change* your business situation to meet your long-range goals. The plan defines *actions* that will bridge the gap between today's results and those desired tomorrow, usually three to ten years from now. A good strategic plan should answer the following questions:

1. *Business definition:* What business do I want to be in? What will be my strategic mix? (See Chapter 1.)

2. *Goals:* What do I want to accomplish? What can I realistically accomplish, both quantitatively (numbers such as return on equity, return on sales, growth, and market share) and qualitatively (corporate image, technical, industry, or community leadership)? By when?

3. *Strategies:* How will I accomplish my goals despite the competition? What competitive weapons will I use — low cost/price, technology, distribution?

4. *Tasks:* Who must accomplish what tasks by what dates?

5. *Resource allocation:* How much money and management talent do I have? How much can I get? What businesses and projects merit money and personnel?

6. *Priorities:* If push comes to shove, which businesses or projects get scarce resources? Which get less, or none at all?

Realistic plans are those that, if well executed, minimize the risk and expenditure necessary to reach corporate goals — and are likely to succeed.

SYMPTOMS OF POOR PLANNING

The following are common symptoms of poor or nonexistent planning.

1. *No Plan:* No one ever did one. The annual budget *is* the plan. Annual product line changes, new manufacturing capacity, additional salespeople constitute "moves for the future."

2. *Lack of Accomplishment:* The company hasn't met long range financial goals for years, and has made little progress in reaching qualitative strategic goals such as the launch of major new product lines. It has lost market share; and shows poor current financial performance.

3. *Same Old Plan:* Old plans are dusted off each year and submitted as new. Goals and strategies don't change with the competitive environment.

4. *Goals Are Only Numbers:* They consist only of projected P&L performance and spending levels. Strategic tasks necessary to realize the numbers are an afterthought — or absent.

5. *Little Organization Involvement:* A planner or the CEO/GM writes a top–down plan without consulting key managers.

6. *Poor Employee Attitude:* Employees consider the plan a paperwork exercise that doesn't help the organization and its personnel achieve their goals, doesn't affect activities, or doesn't specify priorities. They grumble about

lack of direction sometimes because there is no direction or because it has not been communicated. Good people leave, foreseeing no future.

7. *No Documented Process:* The plan format and information-gathering and decision-making processes are casual and undocumented. It's a forms out— forms back exercise. Little thought is given to minimizing effort (particularly paperwork) and maximizing results through good decisions.

8. *Superior Competition* is outpacing you in profits and/or growth. They're investing more in R&D or market development and, unlike you, are moving successfully into new technologies, product categories, or distribution systems.

9. *No Research:* Critical, expensive strategic moves are based on opinion, not market research or fact.

10. *"Now" Time Frame:* Decisions and business discussions are exclusively short-term.

11. *Indecision on New Opportunities:* Because priorities are unclear, it's difficult to make decisions when new business opportunities such as "walk-in" acquisitions or new product ideas arise.

12. *No Rewards, No Penalties:* Good planning goes unrewarded; poor planning isn't penalized. Pay and position are based on today's performance.

13. *No Delegation or Communication* of goals to lower-level employees who will execute the plan. As one veteran of many managements, many plans, noted, "I submit the paperwork every year and then go on doing whatever I want to do anyway."

THE CAUSE

Why Don't People Plan?

Many high-level managers are directed or feel pressured by top management, boards, or stockholders to achieve short-term results at the expense of the long term. They want to show quick results to gain promotions or bonuses or to appear attractive to outside companies. Some managers simply can't think strategically — or don't care to.

Other managers never achieve the level of training that would enable them to plan effectively. They either accept a "formula" planning system but misunderstand the fundamentals or don't plan at all. There is, finally, managerial complacency. Performance and market position have been good, and management, sometimes certain that more of the same will lead to success, sees no need to plot the future. In the 1970s, for example, Xerox apparently did not develop an effective plan to protect itself against low-cost Japanese plain paper copiers, lost share, and quickly introduced an unreliable product that hurt, not helped, its position. Eventually, increased costs led to massive layoffs. The company evidently did not anticipate the competitive price-cutting strategies necessary to retain share.

Why Don't Existing Plans Work?

They're not right or realistic in light of competitive and market conditions. A plan that assumes that growing volume will be sustained by price cuts when the company is not the lowest-cost producer is unrealistic. A plan that assumes that a major business will be built on a new product whose concept hasn't been tested and, in reality, the consumer doesn't want, isn't right — witness the Edsel and GM's J cars.

Not enough resources, people, or money are allocated to pull off the plan; the time and money required to accomplish a strategic goal are underestimated.

No process has been identified for developing the plan, making decisions, and acting on them.

No controls or follow-up in the form of financial or qualitative checkpoints are established to see that goals are met or midcourse corrections are made.

No specific rewards for achieving strategic tasks or penalties for non-achievement to motivate employees.

No separation of goals/tasks/funds for ongoing versus new business or strategic tasks is specified. Managers, therefore, don't differentiate between today's and the strategic tasks. If in doubt or in time of crisis, which is almost always, they focus on today's job.

The top dog doesn't care. The CEO or general manager who relies on instinct develops formal plans only to keep the organization, stockholders, and financial press happy.

The following are real examples of plans and planning processes whose results are known and have been measured over a five- to ten-year period.

A PLAN THAT WORKED: AN ELECTRONIC COMPONENTS BUSINESS

The Situation

In the mid-1960s, the electronic components subsidiary ("the company") of a major corporation managed a small business in passive components such as resistors, capacitors, and inductors. The business was based on unique internally developed technologies. The company's mission, objectives, and strategies were not defined. Although the company occupied a major position in each of its markets, its products offered few prospects for the major growth desired.

The Need for a Plan

A major revolution in electronic circuitry was underway. The integrated circuit (IC), a tiny fingernail-sized chip of silicon, could be made to perform the functions of hundreds or thousands of transistors, resistors, and capacitors. ICs clearly would profoundly affect the size, design, cost, and performance of all electronic equipment and, therefore, of the passive components it contained.

The need for change in business definition was signaled by the company's sales force, its customers, its scientists, and its captive integrated circuit division, all of whom predicted that many passive components would be eliminated or become relatively unimportant as the use of integrated circuits grew. At the same time, scientific and market sources maintained that because ICs couldn't perform certain electronic functions, segments of the passive components business would grow while the rest of the industry stagnated or declined. These functions were inductance, capacitance, high or precise resistance, circuit trimming or tuning, environmental sensing, and interconnection. The message was clear: If the company was careful and selective, it had a future in passive components.

What Was Done?

A planning department was formed under the direction of a new vice-president and general manager and his director of marketing, and staffed with three MBAs with electrical engineering degrees and technical work experience. Their large annual budget was $350,000 (1980 dollars). The planning department, along with the company's operating management, managed the redefinition of the business, development of a strategic plan, identification of specific new product opportunities, and the execution of major parts of the plan.

The company's mission was defined as marketing of any passive component/package/connector compatible with integrated circuits, and whose usage would go up significantly, not down.

Desired and realistic future goals, including size, growth, and market share, were defined for the base business and all new businesses.

For example, real growth for the total business was expected to exceed 15 percent per year; new businesses were expected to contribute in excess of 50 percent of the division's sales and profits within ten years; no less than a #3 market position was acceptable for a new business, with #1 strongly desired; profitability was expected to improve by 90 percent. Management expanded the routes allowed for entry into new businesses, from internal development alone, to include acquisition, licensing, and joint ventures.

The key strategy was the addition of products that could be sold through the existing first-class nationwide sales force and distribution system to an established customer base. Specific product opportunities were identified through interviews with the sales force, an internally managed Delphi study of the electronics industry, in-depth market research of specific component markets and electronic functions, and a consultant specializing in forecasts of electronic equipment, technologies, and component usage. Ten major target growth markets also were identified, including precision resistors, ceramic, tantalum and electrolytic capacitors, sensors, specialized inductors, and potentiometers.

How Successful Was the Plan?

The company's ten-year sales and profit goals were met. Over an eight-year period, three major new businesses were successfully acquired or developed internally. Sales and profits grew 20 percent per year, 60 percent of which was contributed by new businesses.

In order to successfully enter three new markets, ten markets were studied in depth; entry was attempted into each; over 100 acquisition candidates were examined; a number of internal research or development projects were started; a number failed, and new product technologies were brought into the company from other corporations.

Why Was This Plan So Successful?

The company's plan succeeded because impending changes in the market were identified and documented in time to act effectively and the identified growth markets and entry strategies were correct. The quality and quantity of management needed to execute the plan was in place for a sufficient length of time to complete its execution. Moreover, the general manager of the division involved management at all levels in the planning process, carefully balanced the attention given to the short and long term, and insisted that the plan and its progress were effectively communicated throughout the organization. The chief executive officer of the parent company understood and supported the plan, and organization development consultants helped with planning and provided feedback to management on barriers to the plan's progress.

Problems?

Of course! Some of the more significant problems experienced were that too much money was spent on some acquisitions, and unexpected expenditures for personnel and technical development efforts were needed to make both acquisitions and internal developments viable. In addition, several promising products were dropped because of short-term profit pressures, and several years were wasted deciding to enter a major market using conventional rather than proprietary technology.

A PLAN THAT DIDN'T WORK: A CONSUMER FASHION BUSINESS

The Situation

This example is derived from extensive studies of two strikingly similar companies. In the late 1960s, "the company," an autonomously managed subsidiary of a conglomerate, held the major position in the national branded market for certain expensive, conservatively styled men's and women's clothing and accessories. The company's brands were household words. Its wholesale distribution and retail outlets were the best available.

During the 1970s the consumer changed, but the company didn't. In 1970, their product and distribution potentially reached and appealed to over 90 percent of its potential upper-income consumers. By the end of the decade, it serviced less than 50 percent of its available market. Sales and profits stagnated while competitors capitalized on the following key trends: a shift from traditional to European styling and toward casual lifestyles and clothing; a shift in consumer purchases away from department and specialty stores toward concept stores and captive retail outlets; explosive growth in upscale purchases in suburban malls; consumer acceptance of imports; and brand-building through advertising and promotion.

The company incorrectly defined its business in product terms ("We make XYZ product") and not by target market ("Upper-income professionals who need ABC product category"). Management didn't ask members of the target market what they were thinking/wearing/wanting/purchasing. They ignored changes in distribution channels and stayed with those that were safe, comfortable and known.

Plans

Although thick written plans were dutifully produced each year, they resulted in neither change nor progress. Each year's plan, which was not reviewed from one year to the next, was developed by the company's general manager with little input from other managers. Because the company intended to abide by existing policies, plans were considered a paperwork exercise to "satisfy corporate"; corporate management, meanwhile, did not give direction on whether the plans were acceptable. Although the plans sometimes acknowledged the existence of new competitive threats and market opportunities, no programs were developed to combat or exploit them. In general, the plans were unfocused, and had unrealistically high financial goals and promises to execute ambitious programs in unrealistically short time periods. As would be expected, profits stagnated, then deteriorated.

The Need for Change

New management brought in to fix the "profit problem" recognized the need for effective planning. Over a three-year period, the following actions were taken to prevent further erosion and rebuild the business:

Managers who could "think marketing" were recruited to fill key positions.

A strategic plan was developed.

The basic product line was revamped to reflect current tastes, while entry into the European and casual market segments were studied.

Captive outlets were opened.

Studies were undertaken of distribution and the end consumer's needs.

Advertising and brand-building were revitalized.

Outside advisors were brought in to help with fashion design and distribution channels.

How Successful Were These Efforts?

It's too early to tell though current trends are encouraging. Profits have been significantly bolstered by the captive retail outlets, and fresh styling has prevented erosion of the basic product line. As in most turnaround or repositioning situations, it will take four–six years to implement the new plan and eight–ten years to see results.

Whether or not the plan succeeds, it will be expensive to implement. The company will not be as big or as profitable as it could have been if it had changed before or with the market. It is spending a substantial amount of "one-shot," "up-front" money on "catch-up work," including surveys of the target market, development of new distribution channels, product changes and promotional packages, developing and tooling new products, test marketing, and restaffing.

Could This Problem Have Been Avoided?

The answer is very likely, had there been a marketing-oriented management team that employed proven monitoring techniques. The company should have watched (which they did, to some extent), and acted on (which they didn't), leading indicators of change in product styling and purchase behavior including consumer lifestyle studies; Europe's fashion leaders; avant-garde outlets in the United States which lead conventional outlets in styling and display; fashion consultants who are quick to pick up and interpret advanced style, color, and material trends; competitive moves; and purchase panel trends. Effective strategic planning could have capitalized on market trends.

FINDING OUT IF YOU HAVE A PROBLEM

You can quickly assess the quality of your company's planning — and, at the same time, determine if your business definition is correct — with an audit. The audit, which can be conducted by a skilled planner, marketing manager, or outside consultant, includes an evaluation of accomplishments under the prior plan and potential improvements; documentation of the current planning process and identification of potential bottlenecks; evaluation of managers' and employees' attitudes toward the plan; and an assessment of the real and perceived rewards of good planning.

The auditor should be sensitive to the following problems, all of which can undermine the success of a strategic plan.

Unrealistic goals. Promising too much too soon usually results from over-optimistic management; poor estimates of the time and resources required to accomplish major strategic goals; poor or nonexistent assessment of competitors' current and future strengths and strategies and how they can thwart your plans; or poor research and estimates on the size of future markets and your potential share.

Poor strategies. An ineffective strategic plan is based on past experience, instead of on market research geared to the future needs of your target market.

Poor execution. Even if goals and strategies are technically right, poor management can result in poor execution. Trouble can stem from management in-experience; from having the wrong people with the wrong skills in key leadership positions, or a shortage of essential skills; from inadequate management information; insufficient internal communication; and from managers who don't make critical decisions or mid-course corrections in the plan, quickly, appropriately, or at all.

Table 2-1 summarizes areas to be audited, questions to be asked or information obtained, and the likely source of the information.

Table 2-1. Auditing the Company's Planning Process

Area/Objective	Questions/Information To Get	Sources
Old Plans		
Evaluate performance to plan	Compare actual to planned financial performance for past five years: Separate ongoing businesses from new Audit key numbers — sales, growth, NPBT, return on investment	Old plans (everyone keeps them around, if only for window dressing) Controller or financial function for history of numbers
	Identify high-impact goals and qualitative strategic events for the business and by function (manufacturing, marketing, sales, etc.). Typical examples include a new plant, new product line, changed distribution.	Interviews with key managers from the marketing, manufacturing, R&D, human resources, sales departments

Table 2-1. Continued

Area/Objective	Questions/Information To Get	Sources
	Find out which goals were achieved, and which events were accomplished on time. Why? Find out when events met their time–cost–profit targets, which didn't, and why.	Interviews with members of the trade, industry experts, and examination of market data research where necessary
Look at year-to-year changes	Identify major changes in objectives, strategies, and programs from year to year. See if there are good strategic/ competitive reasons behind the changes.	Review of plans for changes; interviews with key managers for reasons
Research	Find out what research has been done or was planned to justify major strategic moves. How well was it done? What happened?	Interviews with the marketing department staff
	Evaluate research on competitive strategy, if any. See if strategies pursued make sense in light of research or sound internal opinion.	
Process		
What Planning Process Is Used?	Chart who does what and when to produce the plan. Pay particular attention to who makes critical decisions and establishes overall goals and priorities. Does it occur at the right place in the planning cycle? Is there duplication or conflict with budget or operations plans?	Review prior plan procedures. Interview GM and person(s) responsible for planning
	What is the format? How well has it worked? What changes have there been, plus and minus, over the years?	Interview with key managers in all functions at all levels
	Who at what level participates; how?	

Table 2-1.   Continued

Area/Objective	Questions/Information To Get	Sources
	How are strategic goals and tasks delegated to levels below the CEO/GM? How far down do they reach?	
	How frequently is accomplishment vs. goal reviewed? How? What kind of changes are usually made?	
Employee's Attitudes	What do key managers, at all levels, think of the planning process and the plan? What improvements have they suggested?	Interview of managers
	What do the "troops" — non-managers, lower-level employees, hourly workers, union officials — know, or care, about company planning?	Interview employees or hold small group discussions
Rewards	How are people rewarded for good planning? How do they *feel* they're rewarded (or penalized)?	Ask CEO/GM, human resources, key managers

If an audit indicates that the plan is not realistic or its execution has been poor, steps must be taken to insure effective future planning and implementation. Such steps may involve changes in management, organization structure, plan review mechanisms, business priorities, and allocation of financial, physical, and human resources. For this reason, plan audits should be done for and subsequent changes made by the CEO and a few top officers or managers — usually after agonizing deliberations over "What went wrong?" and "Where do we want to go?"

If you find that no strategic planning is occurring, see Chapter 3.

Chapter 3

Developing a Healthy Strategic Plan

The Problem

Your company has either no strategic plan or a beautiful planning process that produces nice words, lots of paper and employment for planners — but few results.

MAKE NO MISTAKE ABOUT IT

This is a chapter on mechanics. It includes the flow charts and fill-in-the-blanks forms that the professional planning guru loves and the normal manager hates.

Makes no bones about it: Decisions make strategic plans happen. Filled-out forms don't.

Decisions get made when the manager responsible for strategy is in touch with the market and his or her employees, and the employees are in touch with what's happening in their world. Progress occurs when these people are productively discussing, arguing about, and wrestling with strategy, not shuffling paper. This chapter appears to recommend a lot of analysis and paperwork. Not so. There is a lot of thinking that must go into developing a planning process, particularly for a large, multibusiness corporation. The reader must understand the objectives and mechanics of the planning process, which are detailed in this chapter, then choose the simplest method that will work for his or her particular company, business and industry.

OBJECTIVES OF THE PLANNING PROCESS

Managers employing a *simple* planning process — one that neither interferes with day-to-day business nor creates unnecessary paperwork — will be able to propose realistic strategic options for each business and forecast the financial results; select the best strategies and specify who does what when; review progress and make corrections quickly; and overcome objections to prior planning efforts.

FIXING THE PROBLEM

Determine the reasons that previous plans failed through the methods detailed in Chapter 2. Make sure that the new process and plan address and overcome these problems.

WHERE DOES THE PLAN FIT IN THE BUSINESS YEAR?

Schematically, the strategic plan fits in the framework of the annual business planning cycle as follows:

Business definition and the strategic plan, which are usually completed at the same time, must precede the marketing plan. The operating plan, incorporating the manufacturing and staff department plans, follows the marketing plan and precedes the next year's operating budget, which summarizes expected expenditures and financial results. Individual goals are set for managers and professionals. Frequent reviews insure that strategies and operating goals are met at the business and individual level and that corrective action is taken to prevent deviations from the plan.

Intelligent budgeting separates the P&L and spending budgets for ongoing operations from strategic expenditures (long-term product development, R&D programs, etc.) so that both can be objectively measured. Often, healthy companies suddenly appear sick when they're breaking new ground and attendant losses or expenditures are charged against their basic business. Companies operating on a calendar-year basis usually start strategic planning in the spring, complete the plans during the summer, and require preliminary marketing and operating plans in early fall along with the initial budget submission.

During the first year of the strategic plan, financial estimates should be a manager's best guess at her budget for the coming year if her strategies are accepted. Corporate management is always anxious to have a first look at next year's budget, and you'd better make sure that it's a good one. They'll remember it irrespective of any disclaimer that you or they made at the time of the first "peek."

DEFINING THE PLANNING UNITS

A strategic plan is required for the corporation and for each business, strategic business unit (SBU), and major staff function (such as data processing, R&D, and human resources) within it. The planning units and levels of plans produced within a hypothetical multiple-business corporation are defined below and illustrated in Figure 3-1.

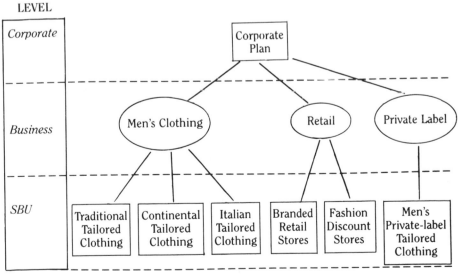

Figure 3-1. Levels of Plans for an Apparel Company

SBUs: A strategic business unit is the smallest unit for which a plan is normally developed. An SBU usually has the following characteristics:

- A business definition — particularly target market, products, services, and distribution channels — that differentiates it from other businesses within a company;
- Its own distinct set of competitors;
- Management and planning largely independent of other business units;
- A single manager with P&L responsibility;
- Direct control of core functions — general management, marketing, sales, and planning — and possibly of manufacturing, sourcing, and product development as well;
- An internal image as a business separate and distinct from others.

Businesses: A single "business" may be made up of one or many SBUs. For example, an upscale, high-price-point apparel company manufacturing suits, sports coats, and slacks may have the following businesses and SBUs principally defined by end-market characteristics:

Business	SBUs
Men's Tailored Apparel	*Traditional clothing* — for conservative, traditionally minded professionals
	Continental clothing — for those preferring the mainstream continental look
	Italian clothing — for the avant-garde dresser
Retail	*Branded retail stores* — full-service stores carrying the company's premier advertised brands, all styles, targeted to upscale men in the top 40 SMSAs
	Fashion discount stores — limited-service stores carrying the company's own private-label brands, all styles, at discounted prices, targeted toward the value-conscious consumer
Private Label	*Men's private label* — makes clothing to order for other manufacturers and/or retail chains for sale under their labels

The corporation, of course, is the sum of its businesses.

A *department* is an organizational unit headed by a manager. Typical marketing departments are product management, creative, wholesale operations, etc.

A *function* is something that a department does. For example, the creative department usually handles the functions of advertising, preparation of collateral material, and occasionally product design. There may or may not be departments or individual managers for each function.

Following is a list of typical marketing departments, in a consumer products firm, whose managers usually report directly to a VP or director of marketing, and the functions that they normally perform.

Product Management
Marketing Strategy
Basic Product-line Management
New Products
Pricing
Terms
Forecasting

Wholesale Operations
Sales
Wholesale Promotion
Order Entry — Service

Creative
Advertising
Collateral
Point of Sale

Retail Operations
Store Operations
Retail Promotion
Merchandising
Order Entry —
    Service

Design
Product Design

Research
Market Research
Strategy Planning

Levels of Planning

For a large corporation, there are three levels of plans and planning activity.

The Corporate Plan consists of the corporation's overall mission, objectives, strategies, key tasks for the coming year, and financial projections. Along with approval of modified plans submitted by individual businesses and SBUs, it includes changes dictated at the corporate level, such as expanding the corporate mission, specifying new businesses to be entered, the old ones to be terminated, or formulating more ambitious financial goals and programs.

The Business Plan, which establishes the overall mission and plan for a business consisting of one or more SBUs, may or may not be the sum of the plans of the various SBUs.

The SBU Plan is developed for every operating SBU and for ones underway.

Staff: Plans for major staff groups generally consist of goals and tasks in support of the operating businesses and tasks with corporate significance or that are unrelated to a given business. Data processing and systems, R&D, and human resources are the groups that require the greatest attention.

The planning process must be structured to incorporate the needs of individual businesses into staff plans. This can be accomplished by developing staff plans after individual businesses have developed their preliminary plans and defined their need for staff services. For example, Data Processing may be designing a new corporate accounts-receivable system for three years hence. A specific division may desperately need a new specialized order-entry system now. Data Processing's plan must reflect both requirements.

STRATEGIC OPTIONS

To develop a workable strategic plan, the head of the corporation and the key managers of each business and SBU must understand the strategic options available and the probable consequences of each.

Business strategy is complex. It depends on the company's position in an industry, the stage of that industry's market, competitive and technological development, and the competitive characteristics of the industry itself. It also depends on the company's internal organization, its finances, and its ambitions.

In general, there are only five overall options open to any given business or SBU:

- Grow
- Grow–Hold
- Milk
- Divest or Shut Down
- Restructure

These options and the circumstances under which they should be considered are summarized in Table 3-1.

Table 3-1.   Normal Strategic Options

Option	What It Means	When to Consider
Grow	Grow to #1 or #2 market position by investing in necessary assets, products, and distribution. Usually requires large infusions of cash plus top notch aggressive management.	Sustained growth market. Large enough to produce desired profit volume. Competitive and financial strength such that company can gain/hold #1 or #2 position. Such advantages include pre-emptive marketing, unique products, low costs, superior brand image, or extensive distribution. Stagnant market with rapid growth segment, untapped geographic area or distribution channels, weak competition with little retaliatory ability, opportunity for technical upset.

Table 3-1.   Continued

Option	What It Means	When to Consider
Grow–Hold	Grow an existing business to the "critical mass" where it becomes a profitable long-term defendable business throwing off cash. Requires infusions of cash for a limited period of time, then good, defensive management.	Business is not a good long-term opportunity (other options are better, poor market position, low growth market, tough competitive situation) but incremental return on investment needed to reach the "critical mass" is high. Can be defended, profitably, against competitors once stabilized.
Milk	Maintain market position or let it deteriorate over time. Manage the business for high cash flow to fund other businesses (or invest). Invest only to maintain desired position. Requires competent maintenance managers.	Stagnant market, poor market prospects, poor position. Competitive strength sufficient to permit maintenance of position without major investments of cash.
Divest or Shut Down	Sell the business or liquidate the assets.	Poor market position, losing money or marginal operation near breakeven, little chance of positive cash flow. Can use assets tied up in business elsewhere. Competitive situation such that maintaining poor position will be tough, expensive. Doesn't fit the company's long-term mission.
Restructure	Combining with another business (inside or outside the company) could put you in the first two categories (above). Combining overhead, manufacturing, sales, or distribution of the operation lowers overall cost, increases profits, and/or market share.	Volume and/or efficiency can be quickly increased by adding high-volume new distribution channels; substantial new categories of product sold through same channels; conversion of all retail properties in an area to one "brand" to obtain geographic management and advertising efficiencies.

Caveats and Exceptions. Managers tend to make two major mistakes in choosing strategic options. First, they always want to grow, get bigger, be better. Who doesn't? Growth is healthy but not always appropriate, particularly when management is not yet skilled enough to manage growth or sound thinking dictates a more appropriate strategy. Choose the correct strategy, not the most popular. Second, managers often interpret conventional strategic options too literally and devote little thought to specific applications tailored to their companies and industries.

The successful companies that ignore the generic strategies discussed above instead rely on one or a combination of four factors or substrategies:

1. Careful market segmentation — picking their shots well.

2. Competitors' weaknesses — capitalizing on someone else's problems.

3. The ability to "create" a market — exploiting a latent need.

4. A better idea — doing it better than the competition.

The following simplified examples illustrate the application of each substrategy.

Segmentation: The market segments in which you participate must be *tightly* defined before you choose your strategy (see Chapter 4). A market with formidable competition may have significant segments ("niches" is the current buzz word) representing large opportunities for growth and profits. For example, the footwear industry has been virtually flat for the past decade, yet despite intense domestic and foreign competition, certain segments have performed admirably. By concentrating on the market for running and athletic footwear, astute companies such as Nike, Adidas, and New Balance built a substantial business in the United States.

Message: Look for the *piece* of the market that represents unexploited opportunity.

Competition: Any strategy must recognize the strength of the competition and your ability to beat them. Companies do succeed in stagnant markets or markets with apparently entrenched competition when their competitors are asleep at the switch.

In the early seventies, Detroit didn't view the Japanese or Europeans as serious long-term competitors in a relatively stagnant domestic car market. The auto companies, seeking profit and remaining indifferent to significant new products or manufacturing techniques, were technically correct, given the state of American competition at the time, but they were not farsighted. The Japanese and Germans, who had enjoyed early limited success in the United States with small fuel-efficient cars on one hand and expensive, luxurious high-performance cars on the other, proceeded to "clean Detroit's clock." They understood the American consumer's desire for such products and benefited from Detroit's inept and hasty attempts to compete. (A J car against a Honda? A Cadillac Seville against a Mercedes? Sheer folly!)

Message: Look for competitors who can't or won't react to your strategies.

Creating a Market: Timberland, a small New England manufacturer of private-label work boots, literally created a market among the general population. It assumed that if a few college kids like their boots, other people would as well. Timberland was right. It established a new category in the shoe industry — rugged indoor/outdoor boots for everyday wear — by marketing an excellent though high-priced product and building a strong brand image with highly creative print, and later TV, advertising campaigns.

Message: If you perceive an unfilled need or trend very early in the game, determine if it's "real" through market research.

A Better Idea: Century 21 changed the name of the game in the fragmented, locally based, often unprofessional real-estate market. It saw the opportunity to build a "brand" where none existed by capitalizing on the fact that a high percentage of real-estate transactions are made by people moving from one city to another. It discovered that consumers have difficulty finding a reputable professional agent, and that their choices were frequently a matter of word of mouth recommendation or chance. Century 21 established a national brand-name through advertising that, like McDonald's for fast foods, stresses high uniform standards. They emphasize service to the customer, professional buying and selling skills, and their ability to sell your house quickly, arrange "creative financing," and find exactly what you're looking for in your new location. It franchised local firms to use their name, provided training, and set up a national referral service where one Century 21 affiliate can sell a client's house in one location while another in a different location can help the same client look for a new one. It must work. Century 21 is enormous — and ubiquitous.

Message: Look for leveraged opportunities to move a product or service a quantum leap forward, however exotic or mundane the industry.

Staff. Strategies are not limited to individual businesses. Staff functions also need strategic plans, generally in support of ongoing businesses or corporate-level long-term goals such as:

- *Engineering:* Equipment or process research and development to gain a long-term cost advantage. Chance–Pilkington's development of the low-cost float glass process for producing inexpensive flat glass created a major technical upset in a mature industry.
- *R&D:* Pursuit of basic research or development in areas that could lead to major new businesses, such as genetic engineering.
- *Human Resources:* Recruiting, training, and career-planning programs to provide the quality and quantity of management needed.
- *Systems:* Long-term systems development to provide state-of-the-art financial, marketing, and scientific information and data processing.

- *Manufacturing/Sourcing:* Long-term configuration and vendors needed to meet capacity and cost goals.

Limits. Prior to developing your plan, it's important to eliminate strategic options that are unrealistic for the corporation and each SBU. For example, businesses that won't be allowed to grow because you're "cash shy" should be informed before planning starts.

WHO WILL BE RESPONSIBLE FOR WHAT?

With the CEO's approval, define roles to be played by individual business units, key managers, staff members, and functional departments. Typical roles in multiple-business divisions or Fortune 500-type companies are shown in Table 3-2. For any size or type of organization, you must consider:

- *Strategy Decisions* — Who will make final decisions on strategy and allocation of resources?
- *Preparation* — Who will prepare the plan(s)?
- *Mechanics* — Who will handle the mechanics of planning, such as development of formats, summaries, and timetables?
- *Review* — Who will review progress, at what levels, when?
- *Delegation and Execution* — Who is responsible for distilling overall direction into achievable goals and tasks and executing the plan?

In large firms, individuals or elaborate organizations reporting to the CEO often coordinate planning. In large businesses within companies, planners often report to the general manager or director of marketing, or planning is personally handled by the director of marketing.

In smaller firms, the chief executive with the help of key managers may undertake informal planning.

Be sure to keep planners in their proper place. They are process people enlisted to help those who must prepare and execute their plan. If they start writing the plan, no one owns it and it won't be executed.

Marketing

Marketing should be the central function in developing a plan because first, any significant action ultimately responds to a market need and is affected by competition in the marketplace. This applies to the obvious, such as new products or distribution, and the not-so-obvious, such as mechanization, cost reduction, fundamental R&D programs, or new financial control systems.

Second, poorly conceived strategic moves in the marketplace produce greater losses than internal foul-ups do. The wrong new product introduced with

Table 3-2. Typical Planning Roles in a Large Multibusiness Company

	Corporate Level			Business and SBU Level	
CEO	**Corporate Planner**	**Head of Finance or Control**	**Head of a Business or SBU (General Manager)***	**Marketing Director Within a Business or SBU**
Decides what he/she personally wants from the plan	Develops format/process for CEO	Establishes financial definitions and ground rules for plans, numerical schedule	Proposes definition, goals, and strategies for business	Coordinates preparation of plan with all functions (manufacturing, finance, sales, marketing, R&D)
Approves format, process	Oversees individual business unit plans	Reviews submitted numbers	Oversees plan preparation	Prepares plan
Gives initial direction to businesses on definitions or strategies	Summarizes corporate overview for CEO; evaluates individual business plans	With planner, consolidates corporate plan numbers	Writes personal summary	
Sets overall corporate definition, objectives, and strategies	Arranges and/or conducts training in strategy and plan preparation		Takes strategic direction from CEO	
Sets priorities between businesses, projects			Delegates strategic objectives, tasks, with due dates	
Allocates money and personnel			Executes and reviews plan	
Reviews progress				

*Note: Organizationally, the head of a business or SBU may be a general manager controlling all functions or a lower-level individual (for example, a marketing manager) responsible for an SBU plan but without direct control over functions such as manufacturing, R&D, and finance.

the wrong pricing strategy can have a far more devastating financial and image impact than a late or ill-advised cost-reduction program.

Third, profitable, long-term strategy depends on identifying and satisfying market needs more successfully than the competition. Everything else — technology, manufacturing, cost, R&D, assets, and organization — are only a means to that end.

A competent marketing manager who understands the basic principles of cost, sales, finance, and R&D is in the best position to judge what will or won't work in the marketplace. Such a manager will be able to balance expenditures and priorities between the short- and long-term (i.e., cost reduction vs. new products vs. market development); and objectively coordinate departments with conflicting interests (i.e., manufacturing's time frame is usually *now,* and R&D's time frame is often *whenever*).

PLAN CONTENT AND FORMAT

The Twelve Basic Questions

There are a million plan formats and forms, a million checklists of plan contents, a million matrices to be filled in to describe your strategy. Any of these may result in a good-looking document, but not a good plan. It makes no difference what *format* you use as long as it accomplishes your objectives and *will work in your organization.*

Regardless of the format used, you *must* answer the "Twelve Fundamental Questions of Planning" listed in Table 3-3. These simplistic, common sense questions, rationally answered during the planning process, will result in an achievable plan — if the organization is committed to accomplishing it and sufficient numbers of appropriately skilled people are available to execute it. See Appendix II-1 for a detailed suggested outline of the planning process.

Preliminary Planning

The following three types of preliminary plans are common.

The Detailed Plan

The objective of a detailed plan, completed at the business or SBU level, is to insure that key makers and executioners of strategy make their contributions, that plan goals and tasks have been coordinated between all functions, that areas needing further research are identified, and that key managers are satisfied with strategies and goals and *believe* that they can be accomplished. The detailed plan generally remains a *working tool at the business level;* it rarely goes beyond the general manager and should not be submitted to corporate executives in large companies. It is necessary when an established business is expected to undergo great change or for a new, high-impact business. It is not necessary when change is minimal; in such cases, updates or new data in critical areas usually suffice.

A detailed plan requires sufficient detailed analysis to yield one or more workable strategies. Its format should not concern top management. Marketing management and the general manager of the business, however, should care. They are plotting their future and the future of the business.

The Summary Plan

A short, simple summary plan for each business and SBU, intended for the CEO, is designed to recommend strategy, forecast performance, present comparisons with other businesses, diagnose strengths and weaknesses, and suggest measurable tasks.

Present strategy: Answers to the basic strategic questions highlighted in Table 3-3, if correct, *are* the strategic plan and its justification.

Forecast performance: A three–five year forecast of profit and loss and asset utilization must be made, separating projections for established base businesses from strategic businesses and expenditures. Forecasts usually run three to five years ahead and include a current-year estimate and two-year history to allow for establishment of the business's track. It's very difficult to quickly implement major changes in sales or profit performance. Any break in track requires substantial documentation. Appendix II-2 includes a typical financial forecast format.

Table 3-3. Twelve Fundamental Questions of Planning

1. What business am I in now?
2. How well am I doing? What is the trend?
3. What are my assumptions about the future?
4. Where do I want to be in the future?
5. What do I have to do to get there? What are my major alternative programs?
6. Why will the competition and the marketplace let me do it?
7. How great a risk is there in my plan? Why?
8. Which business and program options should I pursue? With what resources?
9. Where will these choices take me?
10. Are my organization and resources up to the job? Is the timing right?
11. How will I review and control the plan?
12. How and when do I rework the plan?

Comparison with other businesses: The summary plan presents the nature of each business's market and its present and future competitive position if recommended strategies are followed. A simple summary provides the basis for later comparisons and choices. "Competitive matrices," of which there are many, often are used for this purpose; two of the most widely used appear in Figure 3-2.

Matrices should be used with extreme caution, as *one* input into strategic decisions, and only as a starting point for deep discussion of available options. Simplistically used, they can lead management to ignore unpopular but potentially profitable strategies such as investing in a stagnant industry, and jump on popular (or once popular) strategies such as pursuing low cost to gain market share. They don't address the organization's ability to execute the plan in the competitive environment, a major flaw.

Diagnosis of strengths and weaknesses: An awareness of the company's strengths and weaknesses allows the CEO to determine the chances of implementing the plan, the cost of correcting weaknesses, and the existence of potentially fatal flaws. Most managers do a poor job of evaluating strengths and weaknesses, both internal (organization and manufacturing efficiency) and external (brand strength, quality of sales effort). A rating of strengths and weaknesses by strategic area can be singled out using diagnostic questions such as those shown in Appendix II-2 or by surveying internal and important external personnel including customers.

Measurable goals: Each business is obliged to meet a few measurable goals for quarterly review by the CEO. The more specific the goal, the better (i.e., launch a new $60–$100 softside luggage line by a certain date and achieve an annual sales rate of $8mm a year later). The fewer goals, the better — no more than three to five per year per business is recommended. When the businesses' overall goals are approved by the CEO, detailed action plans — tasks and due dates behind the tip of the iceberg — are developed and incorporated into the operating plan.

The chart in Appendix II-2 offers a complete summary plan format.

The Preliminary Corporate Plan

The preliminary written plan submitted to the CEO of a large multi-business company compares common strategic dimensions of all the company's businesses, forecasts the financial gain/drain of each business and for the corporation as a whole, and presents a one-page "quick scan" summary of each business along with its summary plan (see Figure 3-3). The CEO then can decide where to place corporate emphasis and whether to confirm or change strategy for each business and SBU and can set goals beyond existing businesses and business definitions.

Comparing diverse businesses: Comparisons often are made with Growth/

Size/Growth Matrix[1]

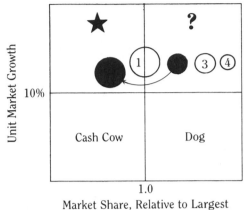

Conclusions: Though we are #2 in this market, we can move to #1 position through new product investments and our distribution strengths. Competitors 1, 3, 4 judged to be weaker.

O = Size of circle indicates annual sales volume
Number = Competitor's number
● = Our company's position
→ = Planned movement in five years

Desirability of Market/Ability to Complete Matrix[2]

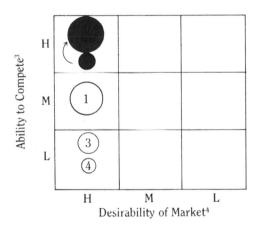

Conclusions: Competitive evaluation shows superiority over all competitors. Two major advantages: Distribution system with developed brand awareness and superior new products; market is highly desirable because of large size, rapid growth, and forecast for sustained life.

H = High
M = Medium
L = Low

O = Competition
● = Our company
→ = Planned movement in five years

[1]Developed by the Boston Consulting Group
[2]Attributed to the General Electric Corporation
[3]Factors include competitive advantages (disadvantages) in product, cost, market share, quality, brand strength, etc.
[4]Factors include market size, growth and maturity, entry barriers, similarity to core company businesses, inherent profitability, technology needed, etc.

Figure 3-2. Competitive Summary for a Single Business

Quick-Scan Summary
Overall Strategy: Grow   Business: Sunglasses

Business Definition   *Target Market:* M/F, 20–49, FI > $25,000, worldwide.
Needs: Superior eye protection; classic to contemporary fashion; features for "active" sport segments.
Products: Sunglasses/shields; outdoor eye protection. $30+ retail.
Distribution: High grade. Sport, tourist, department store, catalog, general merchandise, duty free, boutique retailers.

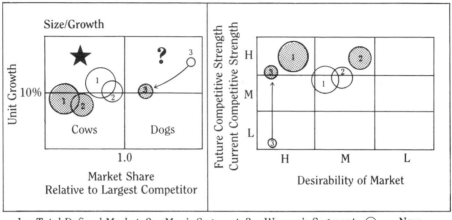

1 = Total Defined Market 2 = Men's Segment 3 = Women's Segment ○ = Now
                                                                  ◉ = Future

Financials ($MM)	−2	−1	0	1	2	3	Δ%/Year 0–3	Major earnings and ROA dilutions years −1 to +1 due to equipment, investment, new product development expenses.
Sales	90	100	120	135	145	155	8.9	
NPBT	9	8.5	11	9.5	13	14	8.4	
ROS %	10	8.5	9	7	9	9	——	
ROA (%BT)	22	18	16	14	19	20	7.7	
Total Assets	41	46	55	67	68	71	8.9	

Figure 3-3.   Quick-Scan Summary

	Plan
Objectives:	Worldwide sales of $180mm by 1989, 20% NPBT, 25% ROA #1 market position, 60% SOM in markets/segments entered, no less than #2.
Strategies:	*Continued:* (1) Retain product function and style leadership through research. (2) Price premium through image/value. (3) #1 brand awareness. (4) Maintain #1 position current channels by giving distribution maximum profit.
	Changes: Penetrate women's fashion/function markets via new lightweight product; department/specialty store, distribution. Penetrate $100+ men's market.
Competitors 1, 2, 3:	Machina (Germany), Samuri (Japan), Schuss (Austria).
Competitive Advantage(s):	Brand awareness; quality image; United States, European, Far Eastern Distribution; R&D effort.
Competitive Weakness(es):	Manufacturing cost; no product above $100; little fashion product for women; weak in department/specialty stores.

Goal	Measurement	Date
1. Profitably enter upscale women's market.	Entry plan approved by CEO	9/1/85
2. #1 position in $100+ men's market.	$10mm sales, NPBT 0	12/31/85
3. Reduce manufacturing cost, update equipment.	Unit cost 8% lower	12/31/86
4. Define strategy in drug/food/mass merchandising market.	Feasibility study complete, reviewed by CEO	10/1/85

Figure 3-3.   Quick-Scan Summary, continued

Share or Competitive Strength/Market Desirability matrices as shown in Figure 3-4. Other matrices are sometimes used to chart other dimensions, such as:

Technology: Sales, investment, and profits versus basic technologies used. Some corporations prefer a balanced portfolio of businesses based on fundamental scientific or manufacturing technologies.

End Industries: Sales, investment, and profits anticipated versus consuming industries, such as scientific equipment, consumer hard goods, retailing, etc. Companies often want to balance investment by industry to minimize effects of the business cycle and to spread risk.

All such fancy comparisons will, of course, be analyzed and reduced to a recommendation that says: *invest* here, *hold* here, *get rid* of these, or I want *more information* here.

Financial Forecasts: There are no standard formats; most companies have their own. Plan schedules focus on the following financial measurements for each business and for the corporation as a whole:

Sales	Net profit after tax
Gross Margin	Investment
Expense	Return on assets
Net profit before tax	Cash flow

It is helpful if the company's computer system can quickly recalculate financial schedules if the CEO wants to play "what if" or change a business's financial assumptions.

The Corporate Plan: Produced after the CEO and his or her advisors have reviewed and revised the preliminary plan, the final corporate plan usually consists of:

* A statement of corporate business definition, objectives, and key strategies — the "soul" of the business, if you will;
* A projection of consolidated long-term financial performance after plan execution;
* Concise directions (one or two pages) to each business and SBU on expected financial performance; strategic posture (grow, hold, milk, etc.); major tasks (R&D projects, organizational restructuring, entry into a new business, divestment, etc.);
* A few key corporate objectives that are the CEO's responsibility.

Growth/Share Matrix

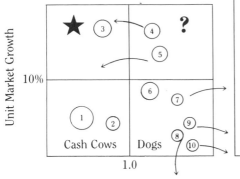

Conclusions: A potentially healthy business if well managed. Includes two cash cows (1, 2) to fund other businesses; a star that will require support to grow, defend its position (3); two question marks (4, 5) where strategic decisions must be made; five dogs that probably should be divested unless they can be turned into a cash source. Planned movement and its financial impact needs in-depth exploration.

Key

○ = Size of circle indicates annual sales volume

Number = Business number

⌣↗ = Direction of planned movement in the future

Desirability of Market/Ability to Compete Matrix

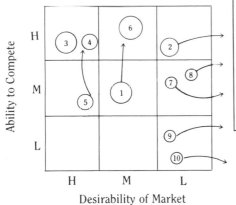

Conclusions: Businesses 3, 4 appear to be winners, grow–sustain. 5 could become a long-term winner if competitive strengths are real. 1, though a cash cow, may require strengthening to maintain its position. How 1 and 5 are to be strengthened must be questioned. 9, 10 should be dumped. 7, 8 should be dumped unless competitive strength is easily increased (unlikely). 2 does not fit company — divest.

Key

See above.

Figure 3-4.   Comparison of Businesses Within a Company

ASSEMBLING THE BASICS INTO A PRODUCTIVE PLANNING PROCESS

Steps in the Planning Process

It's important to determine what steps are to be taken, by whom, and when in the strategic planning process. Sufficient time must be allowed for each step; remember, the key people developing the plan are also managing ongoing businesses.

Table 3-4 graphically depicts the following steps in the planning process:

1.   *Review the Gut Plan:* Most business managers follow a "gut" plan, the strategic course that they're already following, whether articulated or not, until it's changed. The CEO should informally review gut plans, if he doesn't already know them, to understand the current course and prospects of each business.

2.   *CEO's Direction:* The CEO reviews each key manager's plan and explains any preordained strictures on a given business (you can have only X dollars) or the strategy to be followed (you are to run the business for cash). He indicates new directions to be explored during plan preparation (consider expanding into Y category and entering new business Z). In addition, he distributes the usual (but minimal) "plan paperwork," including forms to be completed, due dates, and scheduled reviews.

3.   *Training:* It is unrealistic to send forms to each business unit and expect carefully considered plans in return. Rather, the corporate planner should explain the plan and its format to those responsible for administering each business plan. Continued consulting as questions arise also is necessary. Even more important — and usually neglected — is training in planning, strategic options, and goal setting, which can be accomplished through brief internal seminars followed by individual consulting.

4.   *Detailed and Summary Plan Preparation* by each SBU and business unit is the keystone of the corporate plan. Team meetings led by each general or SBU manager or preferably moderated by a professional facilitator are by far the most effective means of outlining the plan and establishing priorities, critical task assignments, and due dates. Team planning is discussed in detail later in this chapter.

5.   *Preliminary Corporate Plan Review:* At this point, the CEO and the top management team together question individual business plans, consider changes in the corporation's objectives, and determine staff priorities.

6.   *Individual Business Reviews:* When necessary, the CEO discusses a business or SBU plan with its manager to agree upon direction, if it can be decided at this point, and give personal advice and counsel.

7.   *Final Consolidation and Decisions:* Again, a top-team meeting to approve SBU and business plan and to set corporate direction — which is not just the

Table 3-4.   Steps in the Strategic Planning Process

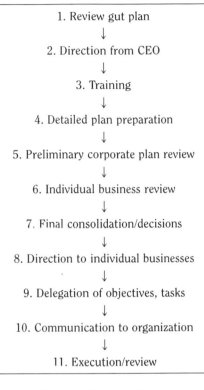

1. Review gut plan
↓
2. Direction from CEO
↓
3. Training
↓
4. Detailed plan preparation
↓
5. Preliminary corporate plan review
↓
6. Individual business review
↓
7. Final consolidation/decisions
↓
8. Direction to individual businesses
↓
9. Delegation of objectives, tasks
↓
10. Communication to organization
↓
11. Execution/review

sum of individual business plans — is very effective when complicated changes in the preliminary plan must be made.

8.   *Direction to Individual Businesses:* Decisions, including approved strategies, prebudget estimates of available resources, and critical events and due dates should be relayed to individual business managers both verbally and in writing.

9.   *Delegation:* Strategic plan objectives and tasks to be accomplished by each business unit should become part of its annual goal setting process. Goals are split between next year — managing the ongoing business, and strategic goals — making the future happen, and passed down to each individual responsible for executing a portion of the plan. Bosses and subordinates must mutually agree that goals are achievable and measurable or modify them accordingly. Table 3-5 shows typical strategic goals delegated to a marketing director.

10.   *Communication:* Employees often complain that their companies lack direction or that their assignments make no sense. Sometimes their accusations are accurate; sometimes their bosses have not effectively communicated the corporate strategy. Business plans are more apt to succeed if all employees are kept

Table 3-5.   Typical Strategic Goals Format for Marketing Director

Strategic Goal	Task(s)	Measurement	Due Date
Product			
Profitably enter market for high-priced ($40 +) high-fashion women's sunglasses	Define needs/potential	Market research complete	9/1/85
	Develop product, distribution concept/ financials	Plan complete	9/1/85
	Test prototype product	Complete competitive design, use, acceptance tests	9/1/85
Profitably gain #1 position in prestige, functional, expensive ($100 +) men's sunglass market	Complete approved plan for introduction this year	$10 mm sales, breakeven NPBT, 30% SOM	12/31/85
		$20 mm sales, 20% NPBT, 50% SOM	12/31/86
Distribution			
Test potential in low-price ($5–15) sunglass market	Test direct sale to/ merchandising of drug/ food stores, mass merchants	Approved plan for Atlanta/Miami implemented. Test sales > $700,000, NPBT loss < $300,000	12/31/86
Wholesale Sales			
Realign territories in proportion to future sales, in line with increased penetration strategies	Consultant's study to recommend realignment, staffing	Plan complete/approved and new people in place	6/15/85
		$15mm annual sales increase in basic business over 1984	9/31/86
Advertising			
Build brand awareness to #1 position in each price-distribution category	Develop, implement awareness plan for basic $25–70 line	40% unaided awareness	12/31/85
		60% unaided awareness	12/31/86

informed, because people are motivated by the security of knowing what's going on, strong leadership, and they develop a sense of pride in their contributions to a sensible plan. Moreover, if they know where you want to go they may suggest ways to help you get there. (Of course, communications must protect proprietary information and reflect the needs of the audience.)

One particularly effective communications program, for a company that planned significant changes in organization and direction, was initiated when the top management team traveled to each staff and manufacturing location, gave a formal presentation of their plan, and discussed it informally in small group meetings with employees at all levels including hourly and union personnel. Dissemination of information, important at the corporate level, is triply important at the business level, where objectives are implemented and awareness of the plan can influence day-to-day decision making. At this level, small group question-and-answer sessions frequently can identify previously neglected issues and problems and alleviate employees' concerns.

Without follow-through, however, credibility and positive momentum may be lost. Once the plan has been communicated, management's responsibility includes action and feedback based on employees' suggestions and questions as well as periodic reviews of progress.

11. *Execution/Review:* Successful execution requires delegation of strategic goals to the key business managers who must execute them, as well as to all the other levels of the organization. Top level goals therefore are broken up into manageable subgoals and "cascaded" down to individuals responsible for their achievement. The most brilliant and timely strategy remains academic unless goals and due dates are systematically set and realistic and acceptable to all involved.[1] Finally, the following periodic reviews and mid-course corrections are recommended at the CEO and business manager level:

Monthly exception reports, consisting of one or two sentences explaining whether an upcoming goal will be met and flagging any existing problems. Handwritten notes on the original goal sheets work well. Serious problems can be discussed personally.

Quarterly reviews of each individual's progress and a brief review of each business plan with the top management team are effective. Goals, priorities, and tasks are changed if necessary.

Critical reviews are held at critical points in the plan, such as prior to the launch of a new project, investment in plant or equipment, or the institution of an acquisition search.

Dip in and out with informal progress reviews of critical steps (market research presentations, review of cost reduction projects, consumer focus groups, construction progress on new facilities, etc.). Such quality checks can reveal more than a ream of reports.

Reviews of strategic goals for each individual within the organization, of course, are included in the normal management by objectives process by which all companies should be run.

---

[1]For a discussion of the critical processes of setting and reviewing objectives, see: Dowling, Kenneth J., *Managing by Agreement*, Private Publication, University of Southern California, Los Angeles, 1983.

SMELLING A RAT

To judge whether a submitted plan is achievable, look for these symptoms, any of which may represent wishful or superficial thinking:

Numbers

Sales, profits, or cash flow depart abruptly from their historical track.

Financial forecasts specify quick improvements to meet corporate goals.

New products, projects, and businesses quickly become profitable.

Financial performance exceeds that of the industry's top performers.

Competition

The competitive edge through which a strategy will work in the market is not or cannot be objectively documented by tests or research.

Strategy

Submitted strategy is a "me too" imitation of a successful competitor's, except that "we'll do it better."

Competition made similar major moves in the market long ago.

The strategy (for example, growth) doesn't fit the marketplace (stagnant or declining).

Disappearing Problems

A significant problem, such as high manufacturing cost, is "assumed away" without a specific solution.

TEAM MEETINGS: HOW TO MAKE STRATEGY, NOT PAPER

Strategic Teams

The best way to develop workable plans is to institute excellent continuing communications between the general manager of a business and his or her staff. The best way to ensure optimum quality and quantity of communications devoted to strategy is to use team planning.

This section is written from the perspective of the general manager of a single business, whose planning team usually includes the directors of marketing, finance, manufacturing, human resources, R&D, and planning. The team planning process, however, works equally well at senior levels for the CEO's strategy team or at lower levels for an SBU manager and key functional people.

Team Planning

The objective of face-to-face team planning meetings is to develop a workable basic overall business strategy and strategies for each function. The steps in this process, illustrated in Table 3-6, are:

1. *Top Team Training* — train the planning team in planning techniques and goal setting.
2. *Prework* — gather necessary information prior to the meeting.
3. *Strategy Meeting* — make key decisions and establish overall objectives and strategies.
4. *Goal Setting* — establish final business goals.
5. *Plan Review* — general manager's approval of the final goals.
6. *Follow-up Reviews* — periodic tracking of progress.

Table 3-6.   Steps in the Team Planning Process

Top Team Training

↓

Prework

Organization/Market Probes
Employee Questionnaire
Develop Summary Plans
Issues Questionnaire

↓

Strategy Meeting

Answer 12 Key Questions
Produce Draft Plan
Practice Goal Setting
Produce Written Plan/Goals

↓

Goal Setting

Individual Objectives
Action Plans

↓

Plan Review

↓

Follow-Up Reviews

Top Team Training

Strategy team members must be trained in strategic planning principles and techniques, setting individual goals, and effective participation in team meetings. Training is usually conducted by an outside organization development consultant, psychologist, or "facilitator" skilled in strategic planning and organization development.

Prework

Important background planning information is gathered and communicated to the strategy team prior to the team meeting. The information therefore does not need to be presented during the meeting, allowing the team to begin work on the plan immediately.

Five types of prework should be considered, beginning with a confidential *organization probe* conducted by a neutral party such as a facilitator. This inquiry is designed to determine people's feelings about the business's direction and operation and to identify perceived barriers to achieving short- and long-term organizational goals.

Although quantitative measurement instruments have been used, probes should consist of free-form questioning to elicit honest and wide-ranging opinion from a sample of people at all levels in the organization. Because some responses come from lower-level employees with limited strategic vision, many will pertain to current problems rather than new strategies. The interviewer must carefully determine which comments represent barriers to long-term strategy (i.e., "we're too overworked to take on anything new") and which to short-term operations. Responses usually fall into the following categories:

- Short-term operations problems (useful in operations planning meetings), such as, "we're running at 115% of capacity, and inefficiencies are killing quality."
- Organizational problems, such as, "the Sales Department is just taking orders and not putting across marketing programs."
- Questions and concerns about strategic direction, such as, "product line X has been falling in volume. Since we're not approaching breakeven, should we really be in this business?"
- Specific suggestions, such as, "we ought to be in X business because we can manufacture the product on the same line as Y at the lower cost than that of the competition."

Table 3-7 is a sample of questions asked and responses received to a probe intended to uncover both operational and strategic problems.

Market probes consisting of interviews with key current and potential customers and industry experts are sometimes conducted to determine the compa-

Table 3-7.   Probe Questions and Selected Summary Responses

Questions	Responses Dealing with Strategy	Responses Dealing with Operations
What is working well? What positive changes have occurred in the past six to 12 months?	Development of better information for use in formulating and implementing business plans (cost data, market research support)	New employees strengthen middle management Improved communication between manufacturing and product management

What barriers do you encounter in getting your work done (corporate; division; departmental)?	Lack of systematic long-range planning
	
	Plans agreed to, not left in place
		Decision making too centralized
		
		"Fire drill" syndrome:
		    Demand for immediate answers
		    Called into "urgent" meetings too often
		    Impact of too many "crash" programs

How do you feel about the division's direction?	Business A is at a crossroads. It must be fully supported or killed	
Do any new directions make sense?	Business X in our division should be combined with business Y in another division because they have better access to our target customer Sales department is inadequate to meet division's long-term needs.	
What changes would make your particular operation more effective?	Manufacturing costs too high; planned reduction needed Outdated materials planning, manufacturing scheduling, forecasting system	More computer support Standard policies for quick approval of new products, pricing, tooling

ny's competitive strengths and weaknesses and potential future strategies from outside points of view.

An *employee questionnaire* should be completed by key employees who will not be directly involved in developing the plan to identify issues that they would like to see addressed, and give them the legitimate feeling of participation in the planning process. The confidential questionnaire is made available to personnel through their supervisor and returned directly to the General Manager's office. Alternatively, meetings can be held by supervisors with their employees to discuss inputs to the plan and summaries sent to the General Manager.

Summary plans in draft form (not detailed plans) for each business function or planning unit, along with a corporate summary, are circulated to the strategic team prior to the meeting. This step is recommended if the business is relatively healthy, leaders are capable of thinking about strategy, and the top team communicates well together. Otherwise, as is often the case in organizationally sick or turn-around companies, the top team may meet first to open up communications and to clarify strategic and operating problems and establish overall direction to assist individual planning units in developing their initial plans.

Finally, *issues questionnaires* are completed by each member of the strategy team soliciting their opinions on:

- the company's strengths and weaknesses; its business definition
- potential strategies
- personnel attitudes that need to be reinforced or changed
- top strategic operations and organizational problems that need to be addressed.

The Strategy Meeting

To keep proceedings on track, effective strategy team meetings should be limited to a few people — usually the general manager, key functional managers, the planner, and a trusted facilitator. Meetings should be held far away from headquarters and last two to three days to allow sufficient time for recreation; a local motel is not effective.

Excellent meetings consist of discussion and decisions establishing goals and priorities, not presentations. A proven sequence of events at strategy meetings is:

Step	What Happens
ANSWER THE PLAN QUESTIONS	• Answer the 12 key planning questions in order
	• List objectives and action steps after each question
	• Rank plan objectives by a) must do, and b) can slip if emergencies occur
	• Set aside operations and other issues

DEAL WITH OTHER ISSUES

- Deal with those requiring immediate action
- Assign other issues to team members for later action

PRODUCE THE DRAFT PLAN

- Produce a draft written plan

SET GOALS

- Produce draft goals for each team member

ESTABLISH FINAL PLAN, GOALS

- Review/revise the final written plan and draft goals

OTHER ACTION STEPS

- Decide on the review process for the overall plan and for individual goals
- List unanswered questions requiring further work. Assign who addresses, when.

Some of the actual issues addressed in strategic team meetings held by two consumer products companies included:

Goals: What volume, assets, profitability are reasonable five years out?

Product/Market: Reaching younger consumers we're missing; what to do about emerging woman's market?; should we be in continental-styled products?; strengthening casual products; need to upgrade, reposition basic line, fill holes.

People: Reorganization to relieve day-to-day pressure on manufacturing director; how to organize sales/marketing.

Sales/Distribution: Retail penetration variable among top 40 SMSAs; owned versus franchised stores — why? where? variation in wholesale penetration nationally; sales coverage in and outside of top 40 markets; store opening schedule next three–four years; role of independent retailer versus own stores; department store weakness — stay in or get out?

Manufacturing: Can't meet three–five year forecast in existing plants; product construction mix will change — to what?

Table 3-8 details typical decisions made at these meetings.

Role of the Facilitator

This individual, who may be the general manager (but only if he or she has been trained to function as a neutral discussion leader) or an independent internal or external professional, must be experienced and must have previously earned the trust of the strategic team. The facilitator's duties include intervening when discussion is unproductive or digressive; clarifying issues when thinking is fuzzy or people are evasive; and ensuring that all participants openly contribute to the meeting.

Table 3-8. Disguised Excerpts of Strategic Decisions Made During a Team Meeting

Can Be Accomplished with Existing Resources	Date	Requires Additional Resources/Approval	Date	What	Budgeted Yes	Budgeted No
		Marketing				
Launch new sport line	9/79	Design, test new top-of-line sport product	2nd qtr. '81	Target market style research		X
Complete analysis of business X (keep or get out); if keep, deliver business plan	1/81					
		Sales/Distribution				
Department store distribution/service plan complete	9/80	Division Sales/Distribution plan integrating all changes needed for all product lines	1st qtr. '81	Consultant to study		X
		Manufacturing				
Plan, add staff to accomplish new product load, cost reduction, plan expanded capacity	4th qtr. '79	Revitalize formal cost reduction program — $5mm annual impact	1st qtr. '80	Engineering staff		X

Planning/Scheduling

EDP system for scheduling of new product cycle	1st qtr. '80		

Finance

Establish in-plant financial organization under plant controller	ASAP	Plant controller	X

Human Resources

Division organization plan including new hires, replacements, succession plan	4th qtr. '79		

Technology

Establish R&D program for product categories A, B	3rd qtr. '80	R&D director plus staff	½* ½

Market Research

Create department and goals	4th qtr. '79		

*Half budgeted, half not

Review Meetings

Abbreviated team meetings are helpful in keeping the plan on track and often combine an operations and strategic review. They are usually held quarterly or semi-annually and, depending on the number of businesses involved, rarely last more than one or two days.

Although any number of people may assume leadership during the discussion/decision/action phases, the facilitator or planner usually is responsible for running the meeting and recording the results.

Goal Setting and Review

After the meeting, individual team members refine their objectives and develop detailed action plans — who must do what, when to accomplish each goal. The objectives are finally reviewed and approved by the General Manager before being delegated throughout the organization for action. The full team reviews the final objectives only if there are substantial changes in goals or allocation of resources between functions.

TEAM AND INDIVIDUAL BEHAVIOR

Team planning requires both attitudinal and behavioral changes on the part of most managers new to the team process. Directive boss-subordinate relationships must be set aside. "My department versus yours" thinking must yield to open communications and to the attitude that team members are equals working together for the good of the business.

The process of building productive team behavior takes one to three years. The General Manager must be committed to team planning and set the behavioral standard for his team mates.

Team members must be willing to:

- confront and resolve conflict between team members or business functions
- learn the "tools" of team behavior including listening, helping others articulate goals, contributing ideas, subordinating departmental or personal needs for the good of the business, and taking personal risks — a willingness to be wrong — in advancing ideas
- be open with and trusting of other team members.

The facilitator should give the team training in factors that help and hinder team and individual effectiveness. He or she will further develop the team's skills during meetings by supporting productive behavior and by showing how to correct behavior that hinders the process.

The boss is still the boss, however. The team is not a voting democracy. After adequate discussion, the general manager may accept the team's recommendations or alter them if her position does not agree with that of the team's. She must, however, behave as another equal on the team until the final decisions must be made.

CONTINUOUS PLANNING

The strategy team may meet frequently — two to four times per month — to resolve critical strategy issues. For example, a Fortune 500 company retained a consulting firm over a nine-month period to decide the future strategy for their bread-and-butter business, a near monopoly for which fierce competition was expected. Continuous meetings involving those who would be implementing the plan ultimately resulted in a successful strategy.

Pros and Cons: The one drawback to team planning — the up-front time it takes — is far outweighed by its time-saving advantages. The process addresses real, not superficial issues critical to a business's success. The resulting plan is doable because each function has accepted its tasks and integrated them into a realistic time frame.

A consensus is established on a common thrust and priorities for the business. General understanding of the plan and the role of each function in its implementation promotes cooperation. People who see the big picture can offer creative suggestions for improvement, and team planning makes possible an early identification of and solutions to problems. The resulting open communications between team members helps resolve the inevitable conflicts. Team planning gives superior business results over other methods.

GETTING STARTED

This chapter presented a sophisticated expensive planning system that takes three–five years to install.

How do you get started simply and practically when the data, planning experience, planners, and time and money — particularly in the case of a small company — aren't available? First, the CEO should answer the strategic planning questions in Appendix II-2, based on her current knowledge and intuition. In short, the CEO should get her "gut" plan down on paper. She should use an excellent process person who is thoroughly familiar with planning as a sounding board and thinker. Next, the CEO should ask her direct reports to do the same, as well as list the three major long-term problems facing their operation and the three major opportunities for growth for the corporation.

Next, a team meeting, led by a facilitator, should be held to:

1. Define your current business — who are you?
2. Define your future business definition, the growth and financial goals you have for the future. Recognize that there may well be parts of your new def-

inition and goals that can be tied down and others that will require further thought and research.

3. Establish specific goals for those opportunities that you *can* act on now, and set a timetable to get answers to questions needed to act on other opportunities and hone your new business definition. Start with small steps forward that your organization can easily accomplish during the first year of planning.

4. Agree on the goals and a timetable with your staff, approve the written goals of each staff member, and insure that they discuss goals to be accomplished by subordinates with them.

Don't worry about company-wide MBO or standards of performance systems to administer goals now if you haven't already installed them. Simply discuss what is to be accomplished, when, by each key person who is assigned a goal, and review it. MBO, like systematic strategic planning, is very worthwhile but takes a long time to install. You don't need sophisticated systems to get started.

How long will it take to complete this exercise? About five days of prework, and five days of meetings — with professional help.

KEYS TO SUCCESS

The Plan

*   *Keep it simple* — Elaborate documents don't get read. Single out the few critical events for review.

*   *Focus on the competition* — Keep asking why you're superior to your competitors, how you know you have an advantage in the marketplace and, especially, whether you're really sure.

*   *Make sure your strategies are right* — If you don't know, do research to find out.

*   *Set priorities* between businesses and communicate key goals. When slippage occurs, employees will know automatically where to place their efforts, and you'll know what tasks require attention and resources.

*   *Follow your instincts* — If you're any good, your gut feelings probably are right. Double-check with research.

Preparation

*   *Demand total involvement* of all key business functions. A one-person plan usually is a one-person failure.

*   *Sounding boards* — Find a neutral one. Use it. Everybody from the CEO on down can become insulated and myopic.

- *Sell upstairs* — If you ensure that your superiors support your plan, you prevent nasty surprises later, particularly if you anticipate a couple of quarters (or years) of lousy performance.
- *Don't relegate planning to financial people* — They understand numbers, not how to make them happen.

Execution

- *Set a realistic pace* — If you're changing direction, don't try to do too much too fast, and don't diversify too radically. Otherwise, you'll overstress the organization and all businesses will suffer.
- *Use the right people for the job* — Don't expect old-line employees to manage a changing "go-go" business (or vice versa).
- *Set regular reviews* — Escape the office hubub to review the plan. Never postpone a scheduled review because of a current problem (unless, of course, it's a genuine disaster).
- *Allow mistakes* — In a supportive atmosphere, schedules and goals are adjustable; after all, not everything can be predicted. A strategic plan, by definition, will change. You *do* want to hear bad news early so you can make good corrections.
- *Install market monitors* — Particularly when embarking on a high-risk, high-exposure strategy in a rapidly changing market, you must react quickly to changes (see Chapter 1).

BASIC PRINCIPLES

The CEO

- *The CEO is the plan* — If he or she doesn't live, breathe, and constantly communicate the plan, it's dead.
- *Paper plans are meaningless* — It's what's in the CEO's gut that counts. If the plans have helped form, change, or solidify his or her gut plan, they've worked. If not, the formal plan is a waste.

Attitudes

- *Inbreeding* — An organization will base its plan on what it thinks is true about the outside world (often wrong or half correct) unless challenged or required to research the market and competition.
- *Gut plans* — People will follow their individual gut plan rather than the official written plan (unless they're one and the same or your managers are committed to altering their gut plans through the planning and review process).

- *Planning is an afterthought* — Most people leave it until the last minute, consider it a bother, do it poorly, dust off last year's plan if it pleased management, and then follow their gut plan.
- *Every business is a growth business* — Even if the market is dropping at an astronomical rate and competition is overwhelming, every manager will forecast turnaround or spectacular growth.
- *Every business will meet corporate goals* — If the CEO desires 20 percent annual profit growth and a 30 percent return on assets, managers will project those goals, even for moribund businesses.
- *Ignoring the competition* — Although most planners pay lip service to marketing strategies designed to counter the threat of competitive products, they rarely spend the time and money required to make those strategies work.
- *If there is a short-term problem, the long-term will be ignored,* because the short-term is much easier to manage. Only reviews and controls can maintain an appropriate balance in a time of crisis.

People

- *People limit your plan* — With their existing employees, most organizations can't execute a plan involving significant change. Growth plans require more people; new directions require new skills and new mind-sets that can't be developed overnight.
- *People are a planning afterthought* — All the great words and super numbers usually fail to address the management and skill changes necessary to implement the plan.

Planners/Strategists

- *A good strategist is an exception* — The person who can think strategy, keep the long-term on track, and run an operation is a rarity. Promote him or her.
- *The best strategists are people with marketing experience* who understand the marketplace and the manufacturing, finance and technical functions. People from the latter functions generally (not always) have too technical and limited a view to be good strategists.
- *Planning technocrats* — Too often, professional planners focus only on producing the numbers or following the correct process and do not involve those who know the business. Remember, you're looking for decisions that alter or confirm the course of your business, not for plans. Line managers plan. Planners only help or facilitate.

Training

- *Training is ignored* — The plan should include training of employees in the new skills needed to realize the plan. If you're switching from manufacturer's reps to a direct salesforce, for example, you'd better teach your sales manager how to manage a direct salesforce.

Time

- *It takes five years* for a plan to get results and convert the skeptics within an organization into believers.
- *Executing long-term plans is the longest, toughest management job* — Making a workable plan involving significant change happen while keeping the basic business on track requires far more management talent — and patience — than simply running a business.

Outside Help

- *An independent facilitator* must be used to effectively start and implement the strategic and team planning processes. Management usually doesn't have the planning or behavioral skills or the unbiased view of their business and organization to do it alone.

Part III

INEFFECTIVE ANNUAL MARKETING PLANS

Chapter 4

Developing an Annual Plan That Works

The Problem

Everybody knows this year's budget, but no one knows precisely what has to be done by whom and when to make the glowing promises happen. Profits suffer, schedules are missed, fingers point everywhere.

For example, a major manufacturer of sporting accessories significantly increased next year's sales budget over anticipated current-year results. Along with heavy sales expected from a new product, substantial increases were anticipated from the sale of existing products to old customers, and through a new distribution channel.

Result? Disaster. The new product wasn't ready for the selling season because product design, manufacturing, engineering, and marketing failed to work effectively together to meet targeted product release dates, and the sales department was not consulted on how sales could be increased to existing customers. Sales and marketing had no firm programs for the new distribution channel before the budget was put to bed. Sales and profits missed budget by a mile; salespeople didn't earn adequate commissions; morale in the sales force fell to an all-time low; and management was embarrassed.

The underlying problem was the absence of a good annual marketing plan specifying goals, tasks, and due dates for every function or operation inside or outside the company supporting the marketing effort.

A MATTER OF DEFINITION

This chapter addresses annual marketing plans: *action* plans whose objective is to achieve *this year's* operating and financial goals and accomplish *this year's* strategic tasks. This is not the same as market planning, which is an analysis that determines what your goals, strategies, and programs *should* be. Unless good market and strategic plans are in place, it's almost impossible to develop a sound marketing plan.

SYMPTOMS

When a marketing organization lacks good marketing plans, the following consequences are likely:

Sales and profits disappoint because:

New sales from new customers are assumed, not planned;

Salespeople, who weren't involved in establishing budgets, complain of unrealistic quotas;

The product mix is significantly different from and less profitable than projection;

The budget is established before timing, cost, and impact of marketing programs is estimated.

High costs due to:

Substantial overruns incurred by design, engineering, and manufacturing in their attempt to expedite new products despite late direction from marketing;

Hand production of salespeople's samples because the manufacturing process wasn't perfected;

Significant overtime needed to produce printed material, displays, commercials, and print ads to meet product sell and advertising closing dates.

Late programs, resulting in:

Products that reach the market late (suicide in a fashion market);

Advertising, promotion, and collateral materials that aren't ready when the product is, thus delaying sales;

Selling programs and pitches, hastily put together for annual kick-off meetings, that aren't as effective as they should be.

Lack of coordination between interrelated functions resulting in:

Marketing, sales, manufacturing, and creative unsure of their joint responsibilities;

Outside agencies — advertising, display, production houses — given insufficient time to do quality work and in need of constant overtime to meet deadlines;

Manufacturing schedules and costs ignored, poor efficiencies as last-minute mix changes are made to rush a new product to market;

Product-line decisions made too late to purchase the raw materials needed to meet targeted releases;

The sales department lacking firm ship dates for samples or orders;

No packaging, labeling, and shipping cartons for waiting products.

Poor Credibility with customers, trade, field forces, and management because:

Creative doesn't have time to research different approaches to advertising and promotion and just slaps something together;

Prices and terms of trade are an afterthought;

Budgets are too high, the product or pricing isn't right, the product is delivered late, and salespeople can't make targeted commissions;

Product reaches the shelves long after ads appear or competitors' products arrive, so that the competition seizes your shelf space, and customers who can't find your product are frustrated.

A Crisis Management Mode:

Managers are always fighting fires, so they can't plan or get ahead of the game.

DIAGNOSING THE PROBLEM

To appraise a marketing plan, first ask to see it. If it's not in writing, there isn't one — mental game plans don't count.

Second, check the budget for the largest categories of sales and expenditures and those showing the largest increases. Explore the programs behind those categories. If you're lucky, a marketing plan may exist in bits and pieces. If you're unlucky, you'll find that substantial changes in sales or spending (or, indeed, maintenance of existing businesses) are not backed up by programs, estimates, program costs and benefits, or specific individuals responsible. Substantial planned decreases must be "real" and fully documented. The following is a list of key departments and functions to probe, and examples of plan contents for a select few. Appendix III-1 is a complete list of functional plans that should be sought and their content.

Department Functions to Probe

Director of Marketing
    Overall marketing plan
Product Management
    Existing product line
    New products
    Pricing; terms
Wholesale Sales
    Sales
    Distribution
    Promotion
    Sales service
Creative/Advertising
    Media
    Co-op
    Collateral
    Displays
    Retail advertising

Design
    New product design
Market Research
    Market research
    Style-use testing
Retail Operations
    Cycle planning
    New stores
Finance
    Sales analysis
    Financial analysis
Human Resources
    Identified staff changes, reorganization

Examples of Plan Content

Director of Marketing
    Overall Marketing Plan
        A written marketing plan covering key goals for each function;
        A master timetable of critical events, and responsibility for them;
        Way plan is to be communicated and reviewed
Product Management
    Existing Product Line
        Qualitative, quantitative line objectives, strategies;
        Competitive objectives;
        Seasonal product offering, positioning, P&L
Creative/Advertising
    Media
        Creative objectives, strategies, schedule, target market, cost effectiveness
Retail Operations
    New Stores
        Plan for year — number, location, financials, demographics

SOLVING THE PROBLEM

To develop or improve on annual marketing plans, determine what you want the plan to accomplish, its form and content; then define the process you'll use to develop an effective plan.

THE PLAN

Objectives

The plan must establish, for the coming fiscal or marketing season, the quantitative and qualitative objectives, strategies, tasks, and due dates for each marketing function, as noted on page 72. It should list goals and due dates for each nonmarketing function that supports marketing (manufacturing, engineering, outside agencies), preliminary budget numbers, and specific goals and dates for each manager involved.

The planning process also should insure that each function, where necessary, prepares detailed plans to guide execution and that all functions plan to complete their tasks in the required sequence and on time. (It's useless if the sales department plans customer calls for a new product before manufacturing can provide samples.) The plan must incorporate mechanisms to review progress in time to correct potential problems and to flag potential plan deviations, positive or negative.

PROCESS AND CONTENT

There are three kinds of marketing plans, each representing a different level of activity. The *keystone plan* sets marketing's overall goals; the *functional plans* summarize the overall objectives, strategies and tasks of each of marketing's ten to twelve functions; and the *detailed plans* direct and control the weekly and monthly actions of most marketing functions. The hierarchy of marketing plans is shown in Table 4-1. The process of developing the annual marketing plan, discussed fully below, is summarized in Table 4-2.

The Keystone Plan

The marketing director is responsible for the development and implementation of the keystone plan, which consists of three simple parts. First, the *statement of overall objectives* reiterates the business's definition and sets key financial and qualitative goals for the coming year (Table 4-3).

Second, the *key objectives to be accomplished* by each function during the next year, beyond the normal maintenance of the business, come from the strategic plan, the marketing department, and the marketing director. Table 4-4 contains excerpts from a functional plan. Strategic goals are always included in the annual marketing plan and implemented and reviewed along with short-term goals.

Objectives are divided into A (top priority) and B (can defer if need be) to facilitate later elimination of projects and identify those from which resources can be shifted if necessary.

Table 4-1. Planning Hierarchy Overview

Who's Responsible	Plan	Objective
The CEO	Strategic Plan ↓	Sets overall strategic direction for the business 3–5 years out.
Director of Marketing	Keystone Plan ↓	Sets overall strategic, short term objectives, timetables, for marketing 12–18 months out.
Director of Marketing, Department Managers	Functional Plans ↓	Set detailed objectives, strategies, tasks, due dates, for each marketing function 12–18 months out.
Functional Managers	Detailed Marketing Plans	Flesh out functional plan objectives in detail for execution.

Table 4-2. Developing the Annual Marketing Plan

Strategic Plan
    ↓
Keystone Plan

Contains
    Business Definition
    Overall Objectives
      Sales
      Profits
    Overall objectives for each marketing function
    Market and planning cycle (18) months

Who Does
Director of Marketing, with direct reports
  ↓
Functional Plans

Contains
Detailed objectives/strategies/tasks/due-dates/cost/benefits

Who Does
Each functional manager. Consults with other functions/agencies upon whom he or she depends
  ↓
Directors Review

What Happens
Marketing Director reviews functional plans with each submitting department head. Modifies as needed
  ↓

Table 4-2.   Continued

↓
Staff Review

What Happens
Director and staff review, modify, and agree upon functional plans, final market cycle.

Output
Published plan to GM, marketing, nonmarketing support functions
↓
Integration

What Happens
Insure support functions include tasks in support of marketing goals in their annual plan.

Who Does
Director of marketing, his staff, and/or GM with outside functional agencies/departments
↓
Financial Impact

What Happens
Calculate rough budget based on plan

Who Does
Controller, director of marketing
↓
Sell Upstairs

Objective
Get agreement to goals and summary financial impact, preliminary budget
↓
Budget

What Happens
Include financial impact, timing in budget proposal
↓
Individual Goals*

Develop individual goals for all managers and professionals who must execute
↓
Detailed Plans*

What
Develop detailed plans for each function for execution.

Who
Functional Manager
↓
Execute/Review

Do it

Review it

Keep it on track

*These steps may or may not occur in this sequence. See explanation on pages 84–85.

Table 4-3.   1985 Keystone Plan/Overall Objectives

Business Definition

Target Market:	Men and women, 20–49 years old, family income in excess of $25,000; international.
Needs Served:	Superior functional eye protection; classic or contemporary fashion; special features for individual active sport market segments.
Products:	Sunglasses; high ($30 +) pricepoint.
Distribution:	Optical, sporting goods, tourist, high-grade department, general merchandise and catalog sales.
Overall Objectives:	Number one in target market, no less than 60% share.

Sales Objectives

	% Unit Increase 84/85	Units 84; Est. 85	$ 84; Est. 85
Wholesale			
Retail			
Old Stores			
New Stores			
International			
Total			

Profit Objectives

	$ Operating Income 84; Est. 85	% Change 84/85
Wholesale		
Retail		
International		
Division		

Key Qualitative Objectives

Reposition, upgrade basic line

Launch expensive top-of-line collection

20 new stores

Establish effective advertising, yielding 60% brand awareness

Define strategy in better-grade women's market

Define strategy in drug/food/mass-merchandizing markets

Table 4-4.   1985 Keystone Plan Overall Objectives by Function*

Product Management

Product	Pricing/Promotions	New Products
Reposition, upgrade basic line quality	Price to meet competition	Launch expensive top-of-the-line men's collection; $1,500,000 first season sales
Add styles/lenses/materials needed to stay current, lead category	Early season load-in promotion to block open-to-buy	
Prune marginal items	Review wholesale terms (discounts, dating, remerchandising, POS, collateral) to insure competitive, supports goals	

Creative

National Advertising	Co-Op	Collateral	In-Store
Build and sustain #1 awareness of our brand against target audience	Meet reasonable competitive offerings, but minimize	Sales presentation for new men's line and catalog, POS, consumer takeaway	Uniform window displays for each of five market cycles. Supporting in-store point of sale
New national umbrella campaign, focusing on classic style performance quality (print)	Cost no more than 2% whosesale sales	Take-away explaining benefits different styles, lenses; when to use; benefits optical quality (B)	Suggestion book for independent retailers with in-store POS available (B)

Retail Ops	Wholesale Ops	Retail Advertising
In new captive or franchised sunbelt stores $300,000 target volume, 45% GM	Achieve 60% category penetration top 40 SMSAs and target classes of trade within them	Retail advertising goal to pull target customers into own stores. 60–70% seasonal frequency — reach in cluster SMSAs; spending = 6% sales
Develop cycle plan for windows, advertising, sales, featured merchandise	Get in top 10 "class" direct mail catalogs (S) (B)	

Design	Research	International	Organization
Complete design of women's line (S)	Complete style/use/concept testing of women's line; give final recommendations (S)	Establish, test captive stores in Carribbean (S) Europe (S)	Add two regional sales managers
			Add one advertising assistant (B)

Key:
S = Strategic goals from strategic plan.
B = Secondary priorities. All others A.
*Selected. Each function would normally have four–six major objectives.

Third, the *approximate timetable* to be followed for the next 18 months in developing and executing the plan (Figure 4-1) indicates, for the coming year, when plans and budgets are due, when departmental objectives are to be accomplished, and when normal events not included in departmental objectives are to occur. Typical normal events are sales meetings, preparation of advertising campaigns, and the start sell of the new line. A separate timetable would be included for the remainder of the current year.

The realistic keystone plan shown in Tables 4-3 and 4-4, and in Figure 4-1, is based on a hypothetical sunglass company selling through captive retail outlets and independent retailers serviced by a network of wholesalers.

Who prepares it? The keystone plan is best prepared through team meetings, structured like the strategic planning meetings described in Chapter 3, with the marketing director and his or her immediate subordinates. Prior to the meeting, the marketing director distributes a list of proposed numerical and qualitative goals (Table 4-3) and a tentative timetable for the planning process and key events (Figure 4-1). The managers responsible for each function prepare their tentative functional goals (Table 4-4) for circulation before the meeting.

At the planning meetings, which often last several days, participants develop the final plan objectives and programs (including detailed functional goals) and a realistic calendar of events.

Team planning is recommended if the marketing team is willing and able to develop objectives as a team and if the marketing director feels the need for improved communications and team building.

Alternatively, the marketing director can personally write the keystone plan, including tentative functional goals, after consulting with all department heads regarding their overall objectives for the coming year. The plan then is discussed and modified as needed either in a team meeting or individually with each staff member. The resulting keystone plan gives each department sufficient direction to permit development of their detailed functional plan.

This method is less effective than team building because it lacks interplay between functions. It's commonly used when the top marketing team is new and unfamiliar with team planning or by an authoritarian boss who prefers to dictate rather than listen.

With either method, a knowledgeable, goal-oriented marketing director and support staff can quickly assemble a preliminary plan. Consequently, they can spend much of their time in keystone plan meetings tackling thorny new situations or potential problems.

Because planning normally starts six months before plans are to be executed, the standard time period covered by the plan is 18 months. Keystone plans usually are given to nonmarketing functions and outside agencies for help in implementation.

Contingency Plans: Contingency plans, which usually are discussed during development of the keystone plan, are necessary in case of the failure of key marketing programs or changes in the assumptions underlying the plan, such as the level of general economic activity. A critical few contingency plans in skeleton form should address potential error or failure in the company's critical assumptions or high-impact programs. They are incorporated in the functional plans and fleshed out only if needed.

For example, if a major new product launch is critical to next year's plan but the product probably won't be ready in time, two contingency programs might be developed. First, a simpler new product already designed and tooled may be substituted for the late product. Contingency plan action may require only the design of selling, advertising and collateral materials and the stocking of long-lead-time production materials to allow timely launch of the contingency product. Alternatively, promotional programs for existing products may be developed to increase sales and fill the void left by the deferred new product.

The Functional Plans

After general direction is set by the keystone plan, short functional plans for each key function are prepared by the department managers and their staffs for use by the marketing director in measuring their progress. These plans include overall objectives, strategies, tasks, due dates, designation of people responsible for implementation, and rough estimates of cost and potential financial return from each area (usually the incremental return below or above the estimated results for the current year). Table 4-5 is a typical functional plan for new products in a fashion apparel and accessories business with two annual selling seasons.

Before committing to tasks and dates, each manager must consult with other functions or agencies that will execute parts of the functional plan. For a new product line, for example, product management must cooperate with design, market research, engineering, and manufacturing.

Functional plans contain two types of objectives and strategies: *Immediate decisions*, made after careful consideration or detailed analysis during the planning process, are exemplified by the realignment of sales territories based upon a study conducted prior to the planning session, or an agreement on the number of styles to be added to the product line based upon management experience without detailed study. *Deferred decisions*, to be made on future dates established in the plan, occur when objectives cannot be fulfilled because further work is needed to develop adequate strategies.

There are three types of deferred decisions. First, *normal business decisions* regarding maintenance or growth of the basic business that require normal lead time for development of a detailed plan. After the objectives, key strategies, and flight dates for an advertising program are agreed upon, for example, creative must commit to dates for review of detailed creative objectives and strategies,

	January	February	May	June	July	August	November	December
Retail Calendar Retail "On Sale" Dates/ Featured Products	Sale/promo Goods Resort Collection Ski line		tion			Sale	Xmas promo Resort collection Ski line	Complete Budget
Departmental Calendar Overall			Strategic Plan	1986 Keystone Marketing Plan	1986 Functional Plans	Completed Marketing Plan		
Product Management	Ship top of line Ship new items, Basic line	Positioning/product goals for due			Ship special sale goods			
Retail Ops.	Sale ads	Sales Meeting	All stores			Sale ads	local ads promoting featured g	
Wholesale Ops.	Complete sell in 1985 program	Complete sell in 1985 program	Sell fill-ins, Xmas, Ski Plan for territory realignment			Recover Xmas, ski	Continue sell new women's lin Sell in pre-season loader basic line Sell complete 1985 program.	

Figure 4-1.   1985 Abbreviated Keystone Timetable

Creative | Regional Show/Resort Advertising — Campaign — 1985 mechanicals, ski, resort | Creative objectives/ strategies 1986 national retail to agencies | Regional sho resort 1986 mechan

Research | Brand awareness study complete | Mass distribution study complete

Design | Start 1987 design

International

Human Resources | Recruit for Ad. Assistant | Recruit for needed salesmen, sales managers | Test store in place

*A similar timetable is produced for 1984, the remainder of the current year.

Table 4-5.   Typical Functional Plan

1985 New Products, Line Refreshing

	Person Responsible:	John DiMico
Date: 6/1/84	Department:	Product Management

Objectives: Refresh existing line. Strengthen to keep up with style, feature and fashion changes.

Move into new profitable categories as identified and if financially warranted.

Strategy: Semiannual line positioning vs. competition, fashion trends to yield product direction, feature changes, research direction

Implement already identified feature changes needed to upgrade basic product.

Market research for potential new categories

Tasks:

Task	Date/Person	Comments
Basic Line (Operating)		
Ship spring '84	12/15/83	
Positioning for Fall '85	6/15/84	DiMico
Positioning for Spring '86	10/15/84	DiMico
Positioning for new low price line for '85	6/15/84	Dalton
Positioning for Fall '86	6/15/85	DiMico
New Categories (Strategic) Positioning, initial product target market research		
Mid-fashion	4/1/85	DiMico
Fashion-forward	4/1/85	Fashion Consultants, Smith
Continental	6/1/85	Europa Design, Smith

Estimated Impact:

Basic Line: 15–20 of 100 basic styles replaced in '85; 6–8 promo styles added.

New Products: Recommendation on whether or not mid-fashion, forward Fashion, continental make sense for 86/87.

Incremental Financials 1985 over 1984 Est.:

($000)	Sales	Gross Margin	Direct Expense	NPBT	Assets
	3,000	1,800	450*	1,350	750

*Includes samples, research, consultant's fees.

Nonmarketing Functions Involved:

Fashion Consultants: Test sketches, sample designs due to research 10/1/84

Europa Design: Test sketches, sample designs due to research 10/1/84

media options and costs, and mechanicals. Second, *project tasks* often entail detailed study. Although a marketing director may accept the general objective of opening 20 stores with up-and-running sales of $300,000 and 55 percent gross margin, he will certainly demand to see a detailed plan including demographic, strategic, and economic justification for store locations before making lease and construction commitments. Third, *budget-constrained* decisions cannot be made simply because one can't know whether funding will be available for a project until budgets are complete. Advertising experiments and long-term market and strategic research often fall into this category.

In all these instances, each functional plan specifies the overall objective and strategy for the function regardless of the remaining work and establishes firm dates for review of deferred decisions.

Appendix III-1 lists all the one-page functional plans normally required of a combined retail and wholesale marketing department for a company or division with its own manufacturing, financial, and personnel functions.

Director's Review

The marketing director reviews functional plans and additional back-up material with each department manager and determines whether plans from different departments are consistent with one another. This is also the best time to privately counsel managers on improving their plans or incorporating new ideas prior to staff reviews.

Staff Reviews

After functional plans are assembled and distributed to key staff members, a second team meeting is held to resolve any conflicts between departments, ensure that interdependent departments can meet one another's deadlines, and give final approval to overall objectives, functional plans and the 18-month timetable. It is helpful if representatives of support functions such as manufacturing, data processing, engineering, and the advertising agency are present during relevant parts of the review.

Integration

The marketing director or functional managers requiring plan support outside the marketing department should personally touch base with nonmarketing support functions to address their concerns and ascertain that they agree with marketing's goals and can accomplish their assigned tasks.

Financial Impact

The marketing director, assisted by the division or corporate controller, produces a simple quick-and-dirty estimate of the financial impact of the plan. This financial impact statement normally adjusts projected current-year performance for planned changes in sales, margins, prices, and expenses and is accompanied by a sources of change chart specifying which programs or assumptions have what top- and bottom-line impact.

A and B priority programs should be noted in case later cuts are required for strategic or spending reasons. Appendix III-2 shows how a typical plan, including manufacturing, has been turned into a preliminary budget. Connecting the plan with the budget yields good preliminary budget figures and pinpoints areas for modification if goals won't be reached; moreover, it's a powerful tool for selling the plan and the budget because it demonstrates that you've done your homework.

Selling It Upstairs

A well-prepared plan, complete with estimated financial impact, is generally quite convincing to the general manager and, ultimately, the corporation. Although the method of presentation varies from company to company, the thrust of the plan should come as no surprise to the general manager if the marketing director has kept in touch.

Approval of the budget by the corporation should be easy if the numbers are supported by objectives and well-conceived programs with careful financial impact statements. It's those managers who devise the budget first and work out programs later who get into trouble — deep trouble.

Individual Goals

After any budget revisions, functional managers must negotiate the written goals with the subordinates who must execute them. Subordinates then prepare action plans — who must do what, when — needed to accomplish delegated goals. In some organizations, preliminary individual goals are developed prior to or during budget preparation.

Detailed Plans

For many functions, detailed action plans are required to effectively execute functional goals. The VP or director of marketing reviews only the most important of these plans, which typically include:

- *The Sales Plan:* Sales targets and quotas by territory, salesperson, account, and product line by month or selling cycle.
- *The Advertising Plan:* A detailed weekly schedule of ads to be run in various media; expenditures by campaign and month; the production schedule for each campaign from creative strategy through first publication or airing; the collateral schedule from creative strategy through production and shipping.

- *The Product and Product Development Plan:* The number of styles and items to be offered by category and price-point; planned line additions or deletions; detailed product development time-table for additions, including positioning, creative ideas, models, market research, testing, tooling, and manufacture.
- *Retail Sales Plan:* Store product emphasis; window dressing/display; advertising thrust and expenditure; sales quotas; profit goals by store and region, by month or selling cycle.

Appendix III-1 lists the contents of detailed plans usually required.

Though detailed plans are shown as Step 10 of the planning process, they actually are prepared at various times throughout the year. For example, the sales plan probably will precede the budget submission, while the advertising plan will follow it. A detailed plan for opening new, different retail operations may be completed at any time. Because of long lead times involved, detailed new product plans for the coming planning year were probably prepared during the previous year.

Execute/Review

As a result of their day-to-day interplay, the marketing director and his or her staff normally keep the plan on track and fine-tune it as it progresses. There are, however, three types of standard reviews held at the marketing director level.

Regular reviews — one-on-one consultations with each department manager, usually monthly, regarding accomplishment versus goals; also marketing staff meetings to discuss general problems with the plan.

Event reviews — at the completion of a scheduled task such as preparation of the advertising creative proposal.

Total plan reviews — of the director of marketing's staff, sometimes supplemented by non-marketing support functions, normally conducted during a crisis when some or all of the plan is off track or there is a recession or failure of new major product programs. See Chapter 9 for formal controls used to monitor critical plan events.

EARLY WARNINGS

If the marketing director establishes a supportive atmosphere, marketing managers will be encouraged to point out early signs of any failings in the plan. Potential problems should be addressed at the marketing director's regular staff meetings, which usually occur weekly.

MANAGING ON A SHORT LEASH

Marketing programs *do* get into trouble — frequently. It's often because of the failure of major programs, economic downturns or surges, or having allotted too little time to difficult tasks. During such times of crisis, the director of marketing meets with the staff, reviews and revises plans and, if need be, implements back-up plans. Programs should be reviewed weekly until the business is out of the woods.

Table 4-6 is a chart of weekly goals used when revisions of a marketing plan affected other support functions. The goals and accomplishments were reviewed at both the marketing director's and general manager's weekly operations meetings.

Tight control, though generally undesirable, is necessary during times of crisis, particularly when many functions, projects, and rapidly paced decisions are needed to get the business back on course.

WHY DO PLANS FAIL?

The principal reasons for the failure of most marketing plans are as follows:

- Little strategic data to back up key decisions, which leads to unrealistic or incorrect goals.
- Inadequate lead time to prepare and execute a plan to meet management objectives, which tempts managers to overpromise. Long lead time usually is required for new product development and tooling, restructuring of the selling organization or distribution, or hiring and training new people.
- Overcommitment by employees who promise the impossible from a desire to please or excel or from fear of disappointing.
- Underresourced because of typical underestimates of money and personnel needed to do the job. People are reluctant to ask for too much or to lower their financial return, are unwilling to confront problems that cost time and money to fix, and/or are sensitive to a management that stresses doing more with less.
- *a lack of integration* with the operating plans of non-marketing support functions;
- *a failure to communicate the plan* and gain understanding of it by those who must execute it;
- *a lack of follow-up and review* and the making of necessary corrections to the plan.

KEYS TO SUCCESS

The Process

- *Think it out.* Before starting, discuss the planning process with your staff and construct a flow chart of who does what when.

Table 4-6.   Weekly Goals for a Crisis Marketing Plan

	Marketing	Manufacturing	Finance/Planning	Human Resources

Phase I: Critical — 7–14 Days	1. Third-, fourth-quarter promo for Category I, Brand A.
	
	2. Expand direct sell to top 44 customers, all products/promos.
	
	3. Need new 1980 product — Introduction plans and schedules for:
	   New line A
	   New line B
	   Fixed lines C and D.
	
	4. Sales management controls to make second half happen; key account selling general manager, director of marketing, and promotion managers; second-half field quotas; cycle plan.
		1. Bring down broadload — reduce overhead (general manager to give official broadload).
		
		2. Immediately reduce backlog in:
		   Line A
		   Line B
		   Requires schedule.
		
		3. Fix Category VI capacity problem, eliminate backlog, build capacity for product line extension C (requires schedule and plan).
		
		4. Ship style 28.
		
		5. Implement agreed-upon Category A cost-reduction steps immediately.
			1. Redo forecast P&L incorporating all changes in sales and costs agreed upon.
			
			2. Five-year plan Phase I.
				1. Gain approval of marketing changes.
				
				2. Fill critical jobs: Group Production Manager, national sales manager, materials manager.
				
				3. Recommendation on plant team concept.
				
				4. Communications package meeting. Decisions to division personnel.

Table 4-6.   Continued

	Marketing	Manufacturing	Finance/Planning	Human Resources
Phase I continued	5. Program and plan to sell 10,000 of product Z/week.	6. Continue implementation of new engineering inspection and supervision to control variances, excess labor in departments 12 and 17.		
	6. Program and schedule for introduction of new Category VI.	7. Decision on realignment of IE staff; final decision on "team" concept.		
	7. Plan and execution to relaunch — reprice top-of-line style 28, Category VI.	8. Revised IE assignments and cost reduction priorities as a result of Step #7.		
	8. Insure that release schedule is met for remainder of year, Category II: Product 22 (7/7) Product 23 (9/15) Product 27 (10/15). (Requires schedule review.)			

			General Manager

Phase II: 14–28 Days	9. Category IV promo for third and fourth quarter —needs development, review.
	10. Category VI three-year plan to make profit happen; '81 collection; European decision, collection.
	11. Category V sales program ready for '81–'82 sport season.
	12. Audit of retail activity.
		9. Reorder the priorities of the engineering assignments.
		10. Purchasing plan, second half.
			3. Fan out new budgets, review and insure controls are in place to control new targets.
			4. Final standard report format; inventory/ shipping/backlog status of new products.
				1. Proposal for foreign plant.
				2. Far Eastern sourcing.
				3. Other meeting follow-ups:
				   Clear with group vice-president capital approval levels;
				   Clarify what I expect included in capital appropriation requests, pricing approval requests with controller.
				
				   Issue new specifications change procedure after item 15, manufacturing complete.
				
				   Issue new collateral, advertising and field product release guidelines to controller.

Phase III: 28–40 Days, Ongoing Tasks	13. Start direct sell on all Category II products. 14. Strategic decision: Dump/ keep Category III. 15. Trade load-in for Category I for '81; 1981 qualifier plan. 16. New Category I and II new-product schedule and system to make happen; new product early-warning system from Friday afternoon manufacturing meetings.	11. Decide how to handle materials management, forecasting, new product tracking until materials manager–new product planner found; exception reporting; Monday review of broadload; early-warning system, schedule blow-back. 12. Staffing evaluation: Supervision and back-ups; organization seeding. 13. Capacity up to 325,000/ week.	5. Analysis of profitability of Category III business — contribution margin on current line and proposed strategies.	

Plan Development

- *Start early,* right after the strategic plan is submitted and long before budget preparation, so the plan can be considered carefully and background data gathered.
- *Base the budget on the plan* and not vice versa (a sure formula for disaster).
- *Involve all functions,* marketing and nonmarketing, necessary to the success of your plan and its preparation. If manufacturing isn't committed to your delivery dates, it can kill you as surely as a down economy can.
- *Keep "upstairs" informed* so that superiors are familiar with the plan and can make additions.

The Plan

- *Keep the plan short and simple.* Details belong at levels lower than the director of marketing's.
- *Put it in writing,* simply and concisely.
- *Communicate it,* ensuring that everyone involved has a copy and everyone in marketing understands its major thrust.
- *Set A and B priorities* for all goals and projects so staffers know what to emphasize without seeking direction from the top.
- *Don't overpromise,* particularly in high-risk, rapid-change areas; if anything, add slack.
- *Prepare back-up plans* in case of significant downside events.

Execution

- *Review the plan infrequently* except in times of crisis. Aside from enforcing the discipline of reviews (monthly at the director of marketing level, quarterly at the GM level), leave your people alone.
- *Distribute overall goals* to all functions, and see that they're reviewed, understood, revised if necessary, and committed to writing by those who must execute.
- *Check a few lower-level goals* after a few months to see if they've been implemented effectively.
- *Get a firsthand feel* for the plan's progress through informal chats with employees at all levels.
- *Tell your boss* first if there's bad news.
- *Revise if necessary* — don't cling to outmoded ideas.

BASIC PRINCIPLES

- *Always have written plans,* ones that are hard for you or your people to ignore.
- *People won't plan* unless you demonstrate that the planning discipline gets results. Despite complaints about paperwork, don't let them run the business by the seat of their pants.
- *If you wing it,* you're sure to be shot down by someone who plans.
- *Creativity* is increased by formal routinized marketing plans (contrary to popular wisdom). Delegating the routine leaves time for inspiration.
- *A good plan is the best defense* against the overestimates normally produced to placate upper management.
- *Firefighting is inevitable,* even with a plan. Without one, everything is a fire drill.
- *Thick plans* indicate thick thinking. Good plans are crisp, short, and comprehensible.
- *Overcommitment* is to be expected from good people. Cut them back to realistic amounts, timing, goals.
- *Don't shove goals down people's throats.* Otherwise, they'll sabotage the plan and blame you — justifiably.
- *People will work their rears off* if they're involved in developing the annual plans and setting their own goals.

Part IV

FRACTURED PRODUCT LINES

Chapter 5

Positioning Your Products and Profits in the Market

The Problem

The product line is out of date: There are too many items, and not the right items. Unit sales goals are missed, and sales trends underperform the market because the line is unprofitable.

Years ago, when Magnavox ignored the sales shift in television sets from large consoles to small, medium-size, and portable sets, it lost substantial business to Zenith, RCA, and the Japanese.

A major producer of components for sophisticated industrial equipment watched for five years as the competition developed more precise components that would be demanded in volume eight to ten years ahead. The company retained its industry position through a crash development program, but with a much lower share than if it had kept pace with the market.

Timex, as cited earlier, ignored the trend toward electronic and digital watches and slick sports-oriented styling. Its eventual feeble efforts to add trendy new products proved insufficient, and Seiko and Casio dominated the market.

To help you solve or avoid similar problems, this chapter explains how to recognize the symptoms of a failing product line, and pinpoint your specific problems by segmenting the market and then defining your specific target market. Determining why the line is or isn't profitable and where it does or doesn't meet target market needs will help you position your line against the competition.

Establishing realistic volume and profit goals, adding or dropping the appropriate products, and calculating the financial impact of these proposed changes will go a long way toward fixing the problem of a broken product line.

SYMPTOMS OF A SICK PRODUCT LINE

- Loss in reported market share
- Complaints about the line by the sales force and distribution system
- High failure rate of new products or product modifications
- Noticeable decline in sales of traditional best-sellers
- High returns or mark-downs on a new line
- A significant portion of the catalog obsolete early in the selling season
- A drop in inventory turns
- Marked superiority of competitive offerings
- Drastically new directions in style or function taken by competitors

THE CAUSE

All of the above can be blamed on poor or nonexistent professional product management. Specifically, managers often are guilty of building the line haphazardly by relying on only internal opinion or on the personal tastes of product or general managers, influential salespeople or customers, or designers. It is a mistake to copy competitors without evaluating market trends, to play it safe and avoid risks that might produce a competitive edge or, alternately, to whipsaw the line and risk too much through drastic change, thereby losing a traditional market without gaining a new one. Managers sometimes show a lack of objectivity when they deny their errors and refuse to abandon unpromising pet products or projects, and when they refuse either to take remedial action or the financial bath required to purge the line. It takes energy, skill, time, and money to develop the expertise needed to keep a line vibrant. It takes regular procedures to objectively review the product line and answer basic questions regarding external and internal factors affecting performance (i.e., Do we still offer what the customer wants? Do we have a competitive advantage? How can we make more money?)

THE CONSEQUENCES

The obvious consequences of neglecting the line include slow or not-so-slow loss of market position, image, distribution and, ultimately, good internal people, field salespeople, and distribution channels; poor profitability versus what could have been; and a costly rebuilding effort or eventual failure.

SOLVING THE PROBLEM

Table 5-1 charts the analytical steps involved in repairing a sick product line, beginning with:

Table 5-1.   Steps in Fixing the Line

Step	Action
1. Data Collection What information is needed to segment the market, position the line, forecast market and company trends. ↓	Segment the market Collect competitive, market, and internal data

2. Analysis/Goal Setting
 	
What's wrong with our line, goals? What needs changing?
	Complete Analyses
	    Segment and category profit versus goals
	    Price–product
	    Price–margin–volume
	    Product mix
	Re-establish Goals

3. Action Summary
 	
What do we need to change? Why?
	Present
	    New, modified products and SKUs needed, those to be dropped
	    Potential products to explore
	    Cost reduction goals
	    Price changes

4. Profit Analysis How do we profit from proposed changes? ↓	Financial evaluation of all changes
5. Implementation Plans What needs to be done to implement change internally, in the market? ↓	Develop plans for all functions involved — marketing, manufacturing, design, systems
6. GMS Review Does he/she buy the plan? ↓	GM's review of recommendations, implementation programs, P&L
7. Implementation	Execute the plan

DATA COLLECTION

A reasonable amount of internal and external data is necessary to define the market and to perform subsequent analyses. Table 5-2 illustrates the hierarchy of terms that defines and organizes product line data and gives examples from the footwear industry.

Table 5-2.   Terminology

Relationship of Terms	Example
Target Market	
A group of consumers described by demographics, attitudes, that you want as your customer within your business definitions.	*Upscale* men's shoe purchaser 35–55; $40,000 + income in top-50 metro areas. Mental set traditional to continental excluding fashion forward.
Market Segment	
Uniform segments of the target market with common demographics, product needs/attitudes, purchase/shopping habits.	*Traditional:* The conservative dresser who wants traditionally styled shoes.
Product Category	
A uniform group of products serving the market segment based on general styling/ use. There may be many products within a category.	Traditional lace-up shoes.
Product	
A specified product (style) within the segment.	Wing tip, straight tip, plain toe, saddle oxford, etc.
SKU	
The item that the customer buys. Each product may come in a variety of colors, sizes, materials, and prices. An SKU* is a *single* item within the line that the customer buys — a specific style, color, material, and size.	Black wing tip, 9-1/2 D, $130 retail, European calf

*Stock keeping unit. Sometimes called a line item.

Segment and Category Definition

After you've perfected your business definition and identified your target market (Chapter 1), you must divide the market into segments of consumers with a common set of needs and into uniform product categories serving each segment. Table 5-3 breaks down market segments and product categories for a hypothetical upscale men's shoe line.

Each market segment must be separated clearly from other similar groupings of consumers. Segments for fashion products usually are based on differences in taste, fashion orientation, and psychological needs and attitudes. For example, Table 5-3 illustrates how a demographically upscale target market for shoes sep-

Table 5-3.   Segment and Category Definition: Upscale Men's Shoes

Business Definition

Target Market: Professional men 25–55; $40,000 + income; in top 50 metropolitan areas; mental set: traditional to continental (*excluding* fashion forward).

Needs Served: Dress, dress casual, and leisure footwear (*excluding* athletic, outdoor-rugged categories). Customer need for highest quality, fit, service that says "I'm upscale, very successful, have taste."

Distribution: Captive stores, select men's specialty clothing, department, men's and family shoe stores.

Competitive Advantage: Superior quality/durability; brand image; distribution.

Pricing: Top range of each category.

Market Segment Definition

Market Segments Served

   Traditional: Shoes compatible with conservative office, social, and leisure wear. Typically, Brooks Brothers/Paul Stuart type clothing; planned shoe purchases.

   Mid-fashion: Shoes compatible with middle-of-road American designers (Lauren, Klein, Alexander, Halston) and other "crossover" shoes.

   Continental: Compatible with mainstream European designers (Lanvin, Kilgore-French-Stanbury, St. Laurent, Armani, Valentino). Impulse buyer; considers self fashionable, trendy dresser. Shops Barney's or Louis, Boston.

Product Categories, Traditional Segment*

Style	Use Conditions	Typical Style
Lace-up	Office/work/formal social	Wing tip, straight tip, welted (heavy sole) product
Formal slip-on	Office/social	Formal ornamented or unornamented slip-on; welted
Leisure slip-on	Social	Penny loafer, soft, hand-sewn moccasin-toed shoe
Leisure/Outdoor	Around home, outdoor wear, errands	Rugged boot; soft knock-about lace-up; boat shoe

*A similar breakdown would be produced for the mid-fashion and continental segments.

arates into distinct, sometimes mutually exclusive, purchasing segments — traditional (conservative styling), mid-fashion (middle-of-the-road), and continental (European flair).

   Product categories — the types of products sold to a segment — usually are based on style, function, place, or condition of use, and overall price range. As Table 5-3 indicates, both the traditional and continental segments may contain lace-up product categories that include wing-tip shoes for office and formal wear, but styling would differ significantly to complement the consumer's psychological needs, wardrobe, and lifestyle as determined by internal knowledge and market research.

For example, the traditional shoe is durable, looks heavy, substantial, and features rugged construction. It looks as if it could be willed to future generations and says "successful, stable, conservative, good judgment." The continental wingtip looks and is constructed of soft, luxurious materials. The shoe says "I'm with it, creative, and have a live-for-today-with-flair look."

If you can't similarly define your market segments and categories, you need to do some market research. Include focus groups to define segments and develop a hypothesis regarding their buying habits, as well as quantitative research and purchase panels to confirm or refute your hypothesis (see Chapter 1 for market research methods).

Required Data

The sources of information needed for the forthcoming analyses are summarized in Table 5-4 and discussed briefly below.

Competitive information: Through interviews with the wholesale and retail trade, you can learn the identity of your competitors, their prices, terms, often their plans, and obtain samples of their products.

Table 5-4. Sources of Competitive, Market, and Internal Information

	What You Need	Why?	How To Obtain
Competitive	By segment, category and style where possible for top two to three competitors	Allows positioning of your product versus theirs.	Interview key retailers and wholesalers with structured questionnaire to obtain pricing/ literature/future plans.
	# or name top sellers	Pinpoints strong and weak volume areas for competition, your line.	
	Samples/catalogs		Buy product at retail.
	Wholesale/retail pricing		Talk to competitors, ex-employees.
	Retail sales trend		
	Their volume		Pump competitors about plans at shows/ conventions.
	Changes in the line planned		
	What trade likes/ dislikes about product/pricing		Identify competitors and confidants, and cultivate them as a source of information.

Table 5-4.   Continued

	What You Need	Why?	How To Obtain
Market	Current and future sales by segment, category. Sales mix and trend by price point and style. Approximate number SKUs needed by price point and style.	Lets you position your product against the market's future direction. Allows planning of number of styles, products, and items needed.	Interview trade associations. Sales level/mix/trend best obtained from continuing purchase panel. Alternative is sample interviews of trade. Future trends require interpretation of future segment and category fashion, best provided by expert designer. Trade can give opinion of price points, number of styles, SKUs needed.
Internal	Price cost, volume, and margin for every style and SKU in the line. Three-year trend in volume. Forecast product cost if expected to change significantly.	Identify profit winners, losers. Identify current and potential future volume winners and losers.	Internal market and financial data systems, best if computer generated.

Market information: You can best determine current market volume and trend by segment, category, and style through formal consumer panels established for long-term market research (see Chapter 1). Otherwise, sample interviews with key trade members plus intelligent interpretation of internal sales and market data and external fashion trends usually will suffice.

Internal information: Your own firm's data, particularly volume, actual cost and profit margin by product and item, often is the most difficult to obtain. Unfortunately, most data-processing systems are geared to produce financial reports, not marketing information.

ANALYSIS/GOAL SETTING

The following four analyses, based on data recommended above, will pinpoint profit problems and correctly position the line.

Segment and Category Analysis

A profit versus goal analysis for all market segments and for each product category will indicate where you're making money and where you're not. Figure 5-1, a profit analysis for the traditional segment, lace-up shoe category, singles out subdivisions requiring special attention at the product–SKU level and measures profitability by:

> subdividing the category into financial decision-making units (in this case, price range, which is directly related to sales volume, product features, and manufacturing cost);

> establishing or reiterating category volume, profit, SKU, and product sales goals for each subdivision;

> comparing current performance to goal; and

> identifying subdivisions that require increased profitability and volume or decreased manufacturing cost or SKUs.

Price-Product Analysis

Figure 5-2 shows a price–product analysis, often called a product positioning chart, for the traditional lace-up category of the upscale men's shoe market. Market and company offerings are positioned by product style and price versus competition.

The analysis encompasses all styles within the category that are currently on the market, separating existing styles currently marketed by the subject company from products marketed by competitors. Additional information on the chart includes total market volume, volume by price range, relative volume by style within the category, and the market growth trend by style.

From these cold data, one can conclude that the company lacks several significant potential styles; offers too little product in the middle-price point segment ($100–$130), where one finds a high portion of the market volume and an even higher portion of profits; and is potentially cluttering its line with two similarly priced products in two styles (wing tip and straight tip).

Intelligent interpretation: To determine the necessary product changes, the company's strategy versus the competition's must be reviewed. Does it offer superior product at equal prices, equal product at equal prices, superior product at lower prices? Is the line broad or narrow? Is it a style/feature leader or on par with the market?

Segment: Traditional		Category: Lace-up Shoes	

Our Current % Mix: 24%, 10%, 66%

Our % Mix Goals: 20%, 45%, 35%

% Market Unit Volume: 10%, 40%, 50%

$ Retail Price (160, 135, 100, 80)

	Goal	Current Line
V1	= 40,000	25,000
GM	= 60%	60%
SKU	= 20	35
V2	= 8,000	6,000
S	= 2–3	S = 4
V1	= 90,000	10,000
GM	= 55%	27%
SKU	= 35	45
V2	= 8,000	5,000
S	= 5–7	S = 2
V1	= 75,000	68,000
GM	= 40%	40%
SKU	= 20	35
V2	= 25,000	8,000
S	= 3	S = 3

Goal

Overall Goals

    Category Units   205,000

    Gross Margin   50%

Market

    Average Growth – 7% P.A.

    (units)   1985–1987

Key

V1 = Minimum volume for price range

GM = Minimum gross margin percentage

SKU = Maximum SKUs per style

V2 = Minimum volume per style

S = Maximum # styles

Interpretation

$135–$160:   SKUs must be reduced. Drop 1–2 products.

$100–$135:   Area of greatest opportunity. Too many SKUs. Average sales per style too low. Too few styles. Need look at pricing/cost reduction to raise unacceptable margins.

$80–$100:   Overall, OK.

Figure 5-1.   Category Profit Analysis; Goals

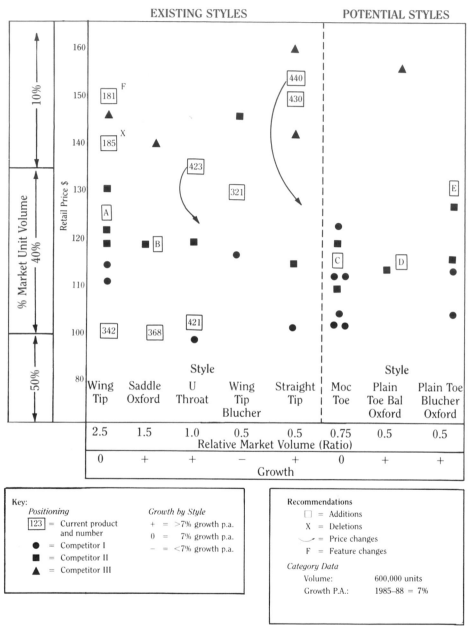

Figure 5-2.   Price–Product Analysis (product positioning) Category: Traditional Lace-ups

Note: This analysis is best presented by overlaying transparencies. First show and explain the axis, then sequentially show your current position, that of each competitor and the recommended changes.

The company's offerings must be compared physically with samples of competitive products. At the same time, management must decide on strategic actions such as adding, dropping, or repricing products; changing materials or features; and injecting new creative design thrust. These decisions usually are reached at positioning meetings attended by product management, design, sales, and manufacturing; results are reviewed by the marketing director and general manager.

Figure 5-2 indicates some of the product and pricing changes in the traditional lace-up shoe line recommended under a blanket strategy of offering a broad line covering most styles with quality and features equal to or better than competition's; pricing equal to competition's; and stressing brand image as the principal competitive advantage. These changes will be consolidated with the results of other analyses in the upcoming action summary.

Three cautions: First, when positioning against competitors, try to forecast their status when your line changes are introduced. Second, note that this analysis simply positions what you have versus what they have and demonstrates where you should be to implement your competitive strategy. It does not test new concepts and products against the target market to help you develop the line significantly beyond competition or radically alter your product strategy. Third, price changes shown here are made to meet competitive price points and may not be an appropriate move (value pricing is explored in Chapter 8). The chart does not indicate whether or where you can make money.

Price–Margin–Volume Analysis (PMV)

The price–volume–margin analysis, which focuses on profitability at the individual product level, will lead to recommendations on products to be dropped, price changes, the future of questionable products, and candidates for cost-reduction programs. Table 5-5 shows a simplified analysis, including recommendations, of several of the shoe styles presented in Figure 5-2 that are slated to remain in the line at unchanged prices.

Product Mix Analysis

At this point, you know how your products should be positioned against competition, which new products to add or drop, and which products are meeting profit goals.

Every product is produced in a number of line items or SKUs: a single suit style comes in a variety of sizes, fabrics, and colors; a single wattage resistor comes in numerous tolerances and resistances; a single one-purpose chemical may come in 25 to 30 slightly different formulations applicable to different manufacturing processes; a single shoe style commonly is offered in two to three colors, three to five widths, and seven sizes, yielding 50 to 100 SKUs. Now, you need to determine how much money you're making on *each* item. The product-

Table 5-5.   Price–Margin–Volume (PMV) Analysis 1985, by Style

Style	Retail Price	Wholesale Price	Manufacturing Cost	Gross Margin			Unit Volume ('000)		SKUs		
				$	%	Goal %	Actual	Goal	Actual	Target	Competition
181	$150	$68	$37.40	$30.60	45%	60%	8	6	40	20	15–25
430	150	68	27.20	40.80	60	60	5	6	35	10	15–25
321	130	62	39.60	22.32	36	55	2	8	45	35	25
421	100	48	29.76	18.20	38	40	16	25	35	20	15–20

Interpretation

Style	Cost	SKUs	Pricing	Other Comments
181	Reduce by $10.20/unit	Reduce by 20	Consider $5 retail increase	Use of unnecessary exotic materials and hand work inflating cost.
430	OK	Reduce by 15	OK	
321	Reduce by $11.70/unit	Reduce by 10	Same as 181	Same as 430 above, plus has features not needed to compete at price point.
421	OK	Reduce by 15	OK	

mix matrix in Figure 5-3 illustrates the profitability and volume of each item in one style of the shoe line under consideration.

Because 70 percent of the items fall below acceptable profit and volume levels, they must be dropped; improved in profit and volume through sales campaigns, price increases, or cost reductions; or, rarely, kept if there is a good strategic reason for doing so. One might maintain a loser when it's absolutely necessary to keep a key customer whose overall business is profitable; when the item is expected to sell profitably at high volume in the future; or when it's a "showcase" product that won't sell but will be displayed and talked about. Typically, 70–80 percent of the volume and profit from a *poorly* managed line comes from 20–30 percent of the SKUs.

For a fashion business relying on service and thus offering a wide selection of styles, colors, and materials, a healthier mix would be 60–70 percent of the profit from 60–70 percent of the SKUs. The remaining 30 percent of the SKUs (which should be at least reasonably profitable) may be required for a full-service upscale supplier or to serve regional needs. Because inexpensive lines often compete primarily on price, the consumer does not expect the selection, service, and brand image associated with expensive lines. Consequently, inexpensive product lines generally are narrow (fewer products per category) and shallow (fewer SKUs per product style). Their lower profitability, moreover, makes it impractical to manufacture, inventory, and sell a large number of SKUs.

A Case History: A well-known manufacturer of fashion accessories recently dropped 35 percent of its SKUs after completing a mix analysis. As a result, delighted retailers could support the same sales level with less inventory. Without short, inefficient runs of low-volume products, manufacturing efficiencies rose by 8–10 percent. Manufacturing cost also decreased because of reduced set-up and run-in time and operator training losses (expenses normally incurred when products are changed on the assembly line). Raw material inventories were reduced by one-third because fewer variations were needed to support the line, and volume didn't suffer at all.

It's too easy to catch "item-itis" and casually add SKUs to a line without questioning their profitability or volume potential. Don't do it! It only leads to product proliferation, high costs, low profits, and high markdowns or write-offs on slow-moving items. Set logical maximum SKU goals for each category and product and stick to them. If you add one SKU, drop another.

How Many SKUs Do You Really Need? Let the market tell you, keeping in mind that everyone wants infinite choices. For each product, compare what you offer versus the competition. Consider the volume it will generate with what your customers say they need against your fully burdened (with fixed overhead allocations) and incremental profit. Then choose.

Generally, low- and high-priced products should carry fewer SKUs than midprice, reasonable-volume products. High-priced items don't have the needed vol-

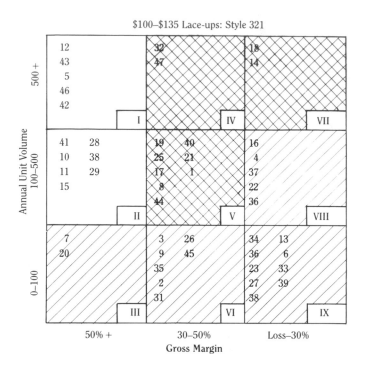

$100–$135 Lace-ups: Style 321

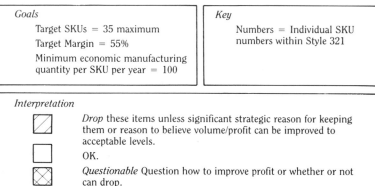

Goals	Key
Target SKUs = 35 maximum Target Margin = 55% Minimum economic manufacturing quantity per SKU per year = 100	Numbers = Individual SKU numbers within Style 321

Interpretation

☑   *Drop* these items unless significant strategic reason for keeping them or reason to believe volume/profit can be improved to acceptable levels.

☐   OK.

☒   *Questionable* Question how to improve profit or whether or not can drop.

Average profit on OK plus Questionable products is shown by detailed analysis to be approximately 48%. Modest price increases or decreases in cost can help line achieve target margin.

Financial Recommendation

1. Keep 20 SKUs in quadrants I, II, IV, V.
2. Cost reduce seven SKUs in IV, V.
3. Drastically improve margins in VII or drop.
4. Drop the rest (III, VI, IX, VIII).

Figure 5-3.   Product Mix Analysis

ume; low-priced items aren't profitable enough to sustain deep inventories. If you're not making or don't expect a substantial *incremental* profit contribution from an item — much less a fully burdened profit — it shouldn't be in the line.

Re-establish Goals

The prior analyses permit resetting of overall product line goals including the product categories that you will participate in and your marketing strategy for each. You then can decide which products will be needed to beat competition, at what price point (as in Figure 5-2), and what your sales volume, gross margin, number of products and SKUs offered should be by price range (as in Figure 5-1).

ACTION SUMMARY

Recommendations: Though the analyses above appear complicated, the recommendations they yield can be simply summarized and presented by a market analyst. Table 5-6 provides a practical format and gives recommendations based on the four analyses presented in this chapter.

Decisions: Determining changes to be made involves intensive work by marketing, product development, and manufacturing functions. The critical questions usually include:

- Can we make cost reductions or increase prices?
- If prices must rise to compensate for cost deficiencies, how much will market share and volume suffer?
- Can unprofitable or marginal SKUs be dropped without harming volume or image? (Usually yes).
- Can product modifications be made or new products developed in time?

Three steps remain before decisions are implemented: proposed line changes must be tested with the trade or consumer; P&L impact on line-change decisions must be forecast; and the final program must be reviewed with the general manager of the business.

Testing: This occurs after the revamped product line is pruned and repriced and samples are available. Though consumer testing generally is unnecessary if line fixes involve only price and minor product changes and deletions, testing with trade and key internal people is necessary. You should prepare a presentation of the revised line complete with pricing, SKU structure, and competitive product and pricing for comparison. Present alternatives — one style variation vs. another, for example — when you haven't reached firm conclusions on a particular product. To ensure adequate time and attention, interview knowledgeable sales representatives, wholesalers, and retailers in a central location, preferably your headquarters. Schedule *individual* interviews, and use a standard questionnaire administered by an objective market researcher, thereby eliminating bias and the

Table 5-6.   Action Summary

Change	Why	Source of Recommendation
Deletions		
Style 185	Similar to Style 183, close in price point. Don't need two in same price range.	Product Positioning Chart (Figure 5-2)
Modifications		
Style 181	To maintain price point, requires upgrading in leathers, finish.	Product Positioning Chart (Figure 5-2)
Style 321	As above.	
Style 440	Must reduce cost, using lower grade materials to meet new price point.	
Price Changes		
Style 423 ⎱ Style 440 ⎰	Reductions needed to be competitive. 423 from $135 to $125. 440 from $150 to $125.	Product Positioning Chart (Figure 5-2)
New Product Additions		
A, B, C, D, E	Adequate volume. Needed to meet competition.	Product Positioning Chart (Figure 5-2)
Products to be Explored		
Style 321, SKUs number 32, 47, 18, 14, 19, 25, 17, 8, 44, 40, 21, 11	Do not meet profit goals but show adequate volume. Should find way to increase profit or consider dropping.	Product Mix Analyses (Figure 5-3)
Cost Reduction Goals		
Style 181	Reduce cost by $10.20/unit or raise price. ⎞ ⎬	PMV Analyses (Table 5-5)
Style 321	Reduce cost by $11.70 or raise price. ⎠	
All $100–$135 shoes	Profits low, costs high. Need to know why, establish profit-improvement program.	Category Profit Analyses (Figure 5-1)
Items to be Added/Dropped		
Style 321 — Drop SKU numbers 7, 20, 3, 9, 35, 2, 31, 26 , 45, 34, 36, 23, 27, 30, 13, 6, 33, 39, 16, 4, 37, 22, 36	Insufficient volume or profit. Drop unless strategic reasons to keep.	Product Mix Analyses (Figure 5-3)

herd instinct characteristic of groups. Afterwards, debate final changes with small groups of salespeople, internal people, and customers. This is especially useful if uncertainty remains regarding recommended actions or you need input on implementation of your line changes.

In addition to the above tests, technical and industrial products often require significant use and technical testing.

Once the line is correctly positioned, subsequent seasonal testing of changes can be accomplished inexpensively and collectively by a handful of sales and marketing personnel at headquarters or by a few knowledgeable retailers and wholesalers in the field.

PROFIT ANALYSIS

Before implementing changes in the line, calculate their impact on:

- Sales (increased by new products and pricing, decreased by deletions);
- Margins (increased or decreased depending on the direction of price changes and cost);
- Costs (decreased by elimination of products, features and SKUs, reduction of carrying charges on lowered inventories, but increased by one-time write-offs of obsolete finished goods, equipment, raw materials, and expenses for new product development, added product features and increased SKUs);
- Depreciation (increased by new equipment, decreased by write-off of old); and
- Assets (raw materials and finished goods inventories increased by product additions, decreased by fewer SKUs of both).

Then calculate the effects on incremental net profit before tax, return on assets, and cashflow, as well as the payback and internal rate of return on any investments. Perform calculations for at least three years to forecast the running profits rate after the first year's extraordinary expenses. This will show whether and when adequate profitability is achieved and the true average return on assets.

A life-of-the-line P&L statement, usually over three–five years, should be done for long-lived product lines and those requiring major changes in assets.

Compare projections for the repositioned line with established goals using the format shown in Figure 5-1.

IMPLEMENTATION PLANS

Implementation may be short and simple if there are few changes in the line, or complex and time-consuming if it's a line relaunch involving many changes.

Table 5-7 summarizes the internal and external factors to be considered in developing implementation plans. It is extremely important to allow adequate time for execution of changes in each functional area. Be especially careful in explaining the benefits of change to consumers and the trade and in coordinating activities by various internal functions.

Table 5-7.   Internal and External Factors Affecting Product Line Changes

Internal

Manufacturing

Time to make new products
Time to build needed inventories
Availability of "old" product until discontinued
Cost of new product
Lead time in acquiring tooling, new raw materials
Disposition of obsolete materials

Design

Cycle time from decision to finished goods
Time to use, style tests
Samples for decision reviews, salespeople

Marketing

Preparation of sales pitch/plan
Customer introduction program
Collateral material availability
Packaging — availability, design, test
Disposition of obsolete merchandise
Trade — consumer tests required

Services

Computer systems for pricing, order entry, warehousing, and training of sales
service personnel

Technical

Technical, materials, environmental, use tests

External

Trade

Timing of introduction to gain acceptance
Benefits to be sold (volume, inventory turns, profit)
Return/disposition of obsolete product
Special terms to propel the change

Consumer

Advising them (as appropriate) of changes and their benefit
In store, POS
Advertising
Promotions
Special incentives to try/examine the refurbished line

Though he or she should be aware of anticipated changes, the general manager usually reviews final plans. Table 5-8 is a review format that can be covered in four to eight hours for a typical fashion product line.

KEYS TO SUCCESS

- *Establish firm line goals,* including profit and volume by product and SKU, based on what's marketable, profitable, and competitive. Challenge products that don't meet minimum hurdle rates.
- *View the line as having a one-year (or one-season) life span;* it must be justified, item by item, annually.
- *Routinize product-line decisions* by establishing an annual or seasonal procedure for careful line analysis and change.
- *Don't authorize lower-level people to give final approval* for price or product changes that they're too inexperienced to decide.
- *Don't ignore peripheral changes* in packaging, customer service, computer programs, advertising, catalogs, etc. The smallest omission, such as a price tag, can cause mass confusion.
- *Base all line changes on the four fundamentals:* what the market wants; what your competition is doing; your stated stratgy; and your defined volume-profit-product line goals.
- *Think ahead* when analyzing the line. Base decisions on the probable situation when your new line hits the market, not on what you see today.
- *Bite the bullet on losers* or products that don't quickly meet profit-volume goals. Otherwise, you'll ultimately write off a backlog of useless products and materials and generate customer ill will.
- *Test changes* in the line, at least with internal people and the trade. Consumer acceptance tests are recommended if changes are drastic; environmental, safety, and use tests are necessary if new materials, construction and performance depart from proven practice.
- *Keep in personal touch with the market* to detect early changes in the business, categories and products. Don't rely on the king's messenger or written reports.
- *Don't become too market-oriented* — keep an eye on the customer and competition, the other on profits. Don't change the line for market purposes if the changes won't boost the bottom line.
- *Don't succumb to short-term pressures* to inflate profits by neglecting to clean up the line. Add products to fill gaps, and maintain quality when reducing costs.

Table 5-8.   Suggested Agenda for Top Management Review of Line Change

Where We Are

Review of business definition, strategy

Goals

Business goals (quantitative, qualitative) now and future

Market Segmentation — market segment and target audience categories, products offered

Category and product goals — profitability, volume, assets, SKUs

Historical performance versus goal

Show and Tell

Physical comparison of old versus new line including styles, price, features, expected volume, SKUs, and profit goals.

Examination of rejected old product, rejected new product ideas, and selected new product along with test results and competitive products

Review of action summary (changes to be made)

P&L

Impact of recommended changes

Comparison to goals

Implementation Plan

All elements, plus timing

Go/No Go

Sign off on plan or alterations to be made, information to be gathered before final decision

BASIC PRINCIPLES

Internal Opinion

- Inside the company, most talk about the line is history. Listen, but don't believe it unless it's confirmed by objective analysis.

Line Changes

- Over time, one-third of any line can be junked without negative effect.
- A narrow line is almost always better for everyone from manufacturer to customer.
- There rarely is strategic justification for retaining a product that is unprofitable or doesn't meet profit goals.

- Gaining a competitive advantage through repositioning and product development is hard. It requires your best people and a lot of money, work, and implementation time and it's worth it.
- Marketers always focus too heavily on the product. Though the supports needed for successful change — including distribution changes, selling programs, advertising, and promotion — often are more important than the line itself; they're frequently an afterthought.

Costs
- When making line changes, marketing capriciously will jerk around manufacturing, purchasing and inventories unless it's held accountable for the cost or lost profits.
- The total cost of a line change (write-off of finished goods or raw material inventories, inventory build-up) is rarely forecast. It must be.
- Actual manufacturing costs always are substantially higher than preliminary estimates.

Testing
- Line changes usually are tested with buddies or vocal members of the company or trade. This is easy, comfortable, and conducive to poor decisions.
- The tough, time-consuming, required product tests — for use, safety, consumer acceptance — often are ignored because they take time and money and delay programs.

Implementation
- Once the need for change is recognized, everyone overcommits to a fast fix, and everything inevitably is late — especially manufacturing in delivering product and marketing in delivering advertising, promotion, and selling materials.
- Marketing and sales don't consider how to explain effectively the benefits of line changes to the customer on the customer's terms.

Tracking
- Keeping a newly positioned line clean is especially tough unless the process is routinized and the general manager demands quantitative measures of the line's content and success. An annual or seasonal line review by the top manager is critical.
- Most people don't — but should — quantitatively track the performance and market positioning of their lines *between* scheduled reviews.

Part V

FALTERING NEW PRODUCTS

Chapter 6

Finding the Causes of Failure

The Problem

You have no new products. Your new products are poorly timed or simply fail. Innovative competitors grab new product opportunities; you don't. Your industry position shrinks as your product line remains static.

After massive investment in R&D and market development, for example, a major electronics manufacturer launched an exotic new computer terminal. When the terminal was predictably outclassed by competitive entries, losses were heavy.

A men's clothing line under the name of an internationally known designer came out late in a saturated market. Moreover, the designs were inappropriate for the target market; cost overruns were extensive; and early warnings by sales management were ignored. The line flopped embarrassingly after a lavish national roll-out.

An important consumer packaged goods firm lost significant market position by neglecting necessary innovations in "standard" categories such as soaps, detergents, and toothpaste, which require constant refreshment to maintain historical profits.

A pace-setting new fashion accessory meticulously tested by a Fortune 500 company met its sales objectives yet failed miserably at the bottom line.

This chapter considers the symptoms and causes of ineffective new product programs, provides diagnostic tools, and offers solutions to a wide variety of new product problems.

115

WHAT'S A NEW PRODUCT?

For the purposes of this chapter, a new product or product line represents:

A major change in direction for your firm, such as a major new product or collection of products in a category new to your company but related to your business definition (i.e., IBM's entry into the personal computer market).

A significant change in your current product offering, such as seasonal changes in fashion lines or periodic changes in automobile styling, engine, suspension, and interior decor. Such new products, which are needed to keep a line up-to-date, invariably entail substantial changes in styling, materials, function, or performance, and they sometimes also require new manufacturing processes and distribution channels and large expenditures for product development and new assets.

A new product is *not* an old product with trivial changes. We are *not* considering products produced through diversification into an entirely different business (i.e., entering the personal computer business from a base in scientific instruments) or an occasional minor new product added to complete a category or update the line.

SYMPTOMS

Organizations that require either an organized new-product program or drastic improvement in existing ones display the following characteristics:

- **Product line not competitive** because *the line is outmoded,* overpriced, deteriorating in quality, and missing critical categories, features, and styles; *the line is churned,* a high percentage is replaced each season, thereby annoying customers and rendering raw materials and finished goods inventories obsolete; there are *no new products* that produce significant sales or profits; there are *too few new products,* compared with competition; *the line missed the market* when the trade disapproved or only a small market segment responded.
- **Costs high and/or unpredictable** because of: *lack of control* when new and in-line product costs continually miss forecast and usually go up; *severe product dilution* due to substantial returns of unsalable product and to quality/performance failures; *cost overruns* involving new product lines that succeed in the market but fail at the bottom line; *sawtooth resource loading,* when critical tooling, engineering, and specification departments are either drastically overworked or idle.
- **Profit goals missed** for new products; failures dilute profits from healthy lines.
- **Stale new products** look like knock-offs of everybody else's line or compete with products in the company's own line; marketable new decorative, mechanical, or technical features are absent — or provided by competitors.
- **Great new concepts fail** because somewhere along the execution chain (design, production, cost, distribution, marketing) a critical link was broken.

- Introductions drastically delayed because of: *missed dates,* usually attributable to engineering and manufacturing; *delayed programs* that damage credibility with senior management and the trade; *technical failures* of safety and environmental tests that can delay a potentially high-profit product for years.
- Inadequate distribution ensures that popular new products fail to achieve expected volume.
- Poor service for in-line products when new products are introduced; stockouts are common for popular new items.
- Low morale in the new product organization, where frustrated employees complain of overwork, too much firefighting, and unclear priorities.

PRIMARY CAUSES OF NEW PRODUCT FAILURE

- The basic business isn't put to bed. The diversion of managerial and technical staff from new product projects because of problems in the company's basic business results in delay and failure.
- Top management lacks a marketing orientation and consequently doesn't react quickly enough to competitive moves or changes in target market needs.
- Goals and plans for new products are missing or they're unrealistic considering the category's life cycle, competition, and available resources.
- No management process for steering new products through the white water of internal development, production, launch, and sustained market and financial success.
- Poor analytical tools for making product, marketing, financial, and investment decisions.
- The organization is inadequate because it's poorly organized or understaffed or its employees lack relevant technical and managerial skills.

SECONDARY CAUSES

- *Management:* A general manager anxious to produce results imposes an over-ambitious new product schedule and demands more sophisticated products than the current organization can produce. Fearful lower-middle management commits to too much too soon. Communication is poor between upper and lower management and between functions at all levels.
- *Decision making:* Most decisions are made at the top with little contribution from the appropriate lower levels. Communications are particularly poor between creative design, product management, and product engineering, which are traditional areas of conflict.
- *Goals:* They're too high and change too frequently; results are expected too soon. Priorities are unclear between new and ongoing businesses and between individual new product projects.

- *Staff:* Mediocre people and low performance standards are too often tolerated for too long. Key functions are ignored at the inception of a project; product and process engineers often, given inadequate notice, are unable to develop a manufacturing process for a product proposed by creative design.
- *Market research:* There isn't any! There's no definition of the target market, new product objectives, positioning, and no trade, consumer, or competitive testing. Top management won't allocate money for necessary data. Arbitrary decisions are made at low levels to launch new products based upon personal taste, short-term fad, or a desire to fill the catalog.
- *Marketing and sales:* Marketing's forecasts of sales volume and mix are inadequate or inaccurate. The marketing function is inexperienced; its planning horizon is a mere six months, and it reacts to competitors rather than plowing new ground. The sales force is unprepared to sell new products because of poor training in selling techniques and in new-product features, benefits, and terms; few sales aids such as audio-visual presentations; no collateral advertising and display packages for the trade; and no specific compensation for success.
- *Design and product development:* Designers, out of touch with the marketplace and disdainful of marketing's needs, often merely copy other firm's designs. Product specifications are unclear. Design, product and process development, and model shop personnel are unfamiliar with the latest new technologies.
- *Performance standards:* Established standards and procedures for laboratory and field testing of product performance, mechanical integrity, quality, and safety no longer apply to new high-technology products. Consumer fit, wear, and use tests, for example, are conducted haphazardly, if at all.
- *Manufacturing and process development:* Substandard process development skills and insufficient time result in delays, failures, cost overruns, and inability to develop cost-effective manufacturing techniques. Inadequate manufacturing methods and early release of a product or process before costs, yields, and quality are proven leads to high costs and delays for repair and redesign; this in turn leads to low profits, late shipment, stock-outs of key items, and customer dissatisfaction. Failure to track the status of critical materials results in late deliveries and delays in product release; unreasonable turnaround times allowed vendors also contributes to delays.
- *Control:* There is no single neutral function responsible for tracking the development, sales or profitability of new products against plan.

SOLUTIONS

Fixes for the aforementioned new product problems appear in Appendix IV-1 to equip you with an understanding of symptoms, causes, and potential solutions and barriers to consider during diagnosis. Once the problems have been identified, the fixes usually are obvious. For example, the remedy for an outmoded line (Appendix IV-1) is to reposition it versus competition and doublecheck your product strategy as suggested in Chapter 4. The solution for being in poor distribution channels is to research new potential channels and design introductory packages to enter those that will pay.

Unfortunately, solutions that are simple in principle often are difficult to execute because of the time, expense, and changes in organizational behavior and personnel required. Repositioning a product line involves both rigorous planning by marketing, product development, and sales personnel who may not be trained for the task, and the expense of market research, redesign, tooling, manufacturing, and relaunching of the revised line. Installing new financial controls may require only a few manually generated reports or complicated, expensive, and time-consuming changes in financial reporting and data processing systems. Therefore, it is crucial that you carefully diagnose the problems specific to your organization to insure that you focus on the barriers to an effective new product program; limit the problems you address to the critical few; propose fixes that can be realistically achieved by the organization and its people; plan execution in detail; and set a realistic pace.

DIAGNOSIS

The process suggested for diagnosing specific new product problems refers to faulty systems that must be redesigned from the bottom up. If your problems are simple or narrowly defined, follow only the relevant steps in the process, which is diagrammed in Figure 6-1.

Problem Definition and Direction

The top managers responsible for new product development, usually the general manager and his or her direct subordinates, must agree on the objectives of the diagnosis and on who will tackle the problems. An interactive top-team meeting, including the general manager, his or her staff and key marketing, product development and manufacturing personnel, is recommended for addressing the following issues:

- What do we think is wrong with our new product programs? (What's *really* wrong may surface only after probes of the organization and the marketplace.)
- What are we getting from the programs?
- What should we be getting? Why?
- How can we determine what we're doing right and wrong?
- What potential solutions should we examine?

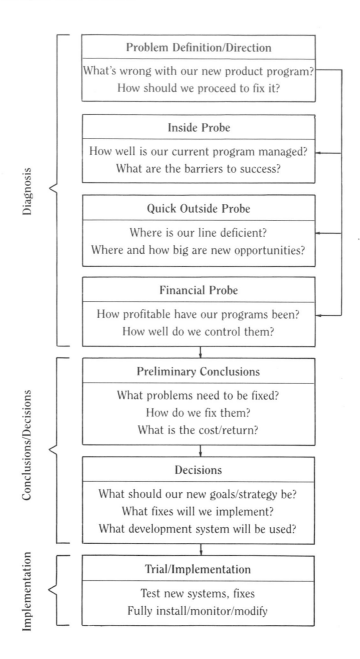

Figure 6-1.   Steps in Diagnosing and Fixing New Product Problems

Because solutions are apt to involve multiple business functions, new product problems should be identified and solutions suggested by a "new products team" composed of seasoned representatives of manufacturing, marketing, finance, product development, engineering, and organization development/human resources. The marketing representative, who often has the most balanced viewpoint, should lead the team.

An alternative to an internal team is an outside consultant or inside individual. This option, however, usually is less effective because teams bring a broad range of functional expertise to bear on problems, know which fixes will work within the organization, and personally are committed to make their recommendations succeed.

Consultants or knowledgeable outsiders are useful supplements to internal teams as sources of new ideas or skills, as objective observers, and as organization specialists who suggest ways of improving team effectiveness.

Data Collection

The new products team should administer three probes required for diagnostic purposes: an inside probe of internal problems, an outside probe of problems and opportunities in the marketplace, and a financial probe to assess the financial performance of previous new product programs.

Inside Probe: This investigation is designed to determine what new product programs have succeeded or failed and why; establish how key new product decisions currently are made; judge the quality of those decisions; and generate ideas for improving the organization and its development system. Consequently, the following questions must be answered:

GENERAL	What do we do or have we done well? Poorly? Why?
	What are the general internal barriers to success in new products? What has blocked specific programs?
GOALS	What are our new product goals?
	How were/are profit, spending, and sales goals for new products set?
	What other criteria (such as target market, distribution channels, potential share of market) are used to select potential new products for development and gauge their success or failure?
OVERALL PERFORMANCE	To what extent have we met our new product goals, financially and in the market place? Where have we failed? Why?
DECISION MAKING	Where, how, when, and by whom are critical, ongoing new product decisions made — initiating a project, approving designs, approving P&L forecasts, tooling, production, launches, etc.? Where should they be made? What analyses are used to make critical decisions?

	What is the quality of decision making? What percentage of key decisions were right? Wrong?
	How good is the linkage between marketing, manufacturing, sales, design, and development.
ORGANIZATION	What functions/people are strong? Weak? Missing?
	What changes in organization, people, assets, spending, management, thinking, and skills, are necessary?
PLANNING/CONTROL	Are there written plans, overall or by project? How are they controlled, reviewed, revised?
	What systems insure that a project stays on track and flag potential deviations from schedule?

Any delicate aspects of the internal probe, such as organization, general barriers to success, and decision making, are best conducted confidentially by a neutral outside party from human resources or by an outside consultant responsible to the new product team. Questions should be phrased to obtain even the most sensitive information, and results should be summarized to conceal sources and discreetly report on personnel issues. This probe is similar to the one used for strategic planning that's described in Chapter 3.

Members of the new product team can determine the correct process for developing new products and consider problems in each functional area. Individual team members usually design and conduct the probe in their own areas of expertise; engineering addresses new product design, finance addresses control, design, creative design, etc.

The team should question a sample of personnel from *all* business functions and levels (from hourly workers to top management) who may have relevant insights.

Quick Outside Probe: The outside probe, which judges the effectiveness of your current new product programs in the marketplace and how you can capitalize on available opportunities, should incorporate the following questions:

PERFORMANCE	How well do we meet the consumer/trade's need for new products?
	What's been good or bad about our new products and the way that they've been introduced to the trade and consumer?
COMPETITION	How do we stack up to our competitors' product innovations, sales rates, profitability, and ability to meet market needs?
	Which competitors do an especially good job in developing/ introducing new products? How? Why?
OPPORTUNITIES	What opportunities are open to us? How big? Single products? Category or line extensions?

How can we more effectively identify market needs and product concepts and judge their worth?

Who are the trend-setters — manufacturers, designers, retailers, and consuming segments to watch in order to spot new product trends and ideas early?

DECISION MAKING

What role does/should the trade and consumer play in the new product development process?

CONSUMER
PERCEPTION

Where does the consumer see us fitting into the market compared to the competition?

What is our brand awareness; our image in comparison to the competition's?

What consumer needs do we meet/do not meet compared to the competition? How can we profitably improve?

What sales, advertising, presentations work?

This probe should be directed by the team's marketing representative and structured and run by a professional market researcher. Techniques for eliciting information from outside groups include field interviews of knowledgeable trade members and industry experts, interactive trade panels and focus groups, quantitative surveys, telephone or in-depth personal interviews with current or potential target customers. Occasionally, outside experts can be invaluable in spotting keys to new product success and pointing out long-term opportunities.

Financial Probe: The financial probe determines your financial status and prospects and the appropriate systems for controlling the development process. It should answer these questions:

DETAILED PERFORMANCE

What was our total financial return on new products and major projects? Which were winners or losers?

What was our track record on the number of new products launched per year? What percent succeeded or failed financially and in the market?

SPENDING

How much did we and will we spend on new products, by department and type of expenditure?

Where and why have there been spending inefficiencies?

How can we increase efficiency?

Where have funds been insufficient to do the job correctly?

POTENTIAL
PERFORMANCE

Based on internal opinion, knowledge of competitive performance, and the performance of our winners, what should our financial return and profit volume be?

CONTROL

What and how effective are our systems for tracking and controlling new product development costs? Post-launch performance?

The financial probe, which should be conducted by a skilled financial analyst, begins with a numerical audit of the costs of getting to market and the subsequent return from each new product program over a number of years. To find the total cost of and return from the program and its percentage of winners, the audit should include new product attempts killed in R&D, aborted at prototype, launched but failed, and launched and successful. Despite the high financial return from winners, when you add the numbers for winners, losers, and those that never reached the starting line, you may find that new product programs are net losers.

The probe next identifies new product development spending rates and staffing by cost center and function and reveals inefficiencies, slack or overstressed resources, excess or tight expense and asset allocations.

At this point, the analyst identifies formal and informal reports that capture and track expense, sales, and financial return versus plan in each function and by product line or project.

All of the above information is gathered through the analyst's interviews of key internal managers in every function devoting money or time to new projects. The final step in the survey — determining how much competitors are spending on new products and their rate of success — depends on inputs from the outside probe and public documents such as annual reports, 10K forms, and speeches to stock analysts.

CONCLUSIONS AND DECISIONS

Using data from the probes, the new products team recommends solutions to identified problems. Appendix IV-2 indicates what input is expected from each member. In deciding which solutions to which problems will be implemented, the team, together with top management, must address, at a minimum, the following issues.

GOALS	Should we change new product goals and strategies? To what?
	How much should we spend on what projects?
ABILITY TO ACCOMPLISH	Are our business and organization healthy enough to allow major new product developments?
PROCESS	What process and controls should we use in developing new products?
PROBLEMS	What problems and barriers must be fixed? How?
ORGANIZATION	How should we be organized? What personnel changes are needed?
CHANGES	How and when do we phase them in?

Answering these questions may take weeks and months of deliberation. The answers, moreover, only set direction (for example, "We will add X dollars in new products within Y years in Z markets," or "Pricing and tooling approvals for new products must be signed by the general manager"). Some recommendations, particularly those involving minor changes in goals and operating procedures, can be achieved quickly, often by a functional manager. The example above, which falls into this category, can be delegated to the financial controller.

Major changes, such as the development of a pilot production line or installation of a complex new product tracking and control system, are considerably more difficult to manage because they require many people (often a multifunctional task force) and much time and money.

IMPLEMENTATION

There are no good comprehensive guidelines on implementing fixes to new product problems. Keys to successful implementation are specific to the organization and problems being solved. The general keys to success are no different than those for managing any change: Plan carefully; make sure you have the right people for the job; introduce changes at a realistic pace; and test major changes on a small scale (or a single new product) to debug them before installation.

Chapter 7

Solving the Four Most Common New Product Problems

This chapter addresses the four most common causes of new product program failure:

- No established goals and plans
- No management process for new products
- Poor analytical tools for new product decisions
- Inadequate organization, structure, and skills

Note that it is pointless to tackle these problems when the basic business is in turmoil or top management lacks a marketing orientation. Such high-echelon organizational and personnel problems are not within the scope of this book.

NO ESTABLISHED GOALS OR PLANS

New product goals exist on two levels: long-range goals (what percent of our sales should come from new products five years from now?) and line-maintenance goals (what portion of an existing line should be refreshed each year?).

Long-range Goals

Long-range goals and plans for internal development should be included in the strategic plan. For optimum growth in sales and profit dollars, the available strategies, aside from diversification into new businesses, are determined by five factors:

1. What are the limits of your business definition? If you're restricted to passive electronic components, you probably don't have the desire or ability to expand into semiconductors.

2. What are the current and forecast sizes of the markets within your business definition and your competitive strength in these markets? If your markets will grow in units by 10 percent over the next five years and all the growth plus 25 percent of the base business will come from new or modified products, it's reasonable to anticipate 10–20 percent growth if you're competitively strong; it's foolish to shoot for 25–30 percent growth under ordinary circumstances, and you need a strong new product development program.

3. How much you can afford and when? As we'll see, profits resulting from expenditures can be calculated. Resources available depend on the priority put on your particular business, your firm's financial condition, and its ability to raise external capital (which may depend partly on the success of your new product programs).

4. How much you can expect to gain financially from both refreshing your line and adding new products? This return, which is constrained by the competitive market, also can be calculated. The profitability of industry leaders is your potential cap unless, of course, you "invent a better mousetrap" in terms of product, cost, or distribution.

5. Are your people able to meet your goals? It's pointless to consider a new product program without appropriate personnel.

Table 7-1 summarizes overall new product goals for an industrial products firm that ultimately succeeded by deciding how big it could be based on industry growth and the growth of potential new product categories, and by assessing how much growth should derive from internal development versus acquisition. This company reorganized its product development and marketing efforts to focus on long-range opportunities identified through research, balancing attention to the basic product line with new product development to insure orderly, profitable growth.

Overall goals *can* be based on management's best judgment (in this case, goals and the analysis inspiring them were developed by a seasoned department of market planning supported by top management) but should not be pursued without confirmation through research.

Goals for Established Products

New product goals for established product lines usually emerge during the annual or seasonal review of the marketing plan and product line. The overall goals that

---

Table 7-1.   Overall New Product Goals for an Industrial Products Firm*

Current Market Outlook

Maturing. Annual growth going from +10 percent to −2 percent

Selling prices declining rapidly

Company Performance

Sales growth slowing, no growth forecast

Profits currently forecast to decline, below target

Profitability cyclical, variable

Selling cost rising as percent of sales as sales increases decline

Becoming less important vendor to key distributors, direct customers; decreasing power in market

Competitive Performance

Total industry sales growth is 6 percent per year (units)

Growth of industry leaders is 10 percent per year

Industry pretax profit 3 percent per year, leaders 10 percent

Opportunities versus New Product Criteria

Research identified ten new market segments or category extensions within our business definition that will grow in excess of 10 percent per year for the next ten years.

They are large enough ($60mm+ each) to be attractive.

They are accessible by either internal development or acquisition. The products can be sold through our existing sales force to existing distributors and direct customers.

Acquisition to be used for short-term growth, internal development for long-term growth.

Component usage will increase with new, growing mechanical and electronic equipment technologies.

We can likely achieve #3 or better position in a number of these markets.

Sales Goals

Grow the overall business by 10 percent (real growth) per years 1969 to 1979.

New business must grow by at least 15 percent per year to achieve this average growth.

---

*Mechanical and electronic components for industrial, computer, telecommunications, military and consumer equipment.

---

limit the addition of new products, such as changes in existing styles or addition of new styles or price points within a product category, normally are established by the general manager and marketing manager. Usually, the goal for a fashion goods line, for example, is expressed in terms of the maximum percent of the number of existing styles in a category that can be changed or "turned" each year to update the line. New products that expand the market — styles and/or price points — are added to the basic maximum number of new products allowed. In both cases, added products are expected to meet volume, profit, inventory turn, and SKU goals. Prudent management will drop a style or product if a new style is not expected to appeal to a new customer or increase sales to an existing one. Figure 5-1 summarizes both the current performance and new product goals for the traditional lace-up shoe segment.

The percentage of a line turned annually depends on the nature of the product. In conservative shoe categories, perhaps 10–20 percent will turn. In a fast-track clothing business, 70–80 percent of the basic line — including styles, fabrics, and colors — may turn, while the number of models and SKUs remains constant. How much a line is turned is dictated by competitive offerings, fashion considerations, and your desire to lead the market with innovative styling. How much you increase the size of your basic line with new styles and price points depends on whether more is needed to meet competition, whether you intend to move the line ahead of competition, and whether you can profit.

The general manager and director of marketing determine goals and line changes during seasonal reviews that follow the format presented in Table 5-8. Changes should be documented, if necessary, with research findings.

No Management Process: Poor Analytical Tools

Realization of new product goals depends upon an established process of internal development with go/no go decision points and basic analytical tools to support decision making. A realistic new product development process, including its objectives, major analytical tools, and instructions for use, is summarized in Figure 7-1 and detailed step-by-step below. This process is adaptable to many consumer, fashion, industrial or technical products, and is useful for those entering the market as well as those concerned with improving an established market position.

CONCEPT DEVELOPMENT

Target Market Definition

The purpose of this step is to identify the current, unfilled needs of your target market, which should have been considered in your business definition. Although you can start from scratch and use only market research to determine unmet consumer needs, you probably will want to test ideas about potential new products during early research efforts. The following six methods can be used to learn what your target market buys and would buy.

First, positioning your line against competitive products will reveal holes in your line (see Chapter 5). Products that the consumer buys but you don't offer allow entry into a category by launching competitive products or improving upon competitor's offerings.

Second, research with the trade and consumer can yield both underlying needs — what consumers want, why they buy, how a product is or will be used — and specific new product suggestions. Structured interviews with the trade are particularly useful for pointing out holes in your line, short-term product trends, and short-term opportunities (they don't have the long view and generally are not creative).

Third, both structured and free-form consumer research provides invaluable information. Consumer focus groups and in-depth one-on-one interviews are superb ways to learn when, where, what and how the consumer buys, how they use products, what they like and don't like, for pinpointing problems with existing items and identifying features of the ideal product. Request reactions to abstract concepts ("What's your opinion of a solar-powered calculator?") and to specific new product ideas ("What's your reaction to the calculator pictured here?"). Free-form research is recommended for eliciting opinions and needs and for generating new product ideas.

Fourth, ranking competitive products according to the reactions of various types of consumers is an excellent way of determining who prefers what features, styles and functions; why best sellers sell, why losers don't. Consumers sometimes are given products for extended use before ranking and interviews. Sample products, such as fashion goods, are suitable for quick testing with techniques such as mall intercepts, in which shoppers are selected and questioned then and there in an isolated room.

Fifth, attribute analyses rely on consumers' responses to detailed examinations of products or sketches and mockups. A computer analysis of their comments indicates what features should be included in your new product and what should be avoided.

Finally, interviews with experts, both within the industry and specialized consultants, are useful for their insight into the future based on knowledge of the past; well aware of trends in product design and customer needs, they often can forecast three to five years ahead.

As a result of any or all of these analyses, you'll be able to focus on consumer problems and unfilled needs, rank them in order of their potential for your business, and direct your technical and creative people to develop unique new products that sell.

Recent activities in the camera market exemplify the different approaches available to manufacturers. As Kodak and the major Japanese manufacturers must have known through their research, the major complaints of the typical point-and-shoot amateur customer include poor focus from three to five feet; inadequate flash coverage and exposure; awkward manual film winding; inability to take rapid-sequence pictures; camera size and weight; and poor picture quality

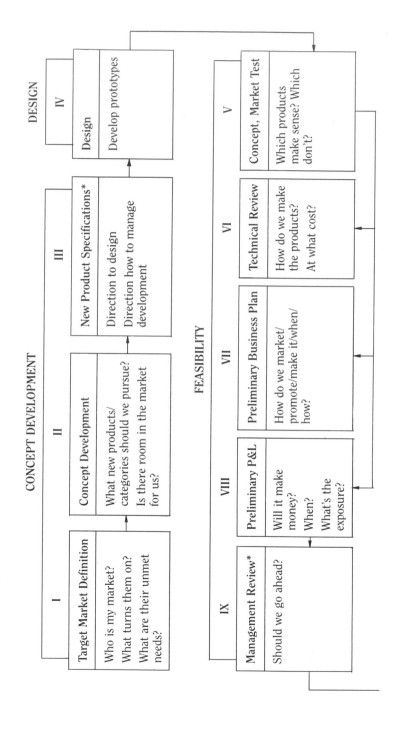

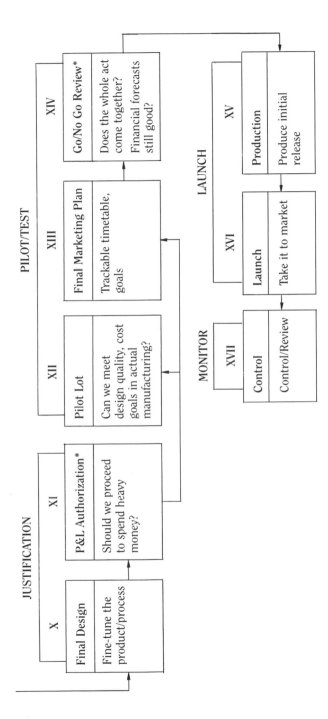

*Key decision points where general management is brought in.

Figure 7-1.   The New Product Development Process

on small-format film. Casual photographers, moreover, had been sensitized by advertising for sophisticated 35 mm cameras that buzz, whir, click, flash and display fancy lights; they probably craved a high-tech camera, but not one as slick, expensive or threatening as the Nikon F3 or Canon AE-1.

Canon, Minolta, and other Japanese companies responded to consumers' complaints with sophisticated auto-focus, auto-exposure, auto-flash, auto-wind 35mm cameras that produce exceptionally high-quality pictures from a relatively large negative. Their products, though expensive, have been runaway best-sellers.

Kodak, in contrast, sought the mass market with an inexpensive new camera, exposure, and film system. The disc camera incorporates all the features of the Japanese entries except for auto-focus and exceptional picture quality, which can't be delivered through the small-format disc negatives.

The market may be expanded later through systems allowing disc negatives to be viewed as positive images on a television screen. The consumer may then be able to select *portions* of the picture to be printed by an automated process that reads the selection from a magnetic strip on the disc.

Another useful example is that of a major women's shoe manufacturer targeting the career professional. Extensive research began when target consumers were shown sketches of shoe styles and close-ups of variations in features such as heel height and construction, toe shape, etc. Computer analysis of their opinions indicated which attributes and styles the target consumer responded favorably to, thereby giving strong direction to the design team.

In a parallel test, many members of the target audience ranked successful and unsuccessful competitive products and specified which styles and features they preferred and why. In addition, focus groups provided strong insight into basic needs and consumer buying patterns and attitudes toward specific brands. Fashion experts contributed creative, long-term thinking on shoe trends.

Concept Development

Intelligent interpretation of research findings by the marketing director and his or her research, product management, and creative team should reveal holes in the current line and new products or categories to pursue. The summary research results for a new shoe line targeted at the professional working woman, and further detailed in Appendix V-1, were:

Target Market:	Career professional women, age 25–45, income $25,000 +, mostly college graduates, shops high-grade department, women's specialty stores
Key Needs:	Fit/comfort; style; suitability with work clothing; usable socially "after hours"
Price:	$110–$140
Work Environment:	Formal office to informal setting

Product: 10–14 styles, principally pumps, slings, and walking shoes for the formal and informal professional

Strategy: Position as the professional working woman's shoe; suitable after hours; brand image, unique design, and distribution key competitive advantages

New Product Specifications

In specifying the new line to be developed, first consider potential competitive positioning in the market. Figure 7-2 shows the overall positioning chart used to position a new shoe line for career women. Competitive price and styling were plotted against the needs of the professional working woman as determined in focus groups. The product market selected included the fashion needs of the target market (traditional through mid-fashion), price–product points where competitors were absent, and direct competition with the most expensive competitive brands.

Business Plan Information: The market research described above is consumer and product oriented. Additional research into the market and its competitive structure is necessary before you develop a marketing plan or devote substantial funds to product development. The answers to the key questions — whether there's sufficient room in the market and whether a particular venture would be profitable — depend on the future size of the market; the strength of your competitive advantage; your potential share and the cost of obtaining it; and, considering distribution and brand awareness, your future competitive positioning versus target competitors. Other relevant issues include the distribution channels and selling effort required, pricing, promotion, and potential key customers and how to cultivate them. This research can accompany early consumer or product research or be conducted independently as needed.

Next, a clearcut statement of objectives, strategies, and delegated tasks plus a timetable are extremely important for new categories and entry into target market segments. Most important, detailed product specifications, along with research results, samples, and the objectives–strategies–tasks statement, should be distributed to each functional group participating in product development from this point on. Table 7-2 is a hypothetical example of the technical specifications that marketing might give to product development at a major camera manufacturer.

A useful technique for conveying design specifications to those developing a product is a "design box" containing written statements of the new product objectives and plan, design specifications, physical samples of competitive product, features to be incorporated, cost goals, and a timetable. A locked duplicate of the box is kept throughout the lengthy design period so that valuable directional materials are available in marketing, design, process development, and manufacturing.

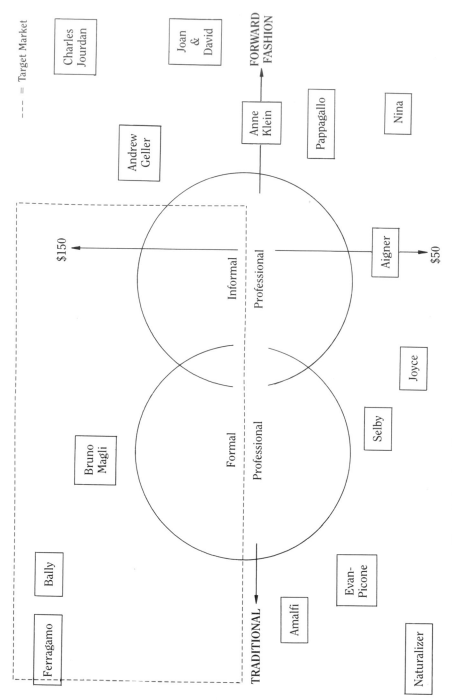

Figure 7-2.   Overall Positioning Chart: New Concept versus Competition

Table 7-2.   Design Specifications, Automatic 35mm Camera

Target Audience:	Ages 19–50, $15,000 + family income. Moderate to heavy travel — family occasion picture taker. Half male, half female users. ¾ male purchasers.
Attitudes:	Aware of advantages of high-technology cameras. Want exceptionally good pictures (reflects on their ability). Don't want point-and-shoot cheapies (poor picture quality, not versatile), don't want expense, yet want sophistication of top-end 35mm.
Price Range (suggested):	$139 Manufacturing Cost: $59.50
Aesthetics:	High-tech look, but uncluttered; looks simple to operate; unintimidating, but impressive
Human Engineering:	Must be superb. Foolproof operation, warnings when any operation incorrectly done, ill advised; controls easily understood. Operated by wide range of male and female hands, broad range of visual acuity.

Technical Features:

Size	120 × 70(h) × 40(w)mm	*Load*	Auto load
Weight	450 grams	*Wind*	Auto advance; motorized exposure at 1 frame per second
Viewfinder	Optical bright frame; low light, in focus, distance indication	*Rewind*	Automatic
Focus	Auto focus 0.6m–∞; focus lock	*Battery Life*	Five rolls with flash; alkaline batteries
Shutter	Programmed electronic speeds, eight seconds to 1/500th	*Lens Quality*	Center resolution 50 lines/mm, edge 40mm @ +5.6; 30mm @ +2.8
Exposure	EV 6–17, ASA 100	*Film*	ASA 25 to ASA 1000
Diaphragm	F2.8/16; auto programmed with shutter for optimum depth of field	*Other*	Self timer; battery check indicator; film transport indicator
Flash	Built-in auto flash; 0.6m–7m, ASA 100; recycle time 1 second	*Case*	Vinyl

Teams: At the concept stage, a permanent development team, led by marketing and including members from manufacturing, product design, product and process engineering, and finance or control, should be appointed for complicated products, those that deviate significantly from existing lines, or those involving unfamiliar or advanced manufacturing methods. Use of a formal team, which manages the new product through launch and turnover to ongoing operating management, has several advantages in overcoming potential barriers to success, especially technical barriers, which can be resolved early on. The involvement of technical and manufacturing personnel at the concept stage permits them to influence product design so that the product can be manufactured at targeted cost and quality; identify required technical advances in materials, process, or construction techniques; discard unworkable concepts; adjust timetables; address technical problems early enough to solve them and prevent expensive errors and the need to play catch-up ball later; and feel responsible for the product's success or failure.

Although the early team effort is principally devoted to product–market development, the presence of a financial person helps assure that cost and P&L information required later will be accurate.

After a poor, untested concept, the second biggest cause of new product trouble or failure is insufficient participation in the development process by marketing, design, and technical functions. Too often, design drops a "final" product in engineering's lap and demands a process to produce it in X months at Y cost. Too often, engineering delivers a jerry-built process that won't meet cost, quality, yield, or production rate goals. Team product development can prevent many of these pitfalls through early, open, and continuous communication.

If you follow the mechanical steps described here, you'll automatically devise a whiz-bang new product concept, right? Wrong! There is no substitute for creativity, particularly in marketing and design. It takes a creative person to determine the pieces of the market to be probed, the concepts to be tested, and the research methods that will get results. It takes a creative marketing and design team to interpret the research, define a workable new product concept, and know at gut level whether the concept is right (irrespective, sometimes, of objective data, which can be wrong because it measured the wrong things).

Market research and subsequent new product specifications only give direction and set limits for the creative design and technical development people. Despite research, design and marketing often are allowed to dictate 5–15 percent of the products added to a line. Success depends on your use of people, not just on the quantity and quality of information that they have.

Design: In designing prototypes for market test, a number of options usually are proposed, modeled, and internally tested for each product. In the sunglass, optical frame and shoe business, for example, three to five prototypes are developed for each product released.

Whether the design cycle is short, as for fashion products, or long, as for technically based products, it's important that sufficient time and resources are allocated for development and reworking of concepts; prototypes are constantly compared to target specifications and shown to the market to insure that designs are acceptable and up-to-date; and process engineering and manufacturing are involved during consideration of new features, functions, materials or manufacturing methods.

Concept/Market Test

Completed prototypes must be tested against the target audience. The tests, described below, are designed to predict product success and sales rate versus competition; select the best prototypes for final development; and reveal potential improvements in style, materials, and function.

Concept tests, involving structured and free-form interviews with the target audience, check whether design is on the right track with words, pictures and mock-ups — and without heavy spending on prototypes. In the early sixties, for example, Corning Glass Works tested consumer reaction to photochromic prescription and sunglass lenses, which darken outdoors and return to a lighter tint indoors, with questions, descriptive words, and photographs illustrating the photochromic effect. At that time, it would have been prohibitively expensive to use the actual product. Corning needed to know whether this unique concept was attractive and, if so, whether the product should be marketed as a comfort glass or a sunglass and in prescription as well as nonprescription lenses. By answering these and other questions, the concept test permitted the company to focus on the most viable product: a prescription indoor–outdoor comfort glass.

Style-feature tests require store-quality prototypes, which potential customers are asked to rank along with best-selling competitive products according to qualities important to the category (style, for example, in apparel or sound quality in audio components). Proven market winners and a few known losers are included, and reactions to each ranked product are elicited. Although sales rates can be approximated by comparing ranking of test prototypes to sales of known best sellers, such projections assume — dangerously — that competitive offerings won't change and that your distribution, brand image, and other competitive dimensions are equal or better.

Prototypes ranked in the top 20 percent of competitive products almost always succeed if the tests are objective and well constructed; they're particularly successful if they differ significantly from top-ranked competitors. Moreover, the ranking of prototypes can be segmented by computer according to many factors, including age, sex, education, location, occupation, income, etc. Often, a product that ranks average will be a real winner in a portion of your target market. Open-toed women's pumps, for example, won't rate well in Buffalo (who wants to shovel snow with her toes?) but will shine in Dallas. A finely crafted optical frame once puzzled design and marketing management by performing poorly overall in a style test. Detailed data, however, indicated that it was top-ranked by men age 50 and up but disdained by their youthful counterparts.

Style-feature tests indicate what will sell today and tomorrow but won't predict the success of advanced products that might establish new trends. Here, creative, intuitive decision making must be used, sometimes combined with testing by known trade and industry experts and individual style leaders.

In *use tests,* which are imperative when new construction or new features are involved, new product prototypes are given to target consumer to use under normal circumstances. Old proven products, if available for comparison, are used by a control group of similar consumers. Differences between the new and control products are carefully evaluated to determine whether the new product offers significant benefits, insure that it functions properly, and uncover any design, construction, and material flaws.

Use tests thus can help improve design and avert disaster — it's hard to duplicate the real world on a laboratory bench. A manufacturer of athletic equipment added a new, low-priced product to an established line to appeal to the budget buyer and infrequent user. Although the new construction technique employed was excellent, in theory and according to inside testing, the product quickly fell apart in the field, and the red-faced manufacturer took large returns. Four weeks of testing with a handful of active athletes would have saved him embarrassment — and money.

Sales tests are excellent when you can afford them and the cost of producing prototypes is low. They are best used for consumer and fashion products; when design or function are new, unique, or controversial; and when going to market entails high risk, such as heavy tooling expenses. With these tests, the sales rate of your product is monitored versus competition in selected stores where your target market shops. Follow-up interviews with purchasers also can be conducted. But because competitive activity, your own promotional efforts, and attention (or, more likely, inattention) by retailers serve to confuse results, it is difficult to judge potential product performance in the selling arena over a short period of time. Sales tests, therefore, are best avoided when other, cleaner options will yield the required information.

Trade tests, in which your new offering is stacked up against competitive products, should be conducted unless there is great danger of competitors beating you to the marketplace and patent office. Interviews with key members of the wholesale or retail trade and their previewing of prototypes may reveal competitive plans and current or future products that will compete with or block yours. Importantly, they can tell you if there's room in the market for your product, whether they're likely to buy it, and under what circumstances.

As for when to stop testing and conducting market research, the answer is never, but research can be reduced substantially as you gain market and product knowledge. Basic in-depth information on your target market is collected only once, then frequently updated with quick surveys aimed to detect change. In-depth testing and ranking of competitive products can be done less frequently with smaller samples as designers and marketing personnel become more knowledgeable, and style–feature–use–sales–trade tests can be scaled down as internal people learn to eliminate "dogs" before consumer testing.

Don't ever get lulled into believing that you no longer need to research the market or test new products — that's probably how your new product program got into trouble in the first place.

Technical reviews combine the results of market tests and early technical thinking and address whether and how a company can make a marketable product, at what cost, with what investment and risks, and whether major technical breakthroughs are still required.

During design and concept testing, technical personnel may have to achieve technical breakthroughs to produce the product. To market its new Naturals™ line for women, for example, Bausch & Lomb successfully developed a thin, extremely lightweight, strong, color-tinted prescription-quality photochromic sunglass lens. Process development, meanwhile, had to determine how to manufacture the product, experimenting with various new processes and equipment. Engineers who devised the Naturals™ lens also were obliged to develop a process for producing more sophisticated, difficult-to-manufacture frames than had been used previously.

At the time of the technical review, technical knowledge should be sufficient to define the proposed production process step by step, put a reasonable plus and minus limit on costs, and establish a timetable from this point into production, specifying hurdles to be overcome.

Technical problems may arise at this point because the task was more formidable than anticipated or, more frequently, because insufficient technical effort was devoted to process development. The latter can be prevented through an established timetable, frequent communication between team leaders and technical members of the team, and assurance that adequate technical resources are available from the start.

Preliminary Business Plan/Preliminary P&L

Marketing is responsible for preparing a preliminary business plan that addresses whether the potential return is high enough and the risk manageable enough to devote more funds to final product and process development. Although minimal detail is required at this point, the plan should cover the items noted in Table 7-3 and in greater depth, the following:

- The product line and its positioning;
- Our competitive advantage and where it will get us (test data available);

Table 7-3.   Go/No Go Review Outline

Marketing

Review of concept, competitive advantage, strategy

Final launch plans, advertising, promotion, POS, distribution, packaging, trade terms

Forecast for line and mix; basis

Review of final line, benefits versus competition

Sales

Key account and territory goals, probability of achieving

Cost

Manufacturing cost by step — materials, labor, overhead, yields, probability of achieving, high-risk steps, potential variances

Cost of critical materials, potential variances

Detailed marketing costs by category, potential variances

Technical

Product performance, wear, use, safety testing summary

Manufacturing

Release/inventory schedule

Identification and review of new and/or high-risk process steps

Pilot line yields

18-month capacity review

Quality standards

Organization

Staffing, additions to staff

P&L

Complete P&L with up- and downside volume and cost estimates, liquidation financials

Risk Summary

Summary of high risks and potential financial impact by function

---

- Marketing and manufacturing steps necessary, timing and costs to launch; costs to date, projected development, and asset investments;
- Key technical and marketing risks and hurdles;
- Anticipated P&L for reasonable life of the product; and
- Staff and organizational barriers to success.

Products often are aborted at this point because costs and risks far exceed potential return; indications of potential success are inadequate; and marketing work is sloppy. The reason that projects that should be *stopped* are continued is that marketing's and management's enthusiasm overrides the subtle or not-so-subtle negative messages. When you've committed weeks, months, or years to a product, it's easier to rationalize insurmountable technical, competitive, or financial barriers and charge ahead than to walk away.

Despite expert advice, internal opinion, early market feedback and common sense, a large company once launched a very expensive piece of industrial equipment incorporating its weak proprietary technology — and missed the market's documented need by a wide margin. The company proceeded and failed because of pride, myopia, and a regrettable lack of expertise and market research.

Management Review

At this stage, the project team must decide whether to proceed. If so, and if large expenditures and new directions are involved, senior management probably will want to formally review the product and business concept, technical conclusions, the anticipated schedule, and forecast financial results and risks. The team should be present at the review, during which representatives of each functional area can present their portions of the project. You may leave the meeting with a clear go-ahead and a commitment of funds to develop the process or product fully; if not, determine why.

If the project's good, sell it. If it isn't, kill it. You'll be a hero in either situation if your management's smart.

Final Design

This is the unnerving time when the big bucks start flowing out while nothing's coming in.

At this stage, changes in consumer products usually are minor and pertain to cost, manufacturing efficiency, new materials, or decorative improvements. Technical products, in which the manufacturing process and technical performance often are interdependent, still may require substantial product development. The major emphasis, however, is on developing a cost-effective manufacturing process, and prototype equipment and soft (limited production) tooling are created. The project does not proceed until process engineering *and* manufacturing agree that the process decided upon can work for volume production, cost goals probably can be met, and quality standards can be maintained. Final prototype product now is subjected to wear, environmental safety, and use tests.

Marketing, meanwhile, continues its launch plans and monitors the marketplace for changes, such as a competitive entry, that affect the game plan. Product design now should be frozen to prevent designers' constant temptation to improve a product up to the day it's shipped.

Product dropouts at this point are rare and usually result from technical and process problems.

P&L Authorization

If you're working on a major line requiring new equipment, you're asking for big dollars now. The job of the marketing manager and marketing team is to provide general management with an honest, factual picture of the project. The general manager's job is to work you over to make sure you've done your homework.

It's advisable to submit a brief written plan before the go/no go review so your boss can raise key issues. And, if you're smart, you'll have identified his or her concerns so you can address them accordingly. Prepare a detailed P&L statement documenting expenses, manufacturing costs, and assets expenditures, and justifying sales. Include relevant research, including process specifications and results from experiments with prototype equipment, and attach for submission or signature any internal paperwork authorizing additional equipment purchases, staff additions, and funding.

Pilot Lot

At this time, major or minor additions to manufacturing equipment are procured or built, installed, and debugged. Pilot lots of the product are run in sufficient quantity and variety to accurately estimate production quality, capacity, yield, and costs; debug equipment with normal production workers at normal rates; train workers and manufacturing supervisors; and produce samples for salespeople, advertising, and public relations.

Final Marketing Plans

Final marketing plans, which are prepared during installation and debugging of equipment, are meant not to rejustify the project but to make it happen. The key elements include:

- Forecasts of sales level, timing, and product mix for manufacturing and finance;
- A sales plan encompassing a calendar for introduction by whom, to whom; goals and timing for key customers by region and sales territory; kick-off sales meetings and training;
- Advertising, point-of-sale, promotional materials — concept, final mock-ups, ready for production;
- Complete up-dated pricing/terms;
- Collateral selling aids, price lists, catalogs at concept or mock-up stage;
- All marketing costs specified for the year ahead;
- A tight timetable for each marketing function;
- Manufacturing plans indicating how much will be delivered to stock and when; and
- Controls to monitor progress versus plan.

Major marketing errors typical at this stage are paying too much attention to product and advertising, too little to the supports crucial to a successful launch, such as sales force training, collateral material, selling aids, pricing, and computer systems.

Go/No Go Review

This anticlimactic review functions as a disaster check or a discussion of previously undeveloped marketing plans with upper management. Abandoning the project at this point is justified only when a process has failed, competition has preempted your market, or the company can't afford to proceed. Table 7-3 outlines the major marketing, sales, organizational and financial points to cover. Production and a date for product shipment are not authorized without satisfactory completion of this review. Top managers from each function — marketing, production, engineering, design — are usually required to sign-off on the plan once approved.

Production

Key problems that arise in early production include production rates too low to meet initial demand or timetable; skewed mix with some products unavailable; below-standard quality; potential late delivery of materials and vendor-supplied parts. Demand weekly, if not daily, production and inventory reports by product and SKU, and monitor work in process. If plant input falls off schedule, you're in trouble, particularly if throughput time is long.

Finally, keep inspecting. Pull product out of stock, watch it in final pack, inspect it along the line. Your interest usually will be appreciated by manufacturing, particularly lower-level supervisors and workers.

Launch/Control/Review

If your plans are well laid, this phase will depend on effective execution and control. Frequent exception reporting on progress versus goal (see Chapter 10) will help keep your launch on track. The most important controls are weekly team communication or meetings to discuss problems and inform the general manager of severe deviations from plan; an automated weekly sales report indicating contacts made, orders taken, and shipments made by key customer, region and territory; and, if your product is sold at retail, reports on how much of what is selling and the reasons for any consumer resistance. Order and sales reporting keeps you on track and also provides real-world information that lets you adjust production levels and mix.

Finally, written monthly exception reports noting what products are missing goals and why are submitted to top management, and quarterly in-depth design reviews are held for all new products to examine forthcoming designs and give direction where needed. Problems typical at this stage include production and/or inventory imbalances; inadequate or ill prepared salespeople; poor quality; late shipment; specific classes of customers (i.e., department stores) not buying to expectation; customers ignoring commitments for displays, retail clerk training, promotions and advertising.

Where Marketing People Fail

Marketing people sometimes fail to develop new products because they remain marketing people and neglect to educate themselves regarding finance, engineering, manufacturing, cost (e.g., how to read a detailed manufacturing set-up), and quality control. Teams are helpful through the interchange of marketing, technical, and financial information during new product development. The marketing leader also should spend time with product and process engineers to learn their procedures and flag potential problems.

Managing Major Programs

For most companies, a new product program perpetuates itself as the existing line is refreshed with frequent introductions and major new products are developed to enter new categories or new businesses. Such companies must carefully schedule their new product load, estimate and manage the resources involved, and examine the cost of creating new products and investments in new product programs versus their return.

Scheduling

Figure 7-3 indicates the development stages for a single moderately complex consumer product and the time and resources required for each step. Slack time is added to allow for inevitable setbacks and time over-runs. Two additional schedules are normally produced. The first, a big-picture summary of the expected key decision points for *all* developmental products. Second, a summary of man weeks required, by quarter, for each critical function, such as design and engineering, to pinpoint the need for additional people or to shift project schedules and "level load" available man weeks. New product development schedules, frequently reviewed, however complex or simple, and as dictated by need, are critical to the success of new product programs for any size company.

Dedicated Resources

Where resources needed for new products such as R&D equipment, manufacturing lines, or people are shared with other operations, make sure that the capacity is adequate and the rules for using them clear. If the potential payoff from your new product can bear the cost, get your own dedicated resources. Sharing rarely works because "today's business" always wins if there is a conflict.

Pre- and Post-launch Problems

Programs frequently become stalled prior to launch as a result of technical failure; too rapid development; failure in market test; or competitive changes in the market. If your new product programs have been properly planned, however, delay is merely a problem, not a disaster. Because your controls are good, you will have spotted the trouble early enough to correct it. Because priorities have been set and slack time allowed, you can shift resources from one program to another. Because you have more new products and ideas in the system than you'll need, you can substitute another product for one that has failed or been preempted. When a dress manufacturer's competitor introduced a new style identical to one he had planned, he simply substituted a product targeted for the same market that was in the works but hadn't tested as positively. The substitute sold well.

After a product has been launched, it's difficult and costly to solve problems. Table 7-4 summarizes the sources and fixes for the following common post-launch problems:

> high costs/low profits
>
> low volume
>
> technical failures
>
> incorrect product
>
> late release to the market

Market Intelligence

Finally, keep your eyes and ears open in the marketplace through your sales and marketing organization to insure that developing products, particularly those with long development times, are still needed and aren't being preempted by competition.

ORGANIZATION STRUCTURE AND SKILLS

A program won't succeed if it's not suited to the structure of the organization or if the employees are incompatible or don't have the skills for the job. This is especially true for a major new product effort designed to change the course of your business (a situation in which help is recommended from your human resources department or outside specialists in organization development and new products). Though there are no simple solutions to these problems, you can identify the type of new product operation appropriate for your people, your business,

STAGES OF DEVELOPMENT	RESOURCE LOAD		
(Weeks 1 2 3 4 ... 23 24 25 26)	Elapsed Weeks Per Step	Man-Weeks for Critical Resources**	Critical Resource***
I. Design			
Concepts*	5	5	D
Design details	3	3	D
First models	4	8	M
Design review	4	1	D
Second models	3	1	M
II. Feasibility			
Market test	5	—	—
Design review	4	1	D
Process review	18	3/6	S/D
Tooling review	1	2	T
Preliminary cost	2	1/1	S/E
Management review*	1	—	—
III. Justification			
Final design	4	2	D
Specifications	8	3	S
Final costs	3	1/2	S/E

	4	2	M
Final models			
P&L authorizations*	3	4/2	S/E
IV. Pilot-test			
Order materials	1		
Tooling	24	24	T
Pilot lot	23	23/6	E/T
Pilot lot review	1	1	E
Pilot lot fix	4	8/4	E/T
Go/no go plan*	3	3/3	S/E
V. Production			
Sales samples	2	—	—
Start sell	—	—	—
Production	15	—	—
Start ship	—	—	—

Key: ⊢⊣ = Time per Step, Months
*Critical management review points.
**More than one person is sometimes required to meet elapsed time requirements. Often there are fewer man-weeks than elapsed weeks because of tasks required that do not use critical resources.
***D — Design (12), M — Model shop (11), S — Specifications (15), E — Engineering (46), T — Tooling (36). Numbers in parentheses are average man-weeks required by each critical function for one product line.

Figure 7-3. Typical Detailed Schedule for One Complex Product (Months)

Table 7-4. Post-launch Problems, Sources, and Potential Fixes

Problem	Source(s)	Fixes
High cost/low profit	Manufacturing costs higher than estimates — usually poor yields, high material costs	Cost reduction team focusing on design, materials, process, product mix
	Overspending in design or marketing — usually on samples and advertising materials	Re-budget, examining return for every dollar remaining in the budget
Low volume	Pricing wrong	Research — correct structure fast; promote if needed to establish new position
	Poor/wrong distribution	If salespeople don't push, give incentive, keep tight-rein, daily quotas; if customers don't have funds to purchase or product not selling, promote or arrange financing
		If wrong channels chosen, get into needed ones fast, even if it's expensive
	Competitive thrust against you	Find their weak point (if any), promote against them, or advertise

Manufacturing behind schedule		Look at scheduling, overtime, outside manufacture or allocation of product to customers; let customers know what they'll get, when
Part or all of line isn't right	Poor style; quality or function doesn't meet standards, market, or competitive needs	Push the part of the line that's right Fix or replace the portion that isn't Dump the line fast if it's a loser and cut your losses
Late release	Many	Defer until next natural release time (season in fashion business), or reserve purchasing dollars of key customers by telling them the product will be late, offering special price or promotional incentives if needed
Technical/quality features	Many	Recall the bad product, replace it fast Withdraw product if not quickly fixable

and your goals by defining the job to be done, defining your options, and implementing the one you've selected.

If you've successfully defined your financial goals, strategies and anticipated new product output and overcome organizational barriers, you'll be able to:

* Establish the volume of necessary new product work;
* Measure the load in terms of the number of new products to be produced and the man-months needed by each function and skill;
* Establish which required technical, professional and managerial skills are currently available and which must be added.

Selecting the Structure

The development of new products can be organized through the following three methods:

The Shoe Horn is applicable when new products come from the organization that runs the ongoing business. Though individuals or departments may specialize in product design and development, all other functions use their day-to-day skills in the new product context. This type of organization is appropriate when the new product effort is low level and consists predominantly of refreshing an existing line (i.e., seasonal changes in style, color, and material) or evolutionary changes in technical products; when the new product cycle is only 8–18 months long; your industry is so slow-moving that people of average ability can handle the new product program, and no new skills are required. Decision making in the shoe-horn mode usually is concentrated at the top because decisions generally are few, simple, and minor, and risks are low.

A Separate Department consisting of all marketing, design, product, and sometimes process development and manufacturing functions usually is headed by a seasoned, technically oriented marketing manager who reports to the general manager. Such departments may take a new product all the way to market when new distribution channels, manufacturing, and marketing skills are needed or else relinquish it to the existing organization for manufacture and launch. Because they're expensive, difficult to staff, and time-consuming to develop, separate departments should be considered as a long-term investment only if the potential payback is very high; the new product effort is large and long-term and demands much time from all functions; the new product direction differs drastically from the current line; existing organization skills are insufficient; and existing technical assets are inappropriate.

New Product Teams, which combine the best of the shoe-horn operation and separate departments, are composed of representatives from all functions relevant to product development developed by team leader from marketing. Teams, which may or may not concentrate full time on the new product, are especially useful when new product decisions must be made rapidly and delegated to lower levels; new products require currently available skills; the new product load changes frequently, so teams can be formed as needed; and technical and managerial competence are high-level. But because teams create unfamiliar relationships and, therefore, stress, they succeed only in a matrix organization in which team members have time and freedom to do their new products jobs. In a matrix organization, a team engineering representative, for example, must perform ongoing duties to the satisfaction of his functional boss and also fulfill his engineering responsibilities to the team.

Teams also must develop open communications and learn to resolve the inevitable conflict between functions and between new products versus the ongoing business. Top management must be willing to manage the teams by reviewing progress against agreed-upon objectives and intervene only when necessary. Finally, teams take time to develop so management must patiently live with the early mistakes resulting from delegation during the team's learning period.

Integration: In any type of organization, integrating the individual functions to work together effectively is a crucial task — and a major factor in new product success. One means of achieving integration is to establish and frequently review new product goals in a preordained format at regular meetings with those involved. Another key is the right organizational spirit, and a third, which requires much time and a tolerance of mistakes, is delegation of decision making to the teams, departments, and individuals assigned to new products. Integrating functions at the top rarely works because it slows the process, diverts attention from the ongoing business and long-term strategy and deprives subordinates of responsibility and pride in their work.

Critical Skills: Organizations establishing or revitalizing a new product program usually lack a progressive, creative marketing thinker combining a "nose" for market demands with knowledge of modern analytical techniques; at least one creative designer who can turn a concept into a unique, eminently salable product; and a technical person familiar with new products who innovates in new materials, product features, and new or low-cost manufacturing technologies.

Ideal? Yes. Impossible to obtain? No.

Pace: Once you've chosen your new product organization and system, decide how quickly you can install it. But don't rush into installation just because the timing and theory are right. For change to work, key managerial skills must be in place and up to speed; key supporting professionals with relevant skills must be available; and goals, strategies, and timing must be realistic and universally understood. When hiring or retraining of existing personnel is necessary, you should ease into the new organization, perhaps by first experimenting with the new structure on limited developments.

New Products in Old-line Organizations

Be especially careful when injecting new products or systems into an old-line traditional organization or making a large new products program the cornerstone of turning around a historically stagnant business. This process demands time — usually three to five years — and patience. People must change ingrained habits and grasp new and sometimes baffling concepts. It is best accomplished by recruiting a few up-to-date thinkers and change agents and training the rest of the organization to do the job if you're confident that it's trainable. If your plans are obstructed by managers who have been doing things the same way for 20 years, your only option is to change them and quickly get on with the job.

Change, which is difficult and threatening, must be managed carefully. Although it represents an opportunity for corporate and personal growth, it has a high potential cost — the possibility of failure. Establishing high-impact new product programs in old-line companies requires carefully thought out changes in direction, personnel, technology, decision-making practices, and communication patterns. The keys to effecting change (and, for that matter, managing any new product program well) are as follows:

Recognize anxiety, individual and collective, induced by change. Personal anxiety concerns potential failure and the loss of position, face, or even one's job. Performance anxiety concerns skills, potential errors, and whether one can prove oneself in the alloted time.

Set a clear direction to minimize anxiety and improve performance. Goals and priorities must be right, few in number, simply expressed, appropriately communicated to all levels, and stable. Any wavering breeds additional destructive uncertainty and lack of confidence in management.

Communicate plans and progress frequently to those involved, and encourage honest feedback. Formal monthly and quarterly progress review meetings with operating managers are essential, as are weekly top-level staff meetings to flag and discuss plan deviations and problems. Informal drop-in meetings with managers bolster morale and help reveal actual progress and problems.

Delegate decisionmaking as much as possible, preferably through a clear written definition of which decisions can be made at what levels.

Set realistic, measurable performance standards for every key employee, and establish periodic reviews.

Provide skill training to give employees knowledge and confidence. The standard requisite technical skills include developing marketing plans, marketing and financial control, market research techniques, cost-reduction programs, and development of performance standards.

Provide counseling, both individual and organizational, with a skilled human resource specialist to help individuals address personal management problems and frustrations.

Implement personnel changes quickly and supportively to demonstrate that while goals must be accomplished, management cares about people. Place valued employees unequipped for the new job where they can contribute, and encourage those who are trainable. Deadwood should be eliminated where possible; replacements should be compatible with the old guard.

Establish a reasonable pace with which employees are comfortable. Too-rapid change results in financial and program failures. If changes are too slow, you may lose corporate support and market position.

Provide a positive atmosphere in which employees are expected to meet standards, understand that errors will be tolerated (within reason) during the learning period, and feel free to discuss issues and problems.

Avoid drastic changes in the organization structure unless you're certain that personnel are ready and your objectives will be accomplished. Without proper timing, training, and preparation, changes in channels of authority can seriously disrupt communciations and trust and actually set your programs back. For example, quickly transforming an authoritarian organization into one that delegates significantly can cause mass confusion.

Communicate with "upstairs" frequently, either to a superior or a board of directors. It is essential that the general manager's superiors understand the program goals, risks, problems and their solutions, timetables, and plans for managing the inevitable stress that accompanies change.

KEY TO SUCCESS

The following operating rules for new product success are worth repeating:

- *Set goals* — Every new product program requires a formal statement of objectives and a positioning statement distributed throughout the organization to ensure comprehension and flush out errors.
- *Establish the right organization* — Don't start a project without a marketing manager for overall direction, a technical team leader, and team members with the technical skills necessary during the development process. Assignment of joint technical and marketing responsibility encourages these two often conflicting functions to cooperate to achieve their goals and emphasizes that any failure is mutual.
- *Get the right people* — Old dogs rarely learn new tricks — at least not quickly. If current employees lack the relevant skills, hire new ones who do.
- *Conduct research* — Don't put products into production without adequate and

positive trade and consumer research; order field and laboratory use and stress testing where necessary. Test summaries must be reviewed by the general manager. Research helps provide assurance that the product is solid and minimizes costly recalls and potential lawsuits.

- *Don't promise new product release dates* until completion of a pilot manufacturing lot and final P&L review with the general manager, and manufacturing has accepted the process from engineering. This precaution permits the general manager to stop any marginal products, yields relatively realistic manufacturing cost estimates, and ensures that the production process is workable.
- *Allow 20 percent slack time* — Unexpected problems can shatter the most meticulous estimates of required time and resources. If you allow extra time for all steps and critical resources, you'll avoid unpleasant surprises later.
- *Know your costs* — Calculate the total cost of a new product program before committing substantial time and money and before making a major commitment to senior management, the public, or the internal organization.
- *Know the costs of each product program* — Calculating all hidden costs and confronting the actual price of a project may reveal that a "sure winner" is marginal and should be scrapped.
- *Put your basic business to bed* — Don't embark on a major new product program unless your basic business is well staffed and managed. Make sure that strategic and operating plan procedures and individual goals throughout the organization are in place. Fix or get rid of problem businesses which, contrary to conventional wisdom, cannot be saved by new products.
- *Fix problems or be fixed yourself* — High-impact new product directions require your best people. Get them. You usually get only one chance with a program vital to your company's future.

BASIC PRINCIPLES

New products are not as quick, easy, or inexpensive to develop as you may think. General management's inevitable tactic of "shoe horning" new products into existing organizations and budgets rarely works.

- *Competition* is the last factor realistically considered in planning and positioning a new product and the first one that will take you down the tubes.
- *Designers,* unless they're motivated or naturally superior, are not truly creative — most are merely technicians who produce more of the same.
- *Market research* is neglected by most managers unless they are those rare true believers or unless they're in deep trouble.
- *Timing* on a new product is always late. Designers hate research, particularly fashion designers.
- *Costs* of manufacturing are always higher than estimated, and marketing always over-forecasts sales and underestimates expenses.

- *The trade* never is as enthusiastic about a product after launch as during research.
- *Engineering* never produces a process satisfactory to manufacturing, and manufacturing never can implement even the simplest process devised by engineering.
- *People* will continue to do their own thing unless you establish goals and a management system and organizational climate that motivates them to cooperate and change.

Chapter 8

Making Sense of Your Price Structure

The Problem

Profits are low; profitability varies significantly from product to product, line to line.

Your product isn't selling, and you suspect pricing is the culprit.

Your price structure seems senseless, and no one takes responsibility.

For example, the previous management of a manufacturer of expensive branded consumer accessories raised retail prices by 35 percent in two years as volume increased substantially. Because the trade predicted volume loss due to higher prices, management accepted mediocre profits despite several years of continuous back orders. Over a two-year period, an overzealous new management raised prices drastically and lowered product quality. Short-term profits increased, but volume suffered. Eventually, after prices were adjusted and product features resurrected, trade and consumer confidence returned as did sales volume and profits.

Although General Motors' J cars were priced competitively with some of the world's best compacts, features, quality, performance, and design were inferior and consumers were skeptical. When the cars didn't sell, GM rolled back prices, largely by eliminating the standard special features still offered by foreign competitors. The cars still aren't selling.

In contrast, a major supplier of a low-price, high-volume industrial commodity consistently gets a 5 percent to 7 percent premium on large contracts because service and quality are superior. A 5–7 percent premium generates considerable cash for investment in product superiority, better service, and the bottom line.

This chapter addresses the symptoms, causes and consequences of poor pricing practices; pricing strategy; the diagnosis of pricing problems; the six steps for solving pricing problems or reviewing an established price structure; and analytical techniques for pricing.

THE SYMPTOMS

Symptoms that may indicate pricing problems include the following.

Complaints

- The trade complains that retail prices are so high that they're losing business. Because margins, advertising allowances and promotional terms are inadequate, they can't make a profit or promote the product.
- Your sales force echoes these complaints.
- Consumers maintain that your products are overpriced — or that they're a fantastic bargain.
- You have no complaints, which means there may be room for price/profit increases.

Volume

- Overall volume changes quickly up or down.
- Volume of parts of the line change quickly, inexplicably.

Margins

- Profitability varies significantly from line to line or item to item within the line, or else it remains uniform.
- Margins, overall or by individual product categories, have been falling.

Prices

- Prices are changed only when costs change or "target margins" are not met.
- They rise less rapidly than costs.
- Pricing is done by cost-plus formula to produce target margins.
- Prices are changed arbitrarily without considering impact on margins, volume, image, competition.
- Increase in profits means increase in price.

- Increase in volume means lowering price.
- Prices vary arbitrarily from customer to customer, salesperson to salesperson.

Product
- Low-priced products cannibalize higher-priced items.
- Similar products cluster around the same price.
- Promising products stagnate or fail.

Competition
- Competitors use price against you with the consumer and to the trade.
- Competitive pricing is a mystery.
- You're ignorant of competitors' motives and operations. You don't know your key price competitors.

Customer Base
- Your customer base changes drastically from year to year.

THE CAUSE

With the exception of superior competition, the following causes of an inadequately profitable or ineffective price structure are within a company's control.

External Factors
- Competition's costs are so low and their market presence so strong that they dictate your pricing.

Internal Strategic Factors
- Failure to relate pricing to profit and marketing strategy.
- Ignoring competitive pricing and strategy when setting prices.
- Pricing is considered apart from the *value* package delivered to the customer.
- No stated pricing philosophy.

Internal Managerial Factors
- No standard procedure for decision making or review and control of prices.
- No organized system for collecting and analyzing market prices and flagging the need for change.
- High cost or margin-hungry management prevents appropriate pricing moves.
- Pricing by cost-plus formula to reach target margins.
- Inadequate rapport with key industry sources or customers who will divulge competitive pricing practices and forecast their moves.

- Inertia allows setting prices how and when it's always been done (usually when the new catalog is due).

CONSEQUENCES OF IRRATIONAL PRICING

- *Low profits,* short or long term, as a percent of sales (you're underpriced);
- *Low profit volume* in total dollars at the bottom line (you're over- or underpriced);
- *Low unit volume* (you're overpriced);
- *Skewed product mix* (because items in your line aren't priced according to their relative value, the market "cherry picks" underpriced products and ignores over-priced ones);
- *Inability to penetrate* some trade channels (your price points aren't right or the price mix or trade terms are inappropriate);
- *Inviting competition* to enter or further penetrate the market (your prices are too high) or inviting financial disaster (they're too low); and
- *Consumer turn-off* when prices are inappropriate (too high for your target audience or too low for upscale customers).

DEFINITIONS

Price

The retail price is what the end user pays for a consumer product. The wholesale price is what the retailer pays the manufacturer, a wholesaler, or a distributor. The term "trade" includes both retailer and wholesaler.

Because the buyer purchases a value package that fills a need, price is only one element in a purchase decision — a point too often lost in establishing price structures.

Value to the Consumer

Value is what the end consumer buys; consequently, price is high or low depending on product, service, and various intangible features. Typical value enhancers/detractors from par price, which is the market average, are:

ENHANCERS	DETRACTORS
Good brand image	Poor or no brand image
Prestige brand	Commodity brand
Peer acceptance	Mixed acceptance among peers
Excellent service	Poor service
Superior function	Adequate or inadequate function

ENHANCERS	DETRACTORS
Superior style/looks	Mediocre style/looks
Convenient distribution	Spotty distribution
Good selection	Poor selection
Ready availability	Spotty availability
Appropriate innovation	Minimal innovation

Strong enhancers translate into a higher price and, of course, cost money. Detractors, which translate into a lower price, save money. These market-oriented factors are crucial in determining a firm's pricing strategy and place in the market. Mercedes cars, for example, offer many enhancers. Based on function and durability, they are probably over-priced considering that certain competitors are roughly equivalent. Yet because target-market prestige, brand image and peer acceptance warrant a 15–25 percent price premium, Mercedes' profits stay up even in a down market. Detroit cars, conversely, have several detractors. As a result of prices above value level, Detroit has lost market share to foreign manufacturers providing par or par-plus value.

In determining strategy, therefore, smart marketers start with competitive value and worry about price later and profits last.

Value to the Trade/Distribution

Value of your product/services to the trade is called profit. Your offering is a "profit package" for which profit, volume and margin are determined by the tangible and intangible factors which are:

TANGIBLES	INTANGIBLES
Product fit with target market	Brand image/prestige
Purchase price	Protected distribution
Resale price	Sales/technical support
Extra discounts for special promotions	Ability to develop special products/ programs
Service-inventory back-up	Training for employees
Return/restocking/merchandising policies	Product/service innovations
Advertising/merchandising allowances	
Special promotional goods	
Dating terms	
Early pay discounts	
Collateral and advertising material provided	
Volume that your total package generates	

For the trade, tangible factors can be turned into a net cost or discount off retail (list) price. For example, a retailer's standard discount may be 50 percent off list, yielding a 50 percent gross margin, but periodic special discounts, return allowances, dating, early pay allowances, free advertising materials and allowances can add 3–5 percent to overall margins.

The intangibles offer additional opportunities for the trade to increase volume and lower costs. The manufacturer providing them may "lock up" a distribution network and lock out competitors.

Competitive Pricing

Competitive pricing does not necessarily mean setting a price equal to competition's. It *does* mean setting a price conducive to accomplishing your goals versus competition. A competitive price may range from a 20 percent premium over competition if your image warrants it and it won't hurt volume, to a 15 percent discount below competition if you want to gain market share or your product or distribution is inferior.

PRICING STRATEGY: AN OVERVIEW

Product and service prices are key strategic and tactical tools that directly affect short- and long-term profits and volume. This chapter concentrates on long-term strategic pricing; short-run tactical pricing will be addressed later.

Price to the Consumer

In general, individual product, product line and brand pricing is a function of, first, *Business Strategy:* Do you want to grow, hold, or divest long-term share? In the entire category or in part? Second, *Business Tactics:* Can you price according to your long-range strategy? Or are short-term deviations needed to gain or inhibit volume, introduce or build the line, thwart a competitor or enhance new distribution? Third, *Competitive Strength:* How good is your product, distribution, and image versus key competitors'? Does your competitive position translate into price advantages or disadvantages? Fourth, *Competitive Reaction:* How will competitors react to your pricing (follow, fight, remain unchanged) based on their long-range strategy, tactics and competitive strength?

Figure 8-1 presents normal retail pricing strategy as a function of long-term business strategy and competitive strength.

Price to the Trade

In addition to the factors applicable to consumer pricing, the price and profit package offered to the trade depends on the extent to which you want to penetrate each trade channel and the extent to which that channel presents a product void.

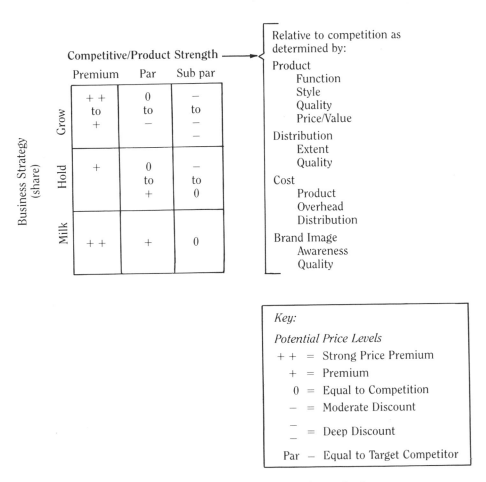

Figure 8-1.   General Retail Pricing Strategies to the Consumer

Figure 8-2 illustrates normal pricing strategies for the trade as a function of long-term strategy and competitive strength. The matrices in Figures 8-1 and 8-2 can be used as guides for planning pricing strategy and market share changes. Consider the extent of changes in competitive dimensions necessary, for example, to gain sufficient strength to move up a cell in share. Estimate the costs and benefits of making the changes.

DIAGNOSING AND FIXING PRICING PROBLEMS

Figure 8-3 summarizes the steps described below for addressing pricing problems. Steps 1–7 are required to fix significant problems and establish routine pricing

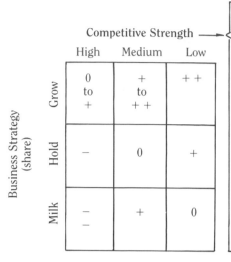

Relative to competition as measured by:

> Demand (real or potential) from
> > The end consumer
> > The trade customer
>
> Need for your specific product/service to
> > fill a void
>
> Service
>
> Price/value
>
> Extent to which line completely meets
> > trade need
>
> Brand image/awareness with
> > Consumer
> > Trade
>
> Product, overhead costs
>
> Product function/style/quality
>
> Marketing support

Key:

Profit Package = Profit as % sales, profit
volume generated by
pricing/terms package

Profit Package Key

+ + = Significantly better than
competition

+ = Better than competition

0 = Equal to competition (par)

− = Below par

$\overline{-}$ = Significantly below par

Figure 8-2. Trade Pricing Strategy:
Profit Package Offered Versus Competitive Strength and Strategy

procedures. Steps 2–6 are routine procedures for companies with correct pricing. Figure 8–4 depicts the four analyses used for diagnosing pricing problems discussed below, Appendix VI-1 provides further detail.

1. **Diagnosing Pricing Problems** Pricing problems indicated by casual internal and market observations can be verified through casual probes inside the company and in the market and a key product trend analysis.

Casual probes Visit the market and test your price/value with distributors and retailers. Visit competitive stores and distributors carrying competitive prod-

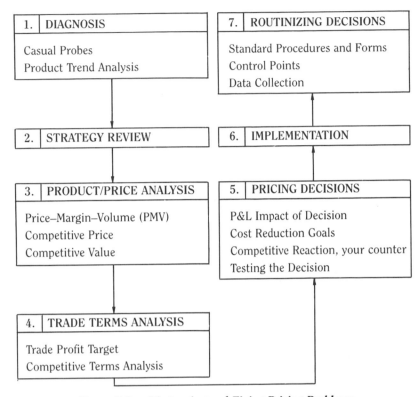

Figure 8-3.   Diagnosing and Fixing Pricing Problems

ucts; collect samples, catalogs, and price/terms sheets. Interview customers in the stores. Then ask your key marketing people the following questions:

What is your pricing strategy versus our top two competitors? Why? What results do you expect?

What competitive terms/services that we lack are valued by the consumer or trade?

How do you establish price levels and line mix at retail?

At wholesale?

How often?

Based on what competitive information?

Based on what non-price benefits offered the consumer or trade?

Who approves the pricing strategy, specific prices and subsequent financial projections? How often?

Ideally, how would you change retail pricing and trade terms?

Even if you delegate the casual probe to others inside or outside your organization, undertake some of the work personally to ensure that reports are accurate.

Product Trend Analysis This analysis yields a broad-based numerical overview of how your prices, volume, market share and costs are tracking the market and allows you to identify categories that merit further attention. The analysis plots for each product category and for three–four years, unit market sales versus your sales; average market price versus your average selling price, the Consumer Price Index versus an index of your manufacturing materials cost, and your unit market share of the category (see Figure 8-4).

The casual probe and product trend analysis will pinpoint 90 percent of your general pricing problems and qualitatively indicate most of the potential solutions.

2.   **Business Strategy Review** Briefly review your business strategy and competitive strength to establish whether you should continue your current strategy or pursue another.

3.   Product/Price Analyses The three analyses discussed below and shown in Figure 8-4 yield recommended retail prices.

Price Margin Volume Analysis (PMV): A PMV compares your actual retail and wholesale prices, gross margin, unit volume, and margin dollars, with targeted volume and gross margin for every product in every category in the line. A PMV should be run at least once annually, or prior to price changes or product introductions. The analysis will reveal which products meet margin or volume goals and suggest potential changes.

Two analyses, the comparative price analysis and value index, compare your prices with those of key competitors and, more important, indicate potential price changes based on the relative value of your product to the consumer.

The Competitive Price Analysis plots the retail price of your product styles versus your competitors'. The analysis not only compares your prices to equivalent competitive product, but points out where you are missing, by style or price-point, products found in the market.

The Price-Value Index representing the weighted advantages or disadvantages of your product (such as quality, style, durability) as perceived by the consumer and trade, and obtained through interviews, shows each of your styles' value relative to competition. The value index when applied to your actual retail prices on the competitive price analysis will indicate where they *should* be, whether they should be increased or must be reduced, or where product features need changing to become competitive.

Price value indices usually are applied across the board to a brand or a major category within a brand, because the consumer's perception of the brand as "premium," "standard," "value," or "cheapie" affects the relative pricing versus competition. Occasionally, indices must be developed by price-point or even individual product when product features and quality differ significantly throughout the line or the target audience varies by price point or product features.

Research techniques that provide solid price-value indices and competitive product-price recommendations include:

a)   Seasoned *management judgment,* which normally is adequate with an established product in an established market, is based on experience, observation of similar product categories, and the marketing savvy of members of the trade. It can be projected, for example, that the 40 percent-plus premiums realized for designer jeans would apply to designer versus non-designer outerwear under $150.

b)   Consumer *price-value-feature tests* are valuable for products or companies new to the market or those making significant changes in lines or pricing structures. Consumers are asked to rank prototype and current products, proven competitive products, and known losers in order of value, discuss pricing issues, and identify features or benefits that placed a product above or below par. Test results indicate absolute prices, prices relative to competitors, and potential volume for each product; the value of specific features; sensitivity of volume to price and/or features; and brand value.

c)   *Value comparisons,* in which consumers rank the value of dissimilar products within the same price range, are particularly useful for new, unproven or unusual products. Men's functional accessories such as attache cases and wallets might be used to price-point a folding umbrella line.

Two other more expensive methods to determine price should be considered only if your strategy is affirmed by basic test results and entails *extremely* high risk (cost of equipment or inventories, loss of share or image). With *simulated store shopping,* consumers are given a fixed amount of money and instructed to buy a product from each of several categories. To judge the effect of price on volume, prices can vary on your and/or competitive products for different consumer groups. Afterward, test subjects provide reasons other than price for their choices.

In *sales tests,* your actual product is put on sale against competitive products at different prices and in comparable locations. Sales at various prices are monitored versus targeted competition. Follow-up interviews with purchasers probe satisfaction with past purchases, intent to repurchase or recommend the product and satisfaction with price and product features. These tests are useful for new products if samples can be made inexpensively, but they're vulnerable to competitive retaliation and the abilities or whims of sales personnel who may prefer a competitor's product over yours or simply don't want to make the effort to sell yours. When producing samples is too expensive, similar products often can be obtained from other countries and modified and branded to suit the local test market.

EXAMPLE 1
PRODUCT TREND ANALYSIS
(Single Category)

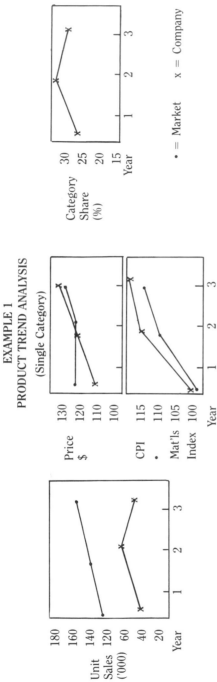

Comments: Apparently increased prices caused lost market share. Need to look at pricing and/or product features to regain share; cost reduction to get profits up.

EXAMPLE 2

PRICE MARGIN VOLUME (PMV) ANALYSIS SINGLE CATEGORY

Style	Retail Price ($)			Wholesale Price ($)			Gross Margin (%)			Unit Volume ('000)			Margin $ ('000)		
	1	2	3	1	2	3	1	2	3	1	2	3	1	2	3
Product A	160	140	150	65	70	75	53	40	40	2	2	3	169	126	207
Product B	79	79	79	41	41	41	38	33	30	15	20	25	450	521	542
Product F															
Category Avg.	110	115	120	55	57	63	50	50.5	42.5	34	44	53	1870	2552	3021
Per Product				Target Gross Margin = 45%					Target Volume = 65,000						

Comments: While margins are meeting targets, volume isn't. Need to investigate product/features and/or price changes to see if unit volumes can be raised along with increased margin dollars.

EXAMPLE 3

| PRICE–VALUE INDEX |

Factors	Our Company	Co. I	Co. II
Quality	3	0	-3
Style	3	0	-3
Features	5	0	0
Image	5	0	3
Service	3	1	0
Average	3.7	.1	-.8
Index (appx.)	120	100	80

Key

0 = Par	-3 = some (-) difference
3 = 10–20% +	-5 = major (-) difference
5 = 25% +	

| COMPETITIVE PRICE ANALYSIS |

Comments: We are under-priced relative to value given compared with top two competitors and can raise prices as recommended without losing share in stagnant market.

*Examples are independent of each other.

Figure 8-4.   Graphic Portrayal of Analyses Used in Diagnosing Pricing Problems*

When to consider each method and its cost for consumer accessories is:

METHOD	WHEN USE	COST*
Management Judgment	Established market, know the market, minor price-product changes	Nil
Price-Value–Feature Tests	Considering major price or price structure changes; new product pricing	Moderate-high, $15–60,000
Value Comparisons	New or novel products	Moderate, $17–20,000
Simulated Store Shopping	As above, with high risk, cash exposure	Expensive
Sales Tests	Considering major price changes; new or novel product; high risk, cash exposure	Very expensive, $30–100,000

Caveat: Note that relative price-value positioning cannot be used to mechanically set prices without considering factors such as:

Projected competitive prices;

Maintenance of "magic" price points (i.e., $99.50) above which consumer purchase resistance increases dramatically;

Price points critical to various retailers' clientele;

Marketing strategy (i.e., initial penetration of a category via price); and

Mechanics of price changes (it's hard to raise retail prices in a recession or trade prices during peak selling seasons).

Relative Value Within the Product Line: The price structure — the relationship of products within a line — must be based upon value delivered to the customer. Even if each product is competitively priced, the structure might be illogical. Consequently, you should insure your products do not compete with one another and that different product prices are warranted by differences in consumer benefits. Check the pricing in your line by answering the following questions:

- Does the price structure accomplish my strategic objectives (grow, hold, milk)?
- Does it accomplish my tactical objectives (grow, hold, or decrease volume across the board or selectively by product, channel, or geography)?
- Is the brand or category's benefit distinct from others offered by the company? Is it wanted?
- Are the prices correct relative to strategy and competition?
- Do prices prevent individual products within the line from competing?

- Are price differences warranted by differences in benefits delivered to the consumer?
- Does the *consumer* consider different prices for different products within the line warranted by different benefits? Why? How do you know?

4.   Trade Terms Analysis Retail prices determine what happens in the marketplace. Wholesale or trade prices and associated terms determine whether a product will reach the market and be promoted once it gets there; your relationship with the trade strongly affects your ultimate market share.

Although the trade sometimes carries prestige brands to build traffic or as loss leaders, retailers and wholesalers base virtually all decisions on potential profit. Before taking on a line, they inevitably consider whether their customers need it, whether it's redundant, and how much money it will generate.

Trade profit is determined by the following formula:

$$\text{PROFIT} = [\text{Realized Resale Price} - \text{Purchase Price}] \times \text{Volume} + \text{Benefit of Nonprice Terms}$$

Realized Price	= Average selling price after deductions for mark-downs, pilferage, write-offs, or clearance of bad merchandise.
Purchase Price	= What was paid for the product, usually expressed as a percent discount from suggested retail or resale price.
Volume	= Units sold.
Benefits of Nonprice Terms	= Reimbursement of expenses or other contributions to profits provided by the manufacturer, such as advertising allowances.

Table 8-1 lists typical price and non-price terms, which vary widely from channel to channel and product to product. Every class of trade (department stores, sporting goods stores, auto parts distributors, etc.) has target profits required to meet profit goals. Check with buyers, publicly available financial statements and private credit reports to determine their goals; some firms will show their audited books.

Competitive Terms: If you're discreet, the trade may provide competitive catalogs, price lists, and published terms. Also seek unpublished terms, such as promotional goods sold below normal price, extra advertising allowances, or bending of rules on minimum orders or payment terms. Your competitors probably consult influential customers regarding pricing-terms programs under consideration; if you cultivate those customers, you may discover competitors' plans.

Target Trade Profit: Once you're aware of competitive discounts and terms and the trade's profit goals, you can calculate the trade target profit, its makeup and the *profit contribution* expected from a supplier as shown in Table 8-2. Target profit, which can be modified to suit your trade strategy and is a powerful tool in selling your programs to the trade, often varies within one channel of trade and

Table 8-1.   Typical Price and Nonprice Terms Offered to Retailers

Price

Standard discounts off suggested retail

Extra discounts for

> Volume — per order or cumulative
>
> Early or preseason order placement
>
> Specific products or product groups

Nonprice Plusses

Financial

> Early pay discounts (2%, 10; net 30)
>
> Markdown allowances
>
> Allowance for returned goods
>
> Rental of counter/display space
>
> Dating (buy now, take merchandise, pay much later)
>
> Anticipation (buy long before need, earlier customer pays, bigger the discount)
>
> Payment for/toward sales clerks
>
> Large or early qualifying buys to earn higher year-long discounts
>
> Consignment (take the merchandise, pay only after it's sold)

Service

> Guaranteed fast shipment from manufacturer's inventory
>
> Special make-up product/labeling
>
> Sales training

Advertising/Promotions

> Cooperative advertising allowances
>
> Straight advertising allowances
>
> Staging of events (celebrity appearances, etc.)
>
> Free collateral material/displays
>
> Catalog participation

Nonprice Minuses

Penalty for late payment of invoices

Restocking charge for returned goods

Tight strictures on advertising presentation, media used

Table 8-2. Target Profit Calculation for a Typical Consumer Product Line (% Sales)

Channel: Department and Specialty Stores

	Store Point of View	Supplier Point of View
Profit Item	Store P&L Statement	Normal "Profit Contribution" Expected from Suppliers
Gross Margin		
Retail Price	100%	100%
Standard Cost	48%	48%
Gross Margin Percent	52%	52%*
Less		
Markdowns	8%	——
Supplier Markdown Contribution	(2)	2
Pilferage	2%	0
Gross Margin Achieved	44%	54%
Supplier Enhancers		
Cooperative Advertising/ Collateral/Display Allowance	2%	2%
Early Pay Discount	2%	2%
Cumulative Volume Discount	2%	2%
Extra Markdown Allowance	1%	1%
Sub Total	7%	7%
*Target Profit Contribution***	51%	61%

*Discounts of 52 percent or mark-up of 108 percent from retailer's cost.
**Product line contribution to profit and overhead.

product category, by size of firm, from corporation to corporation, and geographically.

By comparing your complete trade terms and profit offering with those of your key competitors, you can determine who has the best package, where you're at an advantage or disadvantage, and changes needed to achieve an advantage.

5. **Pricing and Financial Decisions** If you're going to make significant changes after retail prices and trade terms have been analyzed and recommended, be sure to consider potential volume increases or decreases resulting from price changes; increased cost due to improved trade terms; dilution of volume due to similar products within the line; and changes in manufacturing cost if pricing affects volume. Increased volume can reduce cost by spreading overhead; it also can

increase cost through investments in overhead or equipment. Decreased volume usually increases cost because the price of materials rises and overhead is absorbed by fewer units.

Moreover, pricing changes affect selling and administrative costs. Costs not factored into the terms analysis, such as additional service personnel, must appear in the marketing budget as part of the operations planning process or, occasionally, the pricing plan.

If the pricing analysis, which must be run for a sufficient period of time to judge the full P&L impact of contemplated changes, uncovers no strategic flaws and yields acceptable forecast profits, proceed. If not, one or more of the following actions will be required:

Insertions or deletions of products;

Changes in product features to meet or beat competition or reduce cost;

Revision of prices/terms to enhance profitability (almost never to gain share by diluting profits);

A manufacturing cost-reduction program to bolster profits generally and fix unprofitable parts of the line; and

A review of business strategy for the entire category if target profits seem unrealistic, risk seems high, and potential financial rewards seem low

Cost Reduction: Once you know probable margins, you should establish cost goals with manufacturing for *each* product line and significant products within it. Cost-reduction programs are necessary for products not meeting target margins. Marketing, which concentrates on bottom-line profit, should spearhead this effort by establishing product line cost goals and reducing cost prudently in areas under their control such as materials, decorative features, quality standards and size of the line. Manufacturing should accept long-term product-oriented cost goals, and find the cost-reduction methods to meet them.

Countering Competition's Response: Price analyses must anticipate competitive retaliation to your price changes until the market stabilizes. Think ahead by looking back; customers know your competitors' historical responses to similar changes. Key factors affecting that response include the aggressiveness of your move and its effect on their profits; the importance of the line or category to their business; their acceptance with the trade or consumer; their strategy and financial resources, and management's mentality — passive or aggressive. The stronger the competitive reaction, the higher your costs. Your opponents can sabotage your plans (as you can theirs) by quickly meeting or beating your pricing; offering short-term promotions to the trade or consumer promotions at retail; making your positioning obsolete through new products or a restructured line; and increasing advertising.

Testing: Test all significant changes in retail prices or trade terms in the context of the complete market offering (product, pricing, advertising, promotions, and other nonprice programs); consumer testing is needed only for drastic changes in price point or product. Interview salespeople, distributors, or representatives who handle the product, and select retailers from each class of trade affected. Although individual field interviews are acceptable, a complete presentation and review in a central location is preferable. Because competitors will immediately learn of your plans, arrange reviews close to implementation dates.

6. **Practical Implementation** Most industries have product introduction/show/ buy cycles. Implement a strategic price change only when the customer is ready to buy, never in advance. *Sell* the price/terms program as part of a complete trade benefit package (product, profit, volume, image, advertising, etc.), and stress the total profit benefits. Show the trade the profit and volume benefits of an improved price/terms program. Sell your customer on the reasons for cutting benefits such as increased volume and simultaneous introduction of a new product that will add to profit.

Introduce the program quickly, by phone and mail if necessary, to take the competition by surprise. Follow up with personal calls, during which you should seal commitments with key customers. Monitor acceptance of the plan and competitive reaction through sales call reports and frequent personal telephone contact with key customers. In some large firms, a single individual is responsible for collecting and analyzing competitive pricing and terms. Be prepared to change course quickly if early signs, such as loss of volume or crucial accounts, are negative. And be prepared to counter competitive reaction instantly; for example, if you're planning a two-month price promotion in response, make sure all materials are ready when the initial pricing plan is announced.

Use financial reports to track realized prices versus those anticipated in the plan. Immediately after release, reports are often needed weekly, and monthly or quarterly thereafter.

7. **Routinizing Pricing Decisions** Pricing decisions should become part of the annual marketing cycle and incorporate these four elements:

Standard procedures and timing for the annual or semiannual pricing review (which is normally contained in each season's marketing program review) should be carefully considered and communicated in writing. Table 8-3 is a typical sequence.

Standard forms similar to those suggested for pricing and profit analyses insure that you'll consistently obtain the appropriate information.

A control procedure affirms that the numbers are right and responsibility is accepted. Require signature approval by the originator of the pricing scheme, the key financial control, the head of marketing, and the GM. Insure that relevant peripheral functions, including computer operations, credit and receivables, manufacturing, customer service, and advertising, are informed.

Systematic and continuous collection of data on competitive terms and pricing is the responsibility of product management with the help of sales and occasionally market research.

Never gouge the public or the trade when you have a commanding advantage

— they won't forgive you when the market stabilizes. You're in the market for the long pull, so don't take unconscionable profits.

Honda and Mazda, for example, had a very difficult time — after introducing fast-selling models in short supply — preventing some dealers from overcharging for cars or loading them with unwanted accessories for sale to the consumer. This practice hurt disreputable dealers in the long run.

Squeezing Margins

It's appropriate to cut trade profits when you're giving more than the competition is and the product is moving; when you offer a "must have" product; or when distribution is protected so that your product is selectively channeled through a few regional distributors or retailers who get the bulk of your business. Note that selling decreased discounts is hard and commonly evokes emotional outbursts, threats, and high-level power plays from customers. But if you've done your homework, your changes ultimately will be accepted.

TACTICAL PRICING

On a day-to-day basis, you may want to deviate from your established price structure to capitalize on a competitor's weakness or counter a competitive thrust; take advantage of a market surge or protect against a downturn; or stabilize industry pricing after abrupt changes.

Hit your competition when:

1. *They're too weak* to retaliate because their capacity is limited, their product line is narrow and inventories poor, they've alienated the trade, their distribution is inadequate, their management is sluggish or inexperienced, or their manufacturing costs are high.
2. *A hot product* can be used to pull the rest of your line through distribution.
3. *You need volume* across the board or in select categories that are sluggish or unprofitable, scheduled for phasing out, or need a push to become established in the market.
4. *A hole in the market* — an unfilled or new distribution channel — opens up.
5. *They've hit you.*

Counter the threat immediately if the long-term impact of competition's move will cost you more than a retaliatory program. Although tactical moves such as a two-month promotion usually can be quickly matched, strategic moves (a change in their product or price structure, for example) require careful study. If their actions will take time to effectively thwart, consider drastic pricing moves to change the relative value of your product and retain your market position until you formulate a long-term solution.

Confusing the consumer, subtly or directly, about the value of your competition's offering is particularly useful — unless it backfires. Burger King, for example, hit McDonald's hard with effective comparative advertising, alleging that their burgers were better by a scientifically documented taste test. BMW continuously positions their lower price competitors as inferior imitators.

An up-market, when consumers are geared to buy, is a good time to raise prices and introduce new products; the trade approves reasonable price increases that generate more profits. In a downturn, use aggressive price and non-price promotions, selectively launch new products, and prune the slow movers in the line. You can't plan, of course, without forecasting the economy far enough in advance.

If you and your competitors have initiated significant pricing changes, you sometimes can stabilize the market around an acceptable price structure by ignoring their next move and informing your distributors that you're standing pat. It's fine to sacrifice a few share points to attain the desired stable market position.

In general, price structures should not be broken. "Special" deals, which may be illegal, are soon known throughout an industry and can become commonplace. The exceptions are the competitive bids through which many large wholesale or retail chains negotiate contracts. While you might be obliged to break your price structure to meet competition and retain business, try to make as few price concessions as possible; instead, offer advertising allowances, return privileges, paid freight, special packaging and the like. Also, many industrial products are sold on negotiated contracts where deviation is the name of the game.

Beware of predatory pricing, pricing below cost or pricing and/or terms that favor one customer or class of trade. To avoid violation of antitrust laws, review changes in policies with legal counsel.

THE PLACE OF PROMOTIONS

At the retail level, price promotions are necessary to sell slow-moving merchandise and relieve inventories; build store traffic; meet customer expectations during sale periods and tap the buyer who can afford your product only off-price. They usually feature products that are overinventoried or to be discontinued, acceptable second-tier products, and special make-ups that offer fewer features than normal.

The manufacturer should "sell" promotions to the trade and retailer as part of her presentation for the year; she normally gives the trade both price and advertising incentives to promote the desired special products when she wants them promoted. Such products include slow-movers, those overinventoried or to be discontinued, or low cost "make-ups" manufactured only for a promotion. If you don't want a discount image, limit promotional merchandise to a reasonable percentage of sales (10 percent for high-quality products). If you're offering special make-ups, maintain the quality level of the line. Avoid putting best-sellers on sale, and avoid the reputation of a promo house by limiting promotions to short time periods, preferably during traditional sales. When you calculate the P&L for a promotion, indicate both profits from promo goods and profit dilution from lost sales of regular merchandise.

NOTABLE SUCCESSES

Kitchenaid, Maytag, and Amana continuously have maintained price premiums for their products (and probably higher profits) because of their reputation for quality and reliability. Pearl Vision Centers changed the name of the game in the optical world by opening stores for dispensing spectacles, sunglasses, and contact lenses, competing with traditional optometrists and ophthalmologists on price (along with service, frame selection, product guarantees, and advertising). Bausch & Lomb retained its strong market position in the soft contact lens market through carefully thought out, often precipitous, price reductions to counter new entries into the market who were competing principally on price.

KEYS TO SUCCESS

Strategy

Consider strategy, both overall business and marketing strategy, before price. Pricing is only a means to an end.

Tactics

Focus on value when establishing a price structure. Know how much value and profit you must return to the consumer, your retailers and wholesalers to beat the competition.

Don't compete on price. Unless your strategic thrust is exclusively price based on low manufacturing costs. Sell controllable nonprice benefits (image, style, quality) to the trade and consumer.

If you must cut price, keep your basic price structure intact — cut selected items, limit the time period, offer "two for ones," special make-ups, etc.

Think three competitive moves ahead when making price level or structure changes, and incorporate them in your P&L impact statement.

Prepare contingency plans to counter potential competitive price changes.

Competition

Know your competition by regularly gathering market intelligence, catalogs, and price sheets.

Always protect your position.

Don't rationalize competitive price changes that hurt your margins — meet or beat their prices if you must, then determine how to cut cost, increase volume, or develop a better product.

Cultivate field sources, reliable salespeople and members of the trade, who will divulge competitive moves and critique your plans.

Internal Procedures

Systematize pricing — review dates, procedures, and personnel — and develop standard formats for pricing, terms evaluations, and calculation of P&L impact.

Establish a neutral control point, usually a financial controller, to verify the P&L impact of price changes and monitor results. Marketing people tend to overestimate the positive volume and bottom-line impact of programs.

Include manufacturing in pricing discussions; ask them to participate in setting profit-cost goals.

Watch costs, internal and external, materials, labor, and distribution, for increases that may justify price increases.

PRINCIPLES

Pricing

Price should receive top priority. After product, it's the most important factor in the marketing mix, and it's second only to cost in determining profit.

Meet competitive price changes immediately to maintain position.

Ignore "current industry discount practice." Think strategy, value to the consumer and trade, and beating competition.

Personally field-check pricing and acceptance of terms.

To the trade, prices are always too high, discounts too low.

Profit

Poor profitability is your problem — your costs are out of line, your volume's too low, your products aren't right, or distribution is poor. Find out why.

Organization

The COO or GM is responsible for pricing and must review strategy, policy, and impact.

Resist cutting price to gain share or thwart the competition — it's the easy, low-profit way out.

Resist solving short-term profit problems by raising prices or reducing value. It risks long-term damage.

Appreciate the trade's need for profit — they're allies, not adversaries.

Don't base pricing on accounting systems, which rarely produce useful data (real unit cost, marginal cost, cost by product, customer, class of trade). Get it manually until your systems catch up.

Don't let lower level people approve pricing and terms. They are likely to significantly underprice.

Part VII

HIDDEN MARKETING PROBLEMS

Chapter 9

Making Small Changes with Big Impact

The Problem

There are 1,001 pesky little things chewing away at your profits, but you haven't time to fix them. You have too many people, low efficiency, and no backup plans to spike sales in a downturn, combat a competitor, or compensate for a new product failure. Management ignores soaring nonmarketing costs and stagnant sales and distribution channels. Because your company doesn't address customers' nonproduct needs — service, quality, psychological and technical backup — your competitors do just that, and succeed. The business cycle is managing you — maybe right down the tubes.

THE CAUSE

These and other problems often are overlooked because of the universal tendency to focus on exciting new projects or to fight brush fires rather than concentrate on the basic business. Profit improvement in the basic business, after all, is dull, tough, dirty work. Inertia keeps people following standard practices and perpetuating expenditures without justification until disaster strikes. They are indifferent to the cumulative effects of minor actions that can produce bottom line gains as big as those achievable by major new product programs.

In this chapter, you'll find over 35 proven ways for marketing to overcome those pesky little problems and improve profitability. Although not all the suggestions apply to every industry, company, or individual business situation, chances are, if you scan Table 9-1, "Oft Ignored Ways of Making Money," you'll find a few that you've ignored and should explore. Some are quite familiar and, unfortunately, too often forgotten.

PRODUCT

Category Expansions

Quickly moving into categories related to a currently successful business can bring quick profits if the product line is right for the end consumer, if it fits your distribution and image, and if there's room in the market. When both a large publicly owned and a small privately held chain of retail shoe stores began stocking athletic shoes long after that category's growth had peaked, sales and profits increased significantly. Their actions succeeded because customers appreciated the convenience of buying athletic shoes along with dress and casual styles.

Line Extension

Adding product to an already successful line works if you expand the market by stimulating or meeting different customer needs or the extension has been offered successfully by competition. In the early eighties, Bausch & Lomb's profitable Ray Ban™ sunglass line was boosted through development of exclusive new photochromic sunglass lens colors; further development of mirror-coated lenses; introduction of lightweight colored gradient coated lenses; limited introduction of the high-tech look; and introduction of sunglasses color-coordinated with ski fashions.

Special Make-ups

Special make-ups — products briefly sold to increase volume and profits without cannibalizing the standard line — are often items you don't normally market such as low-cost, lower-quality versions of standard styles. These products are usually made with existing equipment so capital investment is negligible. Such black sheep are marketed through normal outlets during off-price sale periods when regular-price goods don't move; overseas outlets or discounters that don't conflict with your standard distribution; and contract sales to wholesalers or retailers who want a special product for private labeling.

Although the profitability of special make-ups might be low, the profit volume and cash flow can be good, especially if make-ups are well-planned factory fillers manufactured when plant volume is low and the added sales absorb substantial fixed overhead. But unless specials are a small part of your line and

Table 9-1. Oft-ignored Ways of Making Money

Product
>   Category expansion
>   Line extension
>   Special make-ups
>   Line pruning

Volume
>   Get volume up by cutting the price

Manufacturing
>   Reduce product cost by marketing direction
>   Schedule for efficiency — not sales
>   Reduce quality standards
>   Reduce inspection

Distribution
>   Channel expansion
>   Channel pruning
>   Weeding out unprofitable outlets
>   Redistricting the sales force
>   Using different selling methods (wholesale)
>   Strengthening weak geographic areas
>   New sales goals/commissions

Advertising/Creative
>   Cut it
>   Cut cooperative
>   Tight expense/project control
>   Chop free product
>   Farm out design
>   Farm out market research

People
>   Cut back/reconfigure

Service
>   Better meet customers' nonproduct needs (service, technical support, etc.)

Inventories
>   Reduce them
>   Configure the line for minimum SKUs

Consultants
>   Cut them out
>   Hold them to their bargain

Vendors
>   Take all you can legitimately get

Price/Terms
>   Extra profit pricing/terms moves

New Products
>   Cut marginal projects
>   Cut sample/development costs
>   Weed out losers early

System
>   Cut unnecessary reports
>   Control DP projects

Repairs/Guarantees
>   Replace it free

Back-up Plans
>   Ready-to-go products
>   Ready-to-go promos

Manage the Business Cycle
>   Cutback early
>   Position for the comeback
>   Act early on the way back

significantly different from your standard products, you'll diminish profits and damage your reputation. If your specials are detrimental to your image, protect your business by distributing them through different channels under another name.

Line Pruning

As discussed in Chapter 4, you can improve profitability, reduce assets and free up cash by maintaining the smallest line consistent with your strategy and unloading poor or unprofitable sellers.

Increase Volume

Volume increases are crucial in a troubled economy, when you aren't meeting budget, your category or line is stagnating, or the market is maturing and you're unprepared to innovate.

Cut the wholesale price for a limited time if your customer will buy a minimum specified quantity of a specified product or a package of promotional goods, but reduce prices only on special make-ups or middle-volume sellers, not top-selling products. Give the trade a strong incentive to maintain suggested retail price through institutional advertising and point-of-safe material. You can get quick results if you offer good product, not junk.

Cut the retail price if the cut is deep enough (usually 25–40 percent) to attract consumers and you can restore the original price without permanently hurting your image. This speedy method is preferable during normal sale period and for nonprestige items such as appliances, tools, and electronic equipment.

Run load-ins or qualifiers — significant discounts to the trade if they buy large quantities before the selling season, often accompanied by increased discounts for six months to a year on rebuys (fill-ins). Such up-front investments limit their purchase of competitors' products, and large inventories encourage quick movement of merchandise. Load-in programs may diminish normal future sales but usually boost the overall sales level.

Promote your high-margin items via point-of-sale material, advertising or adding value (i.e., gift with purchase, special limited editions) without endangering your image with retail price cuts. Coupons, rebates and sweepstakes are effective for high-volume housewares, small appliances and big-ticket hard goods rather than consumer fashions or accessories and industrial goods.

MANUFACTURING

Reduce Product Cost

To accomplish reductions, marketing must set reasonable, lower, product cost goals; compromise on materials, decoration, packaging and number of items in

the line; cooperate with manufacturing, purchasing and product design to identify high-cost components or operations and determine which can be cost-
reduced; and consider cost-effective redesign of old products. It sometimes is
cheaper to manufacture all or part of a product outside your company, particularly low-volume or seasonal items that can be produced more efficiently
elsewhere.

A jewelry manufacturer under severe cost pressure, for example, improved
the corrosion-resistance of its product, reduced material cost and improved manufacturing speed and yields by substituting a less expensive base metal material
that required less gold plating.

Schedule for Efficiency, Not Sales

Marketing must provide a good annual or seasonal forecast for each stable item
in the line. Manufacturing must schedule product as follows:

A — high-volume items run continuously at relatively constant volume

B — moderate-volume items run several times annually at high volume

C — low-volume items run once per year

ABC scheduling or its variations offer several advantages. Continuous high-
volume runs avoid frequent, expensive set-up charges incurred when equipment
tooling is changed to accommodate different products; employees soon become
extremely efficient and don't require frequent retraining; and purchasing can plan
material purchases at optimum prices and minimize inventories. In response to
unanticipated market demand and order patterns, of course, some volume of fill-
ins, quick makes, urgent orders, and new items will inevitably be required and
inefficiently made.

When one manufacturer imposed ABC scheduling on a 3,000+ item line that
previously had been scheduled hand-to-mouth, labor efficiency rose 11 percent,
this translated into a 3 percent unit cost savings. Material usage variances —
waste due to operator error — also were reduced dramatically.

Reduce Quality Standards

Heresy? Not necessarily. Some standards are too tight, especially when set by
technocrats not responsible for P&L rather than by marketing and the marketplace. Compare your quality — materials, defect rate, blemish, or fault frequency
and extent — with competition's and market demands. If in doubt, test different
quality levels to determine what's important to your target market. If you can
lower standards, costs will decrease and yields rise. (But don't reduce quality
below target market requirements just to make money — the consumer will soon
catch on. Remember Detroit's shoddy cars and frequent recalls.)

Despite rigid standards, for example, a manufacturer of high-quality optical goods received many complaints and subsequent returns from Far Eastern and European importers. Because the importers could return unlimited product for credit if vaguely defined standards weren't met, they made returns freely and frivolously. When the manufacturer enforced standards and limited returns from overseas importers, money was saved and consumers remained satisfied.

Reduce Inspection

This isn't heresy either. After marketing and manufacturing establish final product standards, including permissible quality variations and the acceptable quality level (AQL), manufacturing can install a cost-effective quality assurance/inspection program. Inspection costs and the number of inspectors can be reduced without endangering quality if reasonable standards replace informal "ship everything perfect" standards, and if good statistical sample inspections at the appropriate point during manufacture and in final inspection replace frequent 100 percent inspection. The latter, which often is used for expensive products, is ineffective because of inspectors' fatigue and their imposition of personal standards more rigid than those of engineering or marketing. After objectively examining its final inspectors' rejects, one manufacturer found that 35 percent of the rejects were within specification.

DISTRIBUTION

Channel Expansion

Consider quick tactical moves such as selling abroad through agents or piggybacking on establishing American firms selling similar products abroad or obtaining new domestic distribution channels compatible with your current channels (i.e., large high-leverage chains if you're concentrated in specialty stores or smaller operations).

Long-term strategic moves depend on where else your target audience shops and will shop in the future and whether competitors are using any channels of trade that you're not. Changes in distribution must be made cautiously because established distribution channels are economically and legally difficult to cut out. Moreover, the consumer expects to find you in certain channels, and your product borrows the channel's image (that's why you won't find Dunhill lighters in cheap jewelry stores). New channels compete with old, so make sure you're ahead in net sales and profit when you add them.

Consider emerging or newly established channels such as direct mail, cable television, telephone sales, and roving vans, but note that drastic channel changes often involve changes in product design and sometimes in price points.

Levi Strauss, for example, increased immediate jean sales when it moved into mass merchandising via J.C. Penney and Sears. Although the move was made for strategic reasons, filling the pipeline helped short-term results. Hart, Schaffner and Marx has moved into company-owned discount outlet stores selling private-label clothing but not HSM brands. By following their customers, who increasingly buy top brands through off-price and discount outlets, the company protects its market and taps an emerging one. Halston designed a new line for Penney's in order to open up the mass market for his clothing, previously sold only at exclusive specialty stores.

Channel Pruning

Do you have channel or channel-product combinations that aren't sufficiently profitable when their costs are realistically allocated? If they can't be made profitable and won't be particularly important to your target market, think about dropping them.

Store or Customer Pruning

The same goes for individual stores you own or customers you service. Kroger, the biggest and most profitable supermarket chain in the country, is known for mercilessly cutting out stores that don't yield quick profits. K-Mart aggressively expanded its discount stores while closing over half of its Kresge variety stores. Woolworth, in contrast, moved too slowly into discounting and not fast enough in cutting back or improving profitability of their variety stores. Their Woolco discount operations have gone under.

Redistricting and Changing Sales Staff

In most sales organizations, 20 to 30 percent of the sales territories present problems. In the few "sweet" territories with more potential than one salesperson can handle, he or she can skim the high-volume accounts, make lots of money, and leave remaining customers to fend for themselves. Other territories that don't warrant a full-time salesperson are assigned one. Some salespeople are ill-trained to manage their time and customers correctly; some are simply inadequate, but management may be reluctant to remove them for fear of damaging customer relations or because of their age or tenure with the company.

The solution is to identify, periodically, your national potential by geographic area, estimate the man-days required to service your accounts of all sizes and, if necessary, reallocate districts and territories. Retrain or fire salespeople who don't generate expected sales in promising territories, but be fair if their poor performance stems from poor direction, training, product, or service. An electronics parts manufacturer increased sales by 27 percent in one year, for example, after a market survey of sales potential, the subsequent relayout of one sales district, and the addition of one salesperson and a firm of manufacturers' representatives.

Change Wholesale Selling Methods

Now that traditional practices — your own salespeople on the road, perhaps supported by a few independent reps — are very expensive, you must determine the most cost-effective means of closing sales and whether money-saving methods will decrease penetration.

Typical alternative methods include making telephone instead of personal calls (particularly good for low-value items, small customers, and follow-up or service calls); direct mail; independent representatives paid only according to completed sales (but whose work cannot be controlled); a telephone pitch delivered by a skilled telemarketer following a computerized script; and piggybacking with the salesforce of a manufacturer of similar noncompeting goods. Roffe, Dimitri and Smiley, who manufacture color and design coordinated ski wear, ski sweaters, and ski hats respectively, are separate companies that share the same sales organizations. A major book distributor mails catalogs to retail customers and solicits orders only by phone. And many prestigious stores such as Saks Fifth Avenue boost sales through direct mail throughout the year.

Sales Goals/Commissions

Put your sales staff's compensation in line with your goals.

Compensation schemes often depend on sales level or increases, not on marketing's desire to emphasize certain channels, products and programs. Salespeople for a company that offered five lines worked for a flat percentage-of-sales commission and didn't push two of the smaller, less interesting lines. Management consequently lowered the commission rate on the banner line, which almost sold itself, doubled commissions and ran contests with cash rewards to spike sales of the smaller lines.

Strengthening Weak Geographic Areas

Although you may pinpoint weaknesses through the same analysis used for redistricting salespeople, the problems here may be entrenched competition; the wrong product line for the geographic area; and weak terms/pricing or promotional programs.

ADVERTISING AND CREATIVE

Media Advertising

If you have profit or cash-flow problems and your business doesn't demand constant ad pressure, you're unlikely to be hurt by careful cutbacks. Try placing token but high-visibility advertising in key trade and consumer journals to give your salespeople something to talk about and give distributors and customers reassurance that you're still in business. Alternatively, you can cut institutional or brand-building advertising partially or completely for three to twelve months with little effect on awareness or sales. Ask your agency, which will disagree with such decisions, to prove that you'll lose sales — they probably can't.

Cooperative Advertising

Coop is often useless if not harmful. It forms part of your selling-price discount to the customer, rather than effective advertising for you, and communicates the trade's message, not yours. Consider cutting it, offering a slight, temporary increase in discount if you absolutely must to cushion the blow, or withdrawing national programs and participating only in market areas where competition or customers make it mandatory or profitable. If you have no choice, minimize it by demanding ads run on your schedule to tie into national programs; imposing rigid rules and refusing to pay for anything that isn't well documented; refusing to pay more than 50 percent except for exceptional programs; or using it only for special purposes or projects.

Upon discovering that customers were spending coop dollars on ineffective advertising, entertainment, and handouts of pens, a Fortune 500 company with the number-one brand in the category withdrew a $450,000 coop program. Despite the hue and cry from the trade, sales were not affected — but the bottom line was.

Tight Expense, Personnel, and Project Control

Particularly if yours is a small or medium-sized account, your ad, display, and sales promotion agencies might be costing you money through inefficiency or poor management. They're often guilty of overspending budgeted hours and dollars; delivering poor quality; chronic lateness accompanied by lots of overtime; constantly switching account personnel; sloppy media selection; and misbilling. And clients are by no means innocent, either. Be sure to choose your agency carefully, manage them well, and uphold your part of the bargain by giving good, timely direction.

You can save money by using a tight project control system, often called a job jacket system. Define goals for each project; request a timetable and tight cost and time estimates; log in each bill; and inform the agency that you won't pay for over-runs that you didn't order. Always reject the first media proposal and demand 10 percent more audience for the same price — they'll usually deliver. Don't tolerate chronic personnel changes or inadequate agency people; announce that you won't subsidize trainees or notetakers. Issue a monthly report on progress against project goals and expenses. Prohibit overtime, and plan ahead so you can't be blamed for inefficiency. Reject unacceptable work, which should be redone at the agency's expense. And, above all, find an agency that considers your business crucial.

Crack Down on Freebies

If you're in the consumer products business, you're aware that everybody wants one (or a dozen) free. A $50 million business, for example, found it was dispensing $200,000 worth of free products per year to friends, relatives, and customers, sales staff, agencies, and to research firms. Most of such waste can be eliminated by requiring documentation for every free product accompanied by the controller's and the originator's signatures; billing for all loans and samples that aren't returned; establishing courtesy accounts whereby employees or business associates can buy product at wholesale or slightly above; and giving key management personnel a reasonable budget for no-questions-asked freebies.

Farm Out Design

Product, packaging, and graphic design needn't be done in-house, at least not completely. You can cut costs by using an in-house designer-coordinator with one or more outside product designers paid on a minimum retainer and/or an hourly or per-project rate. You also might boost creativity by switching design groups when your direction changes or a group becomes stale.

Farm Out Market Research

Similarly, you can have an in-house coordinator and maybe someone to undertake small or quick-and-dirty jobs and still capitalize on the wealth of product-style-market research agencies available at a relatively modest cost. It's a very competitive industry.

PERSONNEL

Very few organizations, especially in good times, appreciate the value of a lean, well-qualified staff. You can cut costs and improve productivity if you're overstaffed, particularly during a downturn; you've been reluctant to fire poor performers; you maintain unproductive projects and related personnel; or highly paid people are doing clerical jobs.

To eliminate dead wood, ask the human resources department to help you justify every slot and update all performance reviews. Examine the structure of your organization now (which functions report to whom) and consider future needs. Develop key job descriptions and estimate how many people actually are required. Then make all changes warranted, but avoid making disruptive structural changes that will impede progress.

If you must fire people, do it kindly and supportively. Generous severance pay and outplacement services pay off by helping people relocate with minimal financial and emotional trauma and by generating goodwill.

Sometimes personnel increases are warranted. When a national sales manager with a staff of 18 added three district managers, productivity improved far in excess of the $160,000 in cost.

NONPRODUCT NEEDS

Most companies focus on product and/or price offerings and ignore their customers needs in terms of delivery, product service, technical back-up, quality, and pricing. Moreover, they're unaware of how their performance compares to competitors'. One industrial products firm that prided itself on customer service learned from a survey that its image and performance were considered very spotty.

To determine your customers' needs and how you stack up, you could conduct research similar to that done by a major industrial parts manufacturer. Representatives of this company surveyed a large number of decision-makers by mail to obtain their criteria for purchasing from a vendor and opinions on how the company compared to competitors; surveyed a variety of customers in industries that used the company's products; interviewed a large sample of all segments of their industry to discover their competitors' activities and how they could gain an advantage; and developed and implemented a multimillion dollar program to install a new order-entry/inquiry system, fix quality problems, and improve product packaging. They also improved the effectiveness of their distributors and their delivery system. The three to five year improvement program that resulted from this research allowed the company to maintain their #1 industry position and helped propel high annual growth in a highly competitive commodity business.

The study also revealed that it takes time for competitors to recognize service improvements and time and money to copy them and that buyers, particularly in an industrial commodity market, favor the supplier with better service.

By the way, the qualitative "must" needs of the surveyed buying influences were:

BUYERS	ENGINEERS
Meeting delivery promises	Ease of contacting the proper party at vendor location
High quality	Technical information readily available
Assistance in panic situations	Technical support (design help, performance testing, etc.)
Competitive delivery	Receiving information (i.e., specifications) in the form requested
Being advised of potentially serious problems	A good (he/she knows the product, company capabilities) salesperson
Competitive pricing	

The cost of the study, which took nine months of a highly qualified researcher's time, cost approximately $75,000. The payback? Incalculable.

INVENTORIES

To sum up the advice found earlier in this chapter and in Chapter 5, cut the level; cut the SKUs; configure the product line for the minimum SKUs consistent with the market's needs; keep the line clean to avoid accumulated obsolescence; and combine raw materials for different product lines. One manufacturer reduced finished goods inventories by one-third by selling slow-moving or obsolete inventory at distress prices. He also reduced raw material inventories by 30 percent by eliminating unneeded SKUs and near-duplicate raw materials, standardizing materials across product lines, and selling slow-moving materials.

CONSULTANTS

Use consultants selectively and hold them to their contracts.

Consultants can be of great help in improving profits by serving as an objective sounding board, sharing specialized knowledge that can pay off in the short term, and saving your people's time by assembling data and recommendations. They're also useful for leading top team meetings and setting goals and priorities and for justification and development of some of the aforementioned quick profit-improvement programs (line extensions, special promotions, channel expansion, redistricting, sales training, etc.).

To obtain the experience and wisdom for which you're paying, don't accept the services of a $250-a-day newcomer at the $1,000–$2,000 daily rate for seniors. State your goals, establish agreement, get a price for the job, don't pay unless goals are met, and make sure that you approve of the specific people who are to work on your account. Don't accept substitutes — particularly junior people who are just learning.

PRICING/TERMS

Always seek opportunities to raise prices. As advised in Chapter 8, you might consider raising prices on individual items, especially those to be discontinued; eliminating early-pay discounts and expedited freight; charging for quick service, that is, 24-hour shipment; imposing penalty/interest charges on overdue accounts receivable; slightly increasing product quantities to be purchased to gain a specified level of discount. Lots of little charges that customers often ignore can add up to a few percentage points at the bottom line.

VENDORS

Suppliers can make money for you if you stretch out payments within the limits that they allow. If you can, negotiate special terms and cost-saving blanket contracts on items such as printing, displays, and raw materials typically purchased on an as-needed basis. Ask your vendors to carry stocks of raw materials or, indeed, printed materials for you. Where big dollars are involved, get competitive bids and negotiate people down. (Marketing people are the softest negotiators. They should learn from their hard-nosed manufacturing counterparts.)

NEW PRODUCTS

New products, like rabbits, tend to multiply in vast numbers and into all varieties of colors and patterns. List all your new product projects under A (sure winners or tactical or strategic musts); B (probable winners); and C (questionable). Cut out the Cs. If there are screams of protest, examine why (something you should do anyway during new product reviews).

Cut Sample/Development Costs

Consumer products firms will produce three slightly different handmade models to appraise a design when one would do just fine. Marketing will request five times as many models as they'll ultimately take to market. Companies will hand-craft sales samples at twenty times the cost of preproduction test product because manufacturing is running late.

    Sound familiar? You can cut costs if you allow only X number of designs for every product that goes to market (X depends on the novelty of the design); schedule to insure that sales samples come from production; cut the sales staff's sample budget by limiting them to necessities, eliminating customer freebies, and refreshing their sample kits only when required, not upon request. Ask them to return all samples. Instead of a full-blown prototype, use sketches, conceptual models, and partial prototypes to make early design judgments. By making several of these moves, a major consumer accessories manufacturer saved $150,000 out of a $300,000 sample budget.

Weed Out Losers Early

People hang onto their favorite ideas forever, even though prompt removal of ill-advised new products saves time and money. Weed out losers through a consensus among your marketing staffers based on instinct and experience and early "quickie" consumer testing with sketches or prototypes.

SYSTEMS

Although computer-based information systems can be enormously helpful, their development and cost are difficult to control (see Chapter 10). You can improve short-term profits through careful negotiations regarding internal or external systems and rates and subsequent monitoring of rates. Because data-processing people are notorious for poor cost control and accounting and budget overruns, make the DP department absorb any charges in excess of estimate. Eliminate unnecessary reports, and defer development of strategic systems such as shop floor control or a new order-entry system unless you'll suffer competitively without them.

REPAIRS/GUARANTEES

Determine what your product guarantee/warranty, repair and replacement policies are costing, and try to find a less expensive way of meeting your customers' needs. A prestigious consumer accessories firm with a negligible return rate, for example, would carefully examine each product sent in for repair and decide whether liability was theirs or the customer's. In the latter case, if the customer authorized a repair after receiving an estimate, the company returned the repaired product with a bill six to eight weeks later. Eventually, the company eliminated substantial repair, correspondence and billing costs by instituting a free repair or replacement policy and gained immense goodwill from consumers, who got their products back in a week to ten days. Total repair program costs decreased.

BACK-UP PLANS

Ready-to-Go Products

What will you do if a new product fails in test or in the market? What if the economy or category turns sour? One answer is to rely on a back-up — a product or product line that's tested, all or partly tooled, and waiting in the wings for release. (Of course, there must be a need for your product, and it must complement your existing line.)

Don't forget that variations on an already successful theme, such as new shapes, colors, textures and performance features, can increase sales. Detroit often enriches automotive lines with periodic offerings of designer models and interiors or performance packages. After launching a single successful sunglass model, Porsche Carerra quickly increased sales with new frame colors and styles.

Ready-to-Go Promos

As part of your annual marketing plan, determine how you'll react regarding price, product, promotion, and distribution if sales or the economy turn up or down. Although you needn't bother with details for executing these plans, you must establish your basic strategy and basic tactical details and undertake the detail work on long-lead-time items (i.e., design/tooling of special make-ups, details of a sweepstakes, tight detailed layouts of promo materials). Make sure your plans won't become outdated and will remain good back-up for several years or until they're needed as a regular program.

MANAGE THE BUSINESS CYCLE

Whether or not you heed them, the signs of economic downturn and recovery inevitably are there. If you have the insight and courage to act on these signs, you can mint money.

A major manufacturer of highly cyclical industrial parts was so badly burned during the 1966–1969 recession that management conducted an extensive study of their costly mistakes. They concluded that they had ignored clear signals of the downturn until it was too late. Because they tried to maintain efficiency by keeping plants running too long, inventories rose to unacceptable levels; although their customers' inventories also were too high, they hadn't monitored the extent of the build-up. Moreover, they had failed to reduce manufacturing personnel and overhead quickly enough and had not formulated plans to take business from their competitors (admittedly a long shot in industrial businesses with little "promo" leverage).

On the upturn, management saw the signs but was too cautious to act. They delayed necessary capacity expansion and increased production so slowly that inventories shrunk and customer service suffered. When the economy came roaring back, they lost millions of dollars of profits because of business lost to competition and money wasted on overtime and inefficient operation of plants pushed to their absolute limit.

The message, of course, is to cut back deeply and early. When the signals indicate a recovery, act early — spend and position yourself to capitalize on the comeback.

KEYS TO SUCCESS

- *Pay attention to the small things* — you never know when they'll become big and bad. Address a checklist of minor problems periodically at annual operations planning meetings and during budgeting and organization probes.

- *Set priorities.* Focus your efforts on problems that require attention, fixing the most significant ones first.
- *Delegate problem solving.* If the job is crisply defined and they have the time, lower-level personnel usually can handle it.
- *Pay personal attention to the "delicate unmentionables,"* such as sales territory layout, sales compensation, reorganization or reduction in personnel, changes in quality methods and standards, inventories, and system/DP expenditures. They require top-level diplomacy, judgment and, sometimes, toughness.
- *Once you're clean, stay clean.* Divide the checklist among appropriate subordinates responsible for monitoring each area and identifying and fixing problems in their early stages.

Part VIII

INADEQUATE CONTROL

Chapter 10

Controlling the Overall Marketing Function

The Problems

Sales constantly miss forecast. Without warning, marketing costs soar out of control and service deteriorates. New product programs are late; goals are missed; and profitability is poor. Unsaleable assets mount as unexpected lower-level decisions sabotage top-level plans.

You're totally at sea — every month's performance comes as a big surprise.

A junior product manager, for example, drove his small new $1,000,000 line of ski accessories deeply into the red by overspending dramatically on packaging, promotional materials, advertising, and displays. There were no monthly controls to flag the time and money each of this company's businesses was committing to outside agencies, and each product manager's budget was never specified.

Over one-third of the product in an expensive men's accessory line was dead, but no one knew it because management neglected to regularly review line performance versus goal. A consultant's audit revealed that product had been added helter-skelter, slow movers remained in the line, and no goals or controls had been established to determine the size of the line and what gets kept, added, or chopped. Ultimately, a substantial portion of the multimillion-dollar inventory was written off or disposed of at salvage prices. A total of 35 percent of the line was dropped.

199

In late 1982, shortly after giving financial analysts a rosy quarterly and year-end earnings forecast, Warner Communications drastically reduced its projections for sales and earnings of the banner Atari Division. Warner's stock plummeted, and officers who had sold stock immediately prior to the revised forecast were suspected of trading on inside information. Did Atari have the simple controls to show that wholesale and retail sales of video game players and cartridges were falling far short of expectation? Or was Warner too intoxicated with being top dog in a hot new industry to notice the inevitable slow down, shakeout, and increase in competition?

SYMPTOMS

The primary symptom of lack of marketing control is surprise. The more frequent the surprises and the more areas in which they occur, the more out of control your organization.

Adequate marketing controls usually can indicate the following symptoms in time to fix problems or soften the blow.

Sales

Although short-term sales forecasts are missed by wide margins, sales managers can't explain why. They also don't know why some sales territories or stores meet goals while others don't or why top customers suddenly disappear from the top-customer list (if there is one). What's more, the sales mix is unbalanced — oversold in some items, usually high-volume ones, and undersold in others.

Service

The overall service level deteriorates without warning. "Out of stocks" are rampant on specific items; customers are upset; and sales and manufacturing hadn't predicted the problem.

Expenses

Your staff increases, particularly at lower clerical and nonmanagerial levels. Travel expenses as percent of sales continually creep up. Marketing expenses, particularly advertising and promotion, exceed budget. You're not informed in advance of unnecessary travel, collateral materials, publicity events, and customer entertaining or of overspending by advertising and promotion agencies.

Products

You have lots of products, many selling at low volume. New product sales calls and results are behind schedule, and new product service is poor because of manufacturing mix imbalances.

Assets

Lots of unsaleable or slow-moving inventory.

Quality

You learn from the field that your product quality varies all over the map, but you've heard nothing from your inside people.

Receivables

Because outstanding receivables accumulate and large customers are pushing the limits, you're in an unexpected cash bind.

Profits

Formerly profitable products become unprofitable, and you're left with large inventories of unsaleable or slow-moving merchandise.

CAUSES

Inability to control the marketing function usually results from a management that's winging it rather than measuring progress against goals and/or from the lack of money or systems support necessary to establish controls. An organization is liable to lose control if the following commonplace circumstances prevail.

The organization is large, with many decision-making units that often are located in different businesses with different goals. Responsibility for decisions and results is not clearly delegated, and no specific guidelines exist to limit expenditures without upstairs approval. The organization's culture is either swinging or old-line; in either case, it's biased against controls. Because business, program, product line, and individual goals are never set, there is nothing against which to measure performance. If goals are set, progress is neither monitored nor measured. The pace of business is so hectic that there's no time for review (this is most often true of a rapidly growing high-tech business or a fast-moving fashion business). Employees create problems through their tendency to promise too much too soon or commit themselves to unrealistic goals to please the boss; their anxiety about fulfilling these burdensome obligations; and their reluctance to have their performance rated and admit the existence of problems and mistakes.

PURPOSE OF CONTROLS

Marketing controls insure that short- and long-term goals are met by highlighting impending problems requiring immediate attention in time for you to address them, diagnose the problems, and fix them or soften their blow. The earlier the warning, the more specific the diagnosis, the better the control.

Controls are not intended to foster the illness of "management by numbers" — generating lots of numbers pointing out where they're bad, and controlling everything in sight. It's the people, managers, and business thinking behind the numbers that count. Although controls are often used to measure performance, they're not primarily designed for financial reporting or assessment of employee achievement.

ESTABLISHING CONTROLS

Large organizations encompass three levels of responsibility:

Level I: This top level (i.e., VP of marketing) addresses overall performance versus budget and long-range goals; major strategic and policy issues; and integration of programs throughout the marketing functions. Gross, broad-brush controls are used at this level to pinpoint problems or areas, such as sales failing to track forecast, that require further investigation at lower levels.

Level II: On this level, top functional or middle managers, such as director of sales, group product manager, product manager, and creative director, are concerned with developing and implementing detailed programs and making mid-course corrections while executing the operating and strategic plans. More detailed controls are needed here to highlight narrow problem areas and solve the problems (i.e., Why didn't sales track forecast last year in department stores and product lines XYZ?). Level II controls usually are second to be implemented in a new control program.

Level III: Lower-level managers and professional personnel such as assistant product manager, product planners, sales managers and salespeople usually are concerned with identifying and solving short-term problems. The detailed diagnostic controls they require involve extensive data and systems development work and consequently are installed last. Stage III controls let lower-level personnel find and correct specific problems — such as, sales at department store chains A, B, and C are off in products X, Y, and Z; or line X is off because of reduced sales in high-volume products 1, 2, and 3 — often before they're noted by upper-level controls. It's a poor salesperson who doesn't pick up the phone the day that reports show sales are down (then again, it's a poor salesperson anyway who must rely on a report to signal trouble with a major customer).

Table 10-1 lists the areas that most marketing organizations watch and control and typical critical events that control reports should flag. Most flagged events are negative because most businesses set expectations so high that deviations require tough corrective action. Positive events — sales exceeding forecast, costs falling, or new products arriving ahead of schedule — also require flagging and action. If sales exceed expectations, after all, production and inventories must be increased to support them.

Table 10-1. Areas of Control; Typical Critical Events Monitored

Control Area	Events
Overall Financial Performance	Deterioration of sales, gross or by category or line
	Overexpenditure in any major category — usually staff, plant costs, or advertising
Sales/Orders	Falling orders or sales versus prior year, forecast. Overall or by individual categories, products, customer groups, or promotions
The Product Line	Sales–orders–unit costs–mix off, versus goal — in part or all of the line; forecast below budget
	Market share deteriorating in specific categories or lines
	Plant production below required level; mix wrong; cost variances high
New Products	P&L, sales of new launches behind goal; service poor, production mix skewed versus sales
	Products in development behind schedule
Creative	Key programs behind schedule, overspent
Product Quality	Not meeting standards — in general; specific lines
Customer Service	Percentage of product shipped out-of-stock too low, particularly in heart of the line or new or hot products
Inventories	Overall level, percent slow-moving or obsolete too high
Receivables/Terms	Receivables too high with large problem customers
	Special terms offered out of line with policy
Human Resources	Head count too high, can't hire needed people
Expenses	Over budget in some functional areas, underspent in others, indicating lack of progress
Forecast	Forecast of sales, orders, assets, and P&L for quarter, remainder of year highlights problems with sales; gross margin; NPBT; production broad load overall, by category, product; inventories; expenses
Individual Goals	High percentage of individual goals being missed

Figure 10-1 indicates typical titles at each level in the marketing organization, areas normally under that level's control, and an example of problems flagged and the resulting actions.

Because specific marketing controls depend upon the business, its size and its particular goals and programs, there are no instantly adaptable "normal" controls or standard formats. Appendix VIII-1, however, lists common marketing reports and their content, users, and frequency. Useful control reports can be developed from this outline by selecting subjects of critical importance, adding any additional content information suited to your particular business formatting them for your purposes, and selecting the time frame to be covered.

To develop and implement a marketing control program for your organization, assemble a team led by an experienced marketing manager and including a financial controller and a systems specialist from an internal or external data processing group. Then follow the steps described below and illustrated in Figure 10-2.

1.   **Analysis** The basic financial reports available to most companies are of little use to marketing; specialized marketing reports often pertain to the business as it was, rather than as it is or will be. A Fortune 500 consumer products company, for example, could produce an accurate P&L for each business, but not for each product, category or product line, much less each item. As a result, many unprofitable products could not be identified without expensive, extensive manual labor.

To determine what you have, how well it works, and what should be discontinued, gather all reports received by marketing and ask each control level to divide them into the absolute must-have's; those used occasionally; and those that are dispensable.

2.   **Diagnosis** Many organizations employ gross controls (i.e., orders and sales by product line) but lack the detailed controls that warn of subtle trends within a larger category (i.e., sales and orders by item). In such cases, items whose sales rate is outpacing or underselling production input can result in too little to sell or too much in inventory.

To identify your current or potential problems, determine where your company traditionally has lost control and where you've been surprised. Next, establish the controls that will be required in the future due to planned operating and strategic changes. Because control systems, particularly if computer-based, are extremely expensive and take months or years to develop, you must consider future needs. When a consumer products firm abruptly abandoned its "put out a few new products when we feel like it" philosophy in favor of planned, tightly spaced new product introductions, it was forced to develop quickly controls for weekly tracking of sales orders and inventories by product and item and of each salesperson's "hit ratio" by key account.

Level	Control Responsibility	Event (E)/Reason (R)	Potential Action
Level I *VP marketing* Overall goal/strategy/ policy oriented	Identify gross problem areas for attention Integrate solutions across functions Decisions on major policy/strategic issues	E — new product X is failing R — new competitive entry superior	Withdraw spending on product, cut manufacturing schedule, kill at season's end Develop a new product to beat new competitive entry
Level II *Top functional managers, middle management* Problem identification/ solution oriented	Flag specific problem areas within functions Work with subordinates on solutions specific to an individual or the whole function	E — service level fallen from 96% to 86% R — poor forecast; low production, inventories for lines A, B	New forecast, production schedule lines A, B to support new sales rate
Level III *Lower management, professionals* Problem solving/ implementation oriented	Flag, take action or direction to solve specific problems within their control	E — sales, share of customers A, B, C down R — infrequent sales calls, poorer service than competition	Increase sales call frequency Customer service to insure orders shipped on time, give A, B, C special attention

Figure 10-1.   Action to be Taken by Control Level

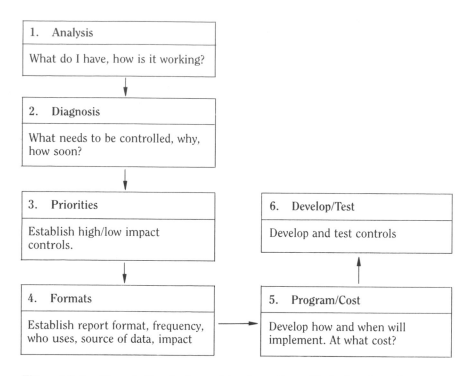

Figure 10-2.   Steps in Developing and Implementing a Marketing Control Program

Finally, request suggestions from all levels of the marketing organization on report formats and improvements in existing controls to obtain earlier warnings or information that better pinpoints specific problems. Ask about the qualitative and quantitative impact and required timing of any recommended changes. And don't neglect the lower-level people responsible for preparing production and inventory forecasts or pricing and margin analyses — they usually need the most detail.

3.   **Setting Priorities** Priorities among reports should be set by organizational level; what's unimportant to the top executive on Level I may be critical to the struggling product manager. Test whether a requested report is meaningful by considering the decisions that can be based on its contents and assessing their importance. Then divide existing or suggested reports into three categories: those you must have, those you need, and those you can do without. Because they're expensive and time-consuming to implement, limit new reports and controls to those in the "must have" category.

It's difficult but often possible to determine the impact, and therefore the cost/benefit, of a report. The importance of some, such as a product line P&L, are dictated by common sense. For others, consider the worst that could happen — and the associated cost — if you lacked the information they provide. For example, you can judge the impact of a profit margin by product line-item report by estimating the number of items below profit goal and the potential profit if they were dropped. Audits of poorly controlled lines have indicated that 15–40 percent of the lines lost money while the lines as a whole showed a reasonable profit.

4. **Establishing Formats** Develop the format and frequency, sources of data, and cost/benefit statement for all required reports. Individual reports are best handled by an expert user and a systems analyst responsible to your overall team. Formats are easy to develop. The most common problems pertain to the unavailability or cost of obtaining historical or current data; anticipating information needed two–five years ahead; defining terms such as "average price;" and confining requested data to a realistic level.

5. **Assembling the Program** After "costing" each report, your team should recommend your program to your general manager by placing new or changed reports in order of sales or profit impact and demonstrating their cost/benefits; estimating the program's completion date; and showing the expense flow for each report and the total program over its proposed implementation. Make sure that all parties — marketing people as well as critical nonmarketing staff — approve the program, then decide what to implement and when.

6. **Developing/Testing the Systems** Control reports normally are developed and tested by a systems person (with needed back-up) and a marketing representative who reports on program progress. Trade-offs are inevitable between the desirable and the possible; this method insures that they're carefully considered.

For best results, use manual reports, where practical, until you're satisfied that a new report is necessary and the format is correct; keep using them whenever a report is needed infrequently. Don't abandon old reports until you're satisfied that the new ones work. Ask the systems/DP department for a monthly report of time and money spent on the total program and on each report, with any overruns flagged and explained. Where possible, use less costly personal computers, and give users on-line control of data (this is especially helpful in pricing analysis, running product line, and new product P&Ls, and examining the P&L impact of expense changes or changes in the product line).

DELEGATION LEVELS

Reports and controls are useless unless the authority to act upon the information they yield is delegated appropriately. How much you delegate depends upon how much authority you're prepared to relinquish, the effectiveness of your organization, and how much risk you're willing to take. If yours is a highly competent organization, in which monitoring and controlling of most activities can be delegated, you should decide exactly which actions/expenditures/events you must approve and which may be approved by others.

Limits on lower-level authority can be established effectively by putting your thoughts into writing and discussing them openly with subordinates to insure that you're delegating sufficiently and that your intentions are clear. Note that initially tight limits can be loosened as your staff earns your confidence. Even if you delegate too generously, however, you're unlikely to lose control. Monitoring of key reports, a good financial controller, and good management by exception — flagging and acting on major exceptions to plan — will keep your finger on the organization's pulse.

Table 10-2 includes excerpts of actual delegation limits, decisions, and approvals reserved for top management, and action steps resulting from a top-level staff meeting on authority limits.

INDIVIDUAL GOALS

The achievement of individual goals — attainment of sales levels, product line margins, spending levels, and timely product launches, for example — often are measured by control reports. Non-numerical goals, such as the completion of a shop floor control program or a significant strategic study, often are strategic in nature and are not measured by standard reports. Progress versus these intangible goals, however, can be reported easily. Asking your staff to submit handwritten progress versus goal statements along with the normal monthly financial and control reports forces them to evaluate their performances, forewarns you of potential problems, and limits discussion in individual and staff reviews to problem areas.

Table 10-3 is a monthly progress report on individual goals.

KEYS TO SUCCESS

- *Consider control's early warning devices* that flag problems or opportunities on which you can act.
- *Decide what critical events need flagging* at all organizational levels before you decide what data and reports you need. The events define the data, not vice versa.
- *Ask your staff,* not just the systems or financial experts, what they need.
- *Start slowly* — the fewer reports, the better.
- *Insure good data is available* before you design a system around it. Garbage in, garbage out — one of the computer era's first truisms — still applies.
- *Don't control through paperwork and manage by the numbers.* Personal contact is best.

Table 10-2.   Excerpts from Approvals Required by VP Marketing

Approvals

The following must be approved by the VP Marketing. Decisions/expenditures within these limits are yours.

Personnel

    Approve recruiting for any replacement or new monthly/management position

    Approve changes in reporting relationship of managers

Expenditures

    Approve and capital or expense items over $5000

Advertising and Major POS/Collateral/Promotions

    Approve written objectives, strategies, and creative proposals including comps, media plan, and cost estimates for programs over $10,000

Consultants/Advisors/Agencies/Market Research/Vendors

    Approve proposal, selection, and cost

Pricing/Terms/Promotions

    Changes in retail/wholesale pricing, terms, P&L impact

Manufacturing Schedule

    Changes in broadload by construction type and plant over 5 percent of current unit volume

Inventories

    Planned changes in targeted turns of raw materials, work in progress, finished goods, retail store stocks over 5 percent of current levels

New Products, Line Additions

    Business and creative objectives, line positioning; models prior to market, trade tests

    Final selection of line — including P&L, market test results

Salaries/Comp

    Increases for direct reports or those over $35,000; any incentive comp plan (salesmen, managers) or special incentive programs

Process/Product Changes

    Any process, material, or specification change likely to significantly change product quality or cost

New Stores/Departments

    Approve target markets — reasons, specific site, and P&L

Quality

    Final quality standards for new products, changes in old

Table 10-3. Reporting Progress versus Individual Goals

Month: December

Goals due this month or carryovers not completed when due.

Goals	Comments
Manufacturing	
Person Responsible: J.A. Johnson	
Carryovers from Previous Month: Finished product meeting the new quality standards established by marketing managers — finish equal to or better than top 3 competitors, lower cost — 11/15/85	Should be complete by 1/15/84
A stable work force, less than 1½% turnover per month, that meets current cost and quality standards — 11/1/85	Complete
Due By 1/1/86: None	
Product Development	
Person Responsible: S.A. Brackett	
Carryovers from Previous Month: None	
Due By 1/1/86: Multiple Sourcing — additional manufacturing source to support 30 dozen per day of Product X by 12/15/85 if sales can support	Capacity — equipment, tooling, materials available. Sales could not support 30 dozen, only 15. Quality poor, not up to standard. Holding at 15 dozen. Working to improve quality.
New/old product cost control — improve profit with better GMA — control GMA on private label to average 38% by 1/1/86	Achieved 38.2% thru December.
Finance	
Person Responsible: C.D. Lane	
Carryovers from Previous Month: None	
Due By 1/1/86: Establish manual manufacturing control system for Plant A	Not done. Plant controller just hired. Will be three months or 4/1 before accomplished.

- *Explain to your staff in writing* what you've delegated to them and what you've reserved for yourself.
- *Truly manage by exception.* Structure your reporting system/personal reviews to highlight major exceptions; delegate the detail, the minor exceptions to plan.
- *Go slowly* when introducing controls to an organization unfamiliar with them. Reassure people that controls help them, rather than spy on them.
- *Schedule regular reviews,* preferably monthly, to discuss results. Otherwise, leave your people alone unless an exceptional event requires urgent action.
- *Demand a cost/benefit estimate* on each report that you install.
- *Avoid computer clutter* — for every report added, consider one to eliminate.
- *Avoid failure.* Negative results are likely if you indulge in overkill on the number of areas monitored, report frequency, or detail; if you prefer expensive, complex computer reports to simple manual ones that do the job; if you focus all reporting and decision making at the top; or if you generate hostility through impersonal management.

PRINCIPLES

- *People ignore expenditures* unless held accountable — it's not their money.
- *Outside agencies are the worst* in living to a budget; staying in control.
- *People hate detail;* unless a system unearths them, significant "hidden" problems will remain hidden.
- *Systematic controls are accepted* by informed employees to whom they're helpful and who aren't overwhelmed by controls and reviews.
- *Marketing controls are hardest to implement* because data are hard to collect and process. Although marketing blunders can be more costly, most companies concentrate on financial or manufacturing information.
- *Controls must identify specific problem areas* early enough to correct problems.
- *Rely on periodic reviews.* Capitalize on the system by allowing subordinates time to take corrective action when numbers are bad.
- *Don't judge without an explanation* of why goals aren't met — the reasons may be convincing.

Appendix I

Exhibit I-1.   One-shot Survey Methods

Technique	What It Is	What It's Good For	When Do You Use It	Information Sources	Typical Cost ($000)	Typical Time	Source* Inside	Source* Out
Internal Data								
Probe inside people	Interviews with key marketing sales and other managers and knowledgeable people Use open-ended questions, structured questionnaires Can be administered by marketing or by neutral confidential inside or outside consultant	Specify the "gut" definition of the business Identify potential changes in the market Determine what businesses people feel the company to be in	First probe	Key internal managers and knowledgeable employees	$3	2 weeks	X	
Evaluate internal data	Collect available internal qualitative (market and strategic studies) and quantitative data	Internal understanding of the company's markets and its position in them	First probe	Internal marketing plans, research studies, strategic plans and studies	$3	2 weeks	X	

Exhibit I-1   215

	Description	Key measures / output	Purpose / comments	When used	Sources	Cost	Time		
		Historical and current financial and marketing data							
External Data									
Evaluate supplier, industry association, periodic studies	Analysis of periodic published studies that evaluate industry statistical trends, forecasts of future	Historical trends of key indicators, including market share, sales, profit, ROI, market segment sales and profitability	Broad overview of business. Such studies rarely give actionable insight, but are good background information	First probe	Industry/trade associations Industry publications Key suppliers	Nil	1 week	X	X
Limited Surveys									
Focus groups	Two-hour discussion sessions with representatives of target audience led by skilled, external, neutral moderator. Questioning directed by structured outline. Responses free-flow, spontaneous.		Qualitatively determining key current and future needs and concerns of target audience (current or proposed) Determining perceptions of problems with the company and competitors	After first probe when internal questions about mission have been raised	End consumers Members of trade, distribution system	$6–25		X	

Exhibit I-1. Continued

Technique	What It Is	What It's Good For	When Do You Use It	Information Sources	Typical Cost ($000)	Time	Source* Inside	Out
	Client observes through mirrored window	Providing data needed to initially define mission, particularly target audience, product, services, distribution, and competitive advantages to be sought						
	Usually three–ten sessions held, six–ten people per session, geographically representative of the market	Provide mission statement, other hypothesis to widely test						

Exhibit I-1   217

Limited field surveys	Limited open-end and structured. Personal and telephone interviews of suppliers, retailers, distributors, real estate developers, OEM customers	Determining, qualitatively, key needs and concerns of target audience, intelligence about competitive strategies, strengths	After first probe when questions about competitive position in the market and mission have been raised	Material suppliers — competitors' strengths, weaknesses, cost-price structure benefits OEMs for industrial markets Retailers/Distributors for consumer markets Real estate developers — competitive strategies, weaknesses, financial strengths, future anticipated actions in consumer business	$10 – 30 +	2–3 months	X	X

Exhibit I-1. Continued

Technique	What It Is	What It's Good For	When Do You Use It	Information Sources	Typical		Source*	
					Cost ($000)	Time	Inside	Out
Extensive Surveys								
Large quantitative field surveys	Surveys of random sample of target audience — trade or consumer

Sample large enough to give statistically significant or "gut" comfortable results

Sample size may range from 50– 2,000 | Confirm or refute hypothesis about target audience and mission

Determine *extent* to which target audience feels positively or negatively about elements of your mission, your company

Obtain additional detail about market demographics, buying habits, needs, competitive strengths, weaknesses, actions | After you have business definition you want to test, have identified key problem areas or opportunity areas where need strength and direction of market opinion

Use if limited survey work does not give sufficient information to act upon | End consumers

Members of trade and distribution system | $ 10– 200 | 3–4 months | | X |

Exhibit I-1   219

| Delphi surveys | Establish a panel of known management, technological, and marketing experts. Develop long-range (5–20 years) consensus on key trends through repetitive questionnaires that Identify important areas to be probed; Identify which areas are important, unimportant; Forecast what will happen in each important area, when, to what extent. Extensive specialized computer programs and expertise are required | Long-range forecasts, particularly: Technological changes in technical industries; Consumer life-style. | Infrequently — every five–ten years. In industries where extensive and complicated changes are anticipated as a result of limited survey work | A small panel of 20–60 experts in technology, consumer behavior, marketing, management. Sometimes run as multiclient studies by consultants to spread high cost | $200+ | 12–14 months | X | X |

*Source = use inside personnel and/or outside experts to conduct survey.

Exhibit I-2.   Examples of Open-Ended Questions to be Used in Internal Probes

Current Mission/Position

1. What business(es) are we in? Describe by target market, distribution channels, products.
2. What strategy (prompt with words such as grow, hold, milk, price, brand, distribution, etc.) do you think we're following in the market?
3. Where are we strong or weak in the businesses that we participate in? Why?
4. Which competitors are better/worse? Why?
5. Has our position strengthened/weakened? Why?

Current Mission/Future Position

1. What is the future of our current market(s) — size, growth, competition, threats?
2. Is our current strategy right? If not, why? What should it be?
3. What changes do you see in our markets that could help or hurt us?
4. If we continue what we're doing, where will we be five years, ten years from now? Why?
5. What must we change to maintain our position in each of our markets?
6. What should we change to get more of that market and/or improve the businesses' profits?
7. Are there any markets, businesses, products that we should get out of?

Future Mission

1. Are there existing or emerging markets, categories, products that we should consider adding? Why? How big are they? What would our priorities be?
2. Why is the market(s) attractive? How risky is it?
3. What strategy should we follow?
4. What's our competition doing in these markets? What do we bring to the party? Why is there room for us? Who's likely to emerge as the ultimate leader?
5. Whom else in the company/industry should I talk to?

Exhibit I-3   221

Exhibit I-3.   Continuing Monitors

Technique	What It Is	What It's Good For	When Do You Use It	Typical Cost ($000)	Typical Time (months)	Source Inside	Source Out
Purchase panels	A representative sample of your target audience is polled or keeps a running diary of their purchases and buying habits Often run by independent research firms for a number of clients because of the large number of people and high cost involved	Spotting pronounced long shifts in purchasing behavior and predicting impact on the firm's position Panels, over time, produce historical statistical trends and pinpoint current purchasing habits such as Product and brands purchased; Price-points; Consumer demographics; Styles; Geographic patterns; Where purchased	Yearly normally sufficient	10–16*			X
Focus group updates	See Exhibit 3	Used to update whether or not target market needs have changed since last focus group	Annually	7	2		X

Exhibit I-3.   Continued

Technique	What It Is	What It's Good For	When Do You Use It	Typical Cost ($000)	Typical Time (months)	Source Inside	Source Out
		Excellent for early warning of changes in needs, perceived position of what your company offers (quality, product, service) Can also pinpoint other target markets for your products or services					
Trade probes	Individual interviews of or focus groups/group discussions with representative member of the retail or industrial trade — independent manufacturers' reps, distributors, and retailers	Target market and distribution trends as seen by the trade Key strategic and tactical trends important to the trade, including: Products/services needed; Discounts/profit required; Advertising presence/strategy/allowances;	Annually	6	1	X	X

Exhibit I-3   223

Technique	Description	What it provides	Frequency	Cost			
Supplier probes	Individual interviews of knowledgeable suppliers; interview supplier salesmen when they call, key marketing and technical people by phone or visit	Advances in materials and technology that could produce new products, open up new markets or reduce future costs Competitive activity — level of production, materials, and equipment being used, level of success in the market, expansion plans, strategy and direction	Annually	Nil	Nil	X	X
Retained experts	Annual or short-term retainer for knowledgeable marketing, technical or design experts to consult on your plans	Experts can provide good feedback on your plans and performance; insights into what's happening and likely to happen in your markets, the potential impact on your firm, and what you should do	Periodically as needed, but normally two–three times per year	$500–2,000 per day	Nil		X

Changes in the market mix needed to increase/protect share;

What competitors are doing/likely to do

Exhibit I-3.   Continued

| Technique | What It Is | What It's Good For | When Do You Use It | Typical | | Source | |
				Cost ($000)	Time (months)	Inside	Out
		Experts are particularly effective in: Basic technology; Manufacturing and materials technology; Design; Consumer/trade trends					
Internal probes	Structured and free-form interviews of key managers and nonmanagers at all levels for their observation of external and internal factors affecting the business Most effectively conducted by a neutral, business-oriented organizational development consultant. Can be inside or outside consultant	Same opinions as in all of the above, except from the "internal" viewpoint Opinion on what internal matters affect market effectiveness short and long-term, including: Personnel; Organization; Systems; Intergroup conflict; Direction;	Annually, tied into strategic plan	$6,000		X	X

Exhibit I-3   **225**

			Lack of facilities, resources, technologies			
Technological studies (usually Delphi)	In-depth probe of technical, market and management experts using one-on-one interviews or Delphi method	Spot long-term trends that may affect the business, how they might affect future businesses, and provide better opportunities	Every three–five years, depending on how rapidly markets and technologies are changing or if significant change is signaled by other monitors	$100–300	6–12	X X
Lifestyle/ demographic studies	In-depth probe of end consumers on underlying lifestyle changes (such as values placed on clothing, recreation, education)	Forecasting shifts and the consumer's future need for products and services	As in the above technique	(n.a.)	(n.a.)	X

*If purchased from a service-selling panel, results to multiple clients.

Appendix II

Questions	Considerations
I. What Business Am I in Now?	
1. What is my target market, trends?	Sex, age, geography, style segment, psychological needs, income, occupation
2. How big is it, trends?	Size ($, units), historical and forecast growth, any important trends
3. How is it reached?	Distribution channels, principal communications media used
4. What products are and will be sold to the target customer, trends?	Style mix, price-points, important trends
5. Where will it be ten years from now?	Will my market grow or shrink? Why?
6. What is my current business definition?	Target markets, needs met, distribution channels, product/services provided, technologies
II. How Well Am I Doing? Trend?	
1. How do I measure success?	Financial measures; internal productivity; employee satisfaction
2. Performance	How well am I doing versus my success measures including sales, profitability, ROA compared to plan and corporate goal? If I'm not meeting goal, why not? How do I compare to my competitors?

Exhibit II-1. Continued

Questions	Considerations
3. Market performance	My overall share of target market and trend
	What part of the target market do I serve? My share?
	Share of important geographic, product and distribution segments; trend
	What part of the target market don't I reach? Why?
4. How do I stack up against my competitors?	Share of top three, their strengths and weaknesses versus mine
	Who's gaining and losing strength? Why?
	What are they trying to do in the target market?
5. What are my top three–five internal problems?	Any major problems preventing progress?
6. What are my top three–five problems in the market?	My major problems preventing progress
7. Where will I be in the future if I just keep doing what I'm doing now?	Forecast market trends
	Competitive conditions
	Future market share and financial performance

III.   What Are My Assumptions About the Future?

	Governmental, environmental, economic and social trends affecting the business
	Internal needs of the organization — competence of employees, working conditions, hours, leisure versus work time, retirement age, employee satisfaction versus expressed needs

IV.   Where Do I Want to Be in the Future? Why?

1. New business definition	Target markets, needs met, distribution channels, technologies, products/services
2. Overall strategy	Grow, grow-hold, milk, divest, combine? Why?
3. What target markets do I want to go after?	Define them in detail — demographics, style segment, psychological needs met, etc.

Exhibit II-1   229

Exhibit II-1.   Continued

Questions	Considerations
	Distribution channels
	Product segments
4. Strategic options will consider	Acquisition, internal development, joint ventures, diversification
5. My market position	Share of target market, market position versus competitors, share of any important market segments
6. My objectives	Overall quantitative and qualitative objectives including sales, ROA, NPBT, internal goals
	Are they realistic? Consistent with my trend? Consistent with the nature of opportunities known to be in my target markets?
7. Growth gap	Gap in sales, profits between current trends and objectives

V.   *What Are My Alternative Programs to Get Me There?*

A. EXISTING BUSINESS	WHAT AM I NOW OFFERING? DOING?	WHAT DO I NEED TO DO TO ACHIEVE MY PLAN?	COST/ BENEFIT
1. Product			
2. Pricing			
3. Advertising			
4. Promotion			
5. POS/display			
6. Design			
7. Wholesale Distribution			
8. Stores/Retail Distribution			
9. Service			
10. Physical Distribution			
11. Manufacturing			
12. Cost			
13. Sourcing			
14. Technology			
15. Systems			
16. People			

Exhibit II-1.   Continued

Questions	Considerations

B.   NEW BUSINESSES

List those that have promise, their cost/benefit.

C.   HOW WILL I MEASURE EACH ALTERNATIVE SO THAT I CAN CHOOSE? CONSIDER:

Financial criteria for choosing programs   Probability of strategic success

"Doability" by the organization

D.   WHERE WILL EACH PROGRAM GET ME? COST, GAIN, WHEN?

VI.   Why Will the Competition/Marketplace Let Me Do It?

1. What competitors' weaknesses will let me achieve my goal?

Who is vulnerable? Why? Consider product, brand awareness, distribution/store locations, product, pricing, management

2. What market trends will help (or hurt) me?

Consider growing product or distribution segments, geographic shifts, social or occupational trends, new markets or segments, new consumer/buyer needs

3. The key competitive advantages upon which my success hinges

Superior financial resources, cost, technology, distribution organization, brand awareness, timing of market entry, etc.

4. How are we likely to get killed if we do this?

List all the ways and then see if there is still a competitive advantage, the risk level acceptable, potential setbacks survivable

VII.   How Much Risk Is There in My Plan? Why?

1. How much risk am I taking?

Key elements that could sink the plan; key assumptions that could be wrong

Are the risks high, moderate, low?

If I'm wrong, how much will it cost?

VIII.   Which Options Should I Pursue? With What Resources?

Probability of achieving each option

Cost/benefit of each

Degree of organization's commitment

IX.   Where Will My Choices Get Me?

Will they fill the gap after discounting?

Exhibit II-1   231

Exhibit II-1. Continued

Questions	Considerations
	Are more programs needed to fill the gap or should goals and mission be adjusted downward?
	Can the required dollars and people needed be obtained?
X. *Is the Organization, Are My Resources Up to the Job? Timing?*	
	Number of people
	Level and types of skills needed
	Structure
	Time for training/hiring to get skills needed to lead change
XI. *How Will I Review and Control the Plan?*	
	Goal setting and review methods for organization and individuals
	Methods, timing for regular plan reviews, personal reviews, informal reviews
XII. *How, When Do I Rework the Plan?*	
	Annual or semi-annual reviews to re-examine plan validity
	Crisis situations, exceptional circumstances
XIII. *Action Plan*	
1. What are the three–five critical tasks to be accomplished in the next 12–16 months? When, by whom? How measured?	Select only those key to the success of the plan that should be reviewed by my superior as part of standards of performance
2. What are the three–five critical tasks to be accomplished by each function within the business? When, by whom? How measured? Which are "A" and "B" priority?	Select those that will be reviewed internally as part of each function's standards of performance All standards must be measurable in time, cost, quantity, or quality

Note: This plan is not required by corporate planning. It is an outline of questions that you may want to address in developing your summary corporate plans at the SBU or group level for your own use.

Exhibit II-2. Summary Business Plan Format

Quick-Scan Summary

Overall strategy _____   Business _____

Business Definition

Size/Growth

Unit Growth

10%

1.0

Market Share
Relative to Largest Competitor

Competitive Strength

H

M

L

H   M   L

Desirability of Market

Financials ($MM) YR   − 2   − 1   0 | 1   2   3   Δ % YR 0–3

Sales

NPBT

ROS %

ROA

Total assets

Plan

Objectives:

Strategies:

Competitors 1, 2, 3:

Competitive Advantage(s):

Competitive Weakness(es):

Task	Measurement	Date
1.		
2.		
3.		

Exhibit II-2   233

Exhibit II-2. Continued

SBU _____

1983–1985 Plan	Address These Issues:
I. What Business Am I in Now?	Target market Needs met With what product? Through what channels? Strengths and weaknesses
II. How Well Am I Doing? Trend?	Sales Profitability ROA Market share compared to competition My top three problems Where will I be if I keep doing what I'm doing?
III. What Are My Assumptions About the Future?	Current target market Social/government/environmental Competition
IV. Where Do I Want to Be in the Future?	New business definition Overall objectives Gap between current trend, new objectives Strategies
V. What Are the Alternative Programs to Get Me There?	Marketplace programs Internal programs

Exhibit II-2. Continued

1983–1985 Plan	Address These Issues:
VI. Why Will Competition/the Market Let Me Do It?	My competitive advantage Who is vulnerable? Why? Where? What new need has been found? What new segment has opened up?
VII. How Much Risk Is There in My Plan? Why?	What are key risks? High, medium, low?
VIII. Which Businesses/Programs Should I Pursue? With What Resources?	Probability of achieving each option Cost/benefit
IX. Where Will My Choices Get Me?	Do the discounted programs meet objectives?
X. Is My Organization, Are My Resources up to the Job? Timing?	Skills and numbers of people needed Organization structure
XI. How Will I Review and Control the Plan?	Goal-setting methods Review methods, timing

Exhibit II-2   235

Exhibit II-2. Continued

1983–1985 Plan	Address These Issues:

XII. How, When Do I Rework the Plan?   Regular rework plans

XIII. Numbers ($000, Fiscal Year)

			Estimated			
	1982	1983	1984	1985	1986	1987
1. Net Sales						
2. Gross Margin $ Gross Margin %						

3. Expense Total $
Expense Total %
a.   normal $
b.   extraordinary $*
     i.
     ii.						

4. Pretax earnings $ Pretax earnings %						
5. Accounts receivable $ a. average b. year end						
6. Inventory $ a. average b. year end						
7. Fixed assets (year end) $ a. baseline b. strategic additions/deletions*						
8. Asset additions a. baseline b. strategic						
9. Total assets employed $						
10. ROA %						
11. ROS %						
12. Sales/WC ratio						
13. Cash Flow $						
14. Contribution Margin $ Contribution Margin %						

*Footnote extraordinary expenditures, and additions to or deletions from fixed assets and the reason for them. See details on next page.

Exhibit II-2.   Continued

Financial Footnotes
1982–1984 numbers should be in current (as reported) dollars. 1985–1987 numbers should be in 1984 dollars. Assume no inflation 1985–1987. Any price increases or cost increases should result from strategic moves or changes, *not* inflation.

Line   Explanations

3a. *Normal expenses* are those normally incurred in running the business the way that you do now.

b.   *Extraordinary expenses* are those that you will incur in making *major* strategic changes. Example: significant staff additions, increases in media advertising, development of a new line.

7a. *Baseline fixed assets* are those assets expected to be in place at the end of FY84 and those needed to maintain operations at their current level, net of depreciation.

b.   *Strategic asset additions or deletions* are changes made to grow, contract, or significantly change the direction of the business, net of depreciation, at year's end. Examples include building/purchasing of new stores, new plant and equipment.

8.   *Asset additions* are those assets added during the year to (a) maintain baseline business, (b) change strategic direction. They are *not* net of depreciation.

9.   Total assets employed, average.

12. Working Capital = Average inventory plus average receivables.

13. Cash Flow = Pretax earnings × 0.5 plus depreciation, plus decreases minus increases in inventories and receivables and net change in fixed assets excluding depreciation.

14. *Contribution margin* = Pretax earnings plus all fixed costs.

Allocation of Overhead
Assume that the same corporate overhead dollars are allocated to your group 1985–1987 as in 1984. Assume that the interest charged on assets is the same in 1985–1987 as in 1984 (11% of assets in existence in 1983 and 15% on asset increases beyond 1983 levels).

Budget, Accuracy of Numbers
This is a strategic plan, not an accounting exercise. Your numbers should therefore be reasonable estimates but not a "bottoms up" budget. 1985 financials are, however, expected to be as close as reasonably possible to your expected budget.

Economic Assumptions
Assume that the economy will show real growth of 2% in 1985 and 3% per year in 1986, 1987.

XIV. Questions
All questions concern (a) your *current* position and performance in (b) the business that you *want* to be in.

1.   Definition of my target market:

2.   How big is my target market? Units $
     What is its forecast annual growth ____ % per year in units?
     What is my share now? ____ % What will it be in three years   ? Five
     years   ?

Exhibit II-2   237

Exhibit II-2.   Continued

3. Who are my top three competitors and their share now? What market position will they have in five years? What are their *two* greatest strengths and weaknesses?

	Position			
Competitor	Now	5 Years	Major Strengths	Major Weaknesses
A.				
B.				
C.				

4. *Rate Your Strengths and Weaknesses* and the importance of each strategic element by checking the appropriate number or letter.

    Importance: The importance of this element to my plan is A = critical, B = important, C = so-so, X = not applicable.

    Rating: Relative to my *toughest* potential competitor, I rate my business assets (10 walks on water, 5 is equal to, 0 is a disaster).

Strategic Element	Importance	Rating
Product		
(a) Extent product line meets overall needs of market served	A B C X	10 9 8 7 6 5 4 3 2 1
(b) Product mix	A B C X	10 9 8 7 6 5 4 3 2 1
(c) Quality	A B C X	10 9 8 7 6 5 4 3 2 1
(d) Styling	A B C X	10 9 8 7 6 5 4 3 2 1
(e) Materials	A B C X	10 9 8 7 6 5 4 3 2 1

Exhibit II-2.   Continued

Strategic Element	Importance	Rating
People		
(a) Overall	A̅ B̅ C̅ X̅	10 9 8 7 6 5 4 3 2 1
(b) Marketing	A̅ B̅ C̅ X̅	10 9 8 7 6 5 4 3 2 1
(c) Sales	A̅ B̅ C̅ X̅	10 9 8 7 6 5 4 3 2 1
(d) Manufacturing	A̅ B̅ C̅ X̅	10 9 8 7 6 5 4 3 2 1
(e) Retail	A̅ B̅ C̅ X̅	10 9 8 7 6 5 4 3 2 1
(f) Staff	A̅ B̅ C̅ X̅	10 9 8 7 6 5 4 3 2 1
(g) Systems	A̅ B̅ C̅ X̅	10 9 8 7 6 5 4 3 2 1
(h) Technical	A̅ B̅ C̅ X̅	10 9 8 7 6 5 4 3 2 1
Retail Distribution		
(a) Number of stores	A̅ B̅ C̅ X̅	10 9 8 7 6 5 4 3 2 1
(b) Number of markets	A̅ B̅ C̅ X̅	10 9 8 7 6 5 4 3 2 1
(c) Extent in right markets	A̅ B̅ C̅ X̅	10 9 8 7 6 5 4 3 2 1
(d) Extent cluster	A̅ B̅ C̅ X̅	10 9 8 7 6 5 4 3 2 1
(e) Productivity of stores	A̅ B̅ C̅ X̅	10 9 8 7 6 5 4 3 2 1
(f) Quality of stores	A̅ B̅ C̅ X̅	10 9 8 7 6 5 4 3 2 1
(g) Quality/type of locations	A̅ B̅ C̅ X̅	10 9 8 7 6 5 4 3 2 1
(h) Extent locations/markets/ quality stores match purchasing pattern target market	A̅ B̅ C̅ X̅	10 9 8 7 6 5 4 3 2 1
Wholesale Distribution		
(a) Extent wholesale distribution	A̅ B̅ C̅ X̅	10 9 8 7 6 5 4 3 2 1
(b) Quality of wholesale distribution	A̅ B̅ C̅ X̅	10 9 8 7 6 5 4 3 2 1
(c) Types of wholesale distribution	A̅ B̅ C̅ X̅	10 9 8 7 6 5 4 3 2 1
(d) Geographic distribution	A̅ B̅ C̅ X̅	10 9 8 7 6 5 4 3 2 1
(e) Service	A̅ B̅ C̅ X̅	10 9 8 7 6 5 4 3 2 1
(f) Extent current distribution matches purchasing pattern target market	A̅ B̅ C̅ X̅	10 9 8 7 6 5 4 3 2 1
Advertising/Marketing		
(a) Advertising strategy	A̅ B̅ C̅ X̅	10 9 8 7 6 5 4 3 2 1
(b) National advertising	A̅ B̅ C̅ X̅	10 9 8 7 6 5 4 3 2 1
(c) Local/coop advertising	A̅ B̅ C̅ X̅	10 9 8 7 6 5 4 3 2 1

Exhibit II-2   239

Exhibit II-2.   Continued

Strategic Element		Importance				Rating									
(d)	Spending against consumer	A̅ B̅ C̅ X̅				10̅	9	8	7	6	5	4	3	2	1̅
(e)	Spending against trade	A̅ B̅ C̅ X̅				10̅	9	8	7	6	5	4	3	2	1̅
(f)	Brand awareness	A̅ B̅ C̅ X̅				10̅	9	8	7	6	5	4	3	2	1̅
(g)	Brand image	A̅ B̅ C̅ X̅				10̅	9	8	7	6	5	4	3	2	1̅
(h)	POS promo	A̅ B̅ C̅ X̅				10̅	9	8	7	6	5	4	3	2	1̅
(i)	Trade promo	A̅ B̅ C̅ X̅				10̅	9	8	7	6	5	4	3	2	1̅
(j)	Info about market	A̅ B̅ C̅ X̅				10̅	9	8	7	6	5	4	3	2	1̅
(k)	Product research	A̅ B̅ C̅ X̅				10̅	9	8	7	6	5	4	3	2	1̅

Manufacturing/Sourcing, Internal

(a)	Unit cost	A̅ B̅ C̅ X̅				10̅	9	8	7	6	5	4	3	2	1̅
(b)	Condition of plant and equipment	A̅ B̅ C̅ X̅				10̅	9	8	7	6	5	4	3	2	1̅
(c)	Efficiency	A̅ B̅ C̅ X̅				10̅	9	8	7	6	5	4	3	2	1̅
(d)	Quality	A̅ B̅ C̅ X̅				10̅	9	8	7	6	5	4	3	2	1̅
(e)	Ability to serve three-year volume/product needs	A̅ B̅ C̅ X̅				10̅	9	8	7	6	5	4	3	2	1̅
(f)	Manufacturing technology/ methods	A̅ B̅ C̅ X̅				10̅	9	8	7	6	5	4	3	2	1̅

Sourcing, External

(a)	Ability to serve three-year volume/product needs	A̅ B̅ C̅ X̅				10̅	9	8	7	6	5	4	3	2	1̅
(b)	Unit cost	A̅ B̅ C̅ X̅				10̅	9	8	7	6	5	4	3	2	1̅
(c)	Quality	A̅ B̅ C̅ X̅				10̅	9	8	7	6	5	4	3	2	1̅

Terms

(a)	Pricing	A̅ B̅ C̅ X̅				10̅	9	8	7	6	5	4	3	2	1̅
(b)	Other terms	A̅ B̅ C̅ X̅				10̅	9	8	7	6	5	4	3	2	1̅

Appendix III

Exhibit III-1. Marketing Plans: Where to Look, What to Look For

Department/ Function — Plan	Functional Plan Contents
Director of Marketing	
Overall Marketing Plan	A written marketing plan covering all functions.
	A master timetable of critical events, people responsible for them, for all marketing, nonmarketing functions, outside agencies.
	Evidence that the plan has been communicated, is reviewed.
Product Management	
Existing Product Line	Qualitative product line objectives, strategy.
	Competitive objectives by product category; trade, consumer selling benefits.
	Number of styles, SKUs, to be offered by category. Additions, deletions; P&L impact, inventory impact of changes; margins, volume planned by SKU.
	Forecast volume, mix, agreed upon by manufacturing, sales.
New Products	Overall objectives, strategy.
	Positioning and design direction for new products/modification of basic product, including price, general style, competitive positioning, cost budget; timetable from creative idea through research, testing, manufacture, launch.
	Release schedule and quantities signed off by design, development, manufacturing, sales.

Exhibit III-1.   Continued

Department/ Function — Plan	Functional Plan Contents
Pricing/Terms	Objectives/strategy.
	Pricing and competitive positioning by category and product; margins. Comparison of trade term versus key competitors. Recommendations, volume, and P&L impact of both.
	Price–margin–volume schedules with costs agreed upon by manufacturing, prices based on analysis.
Wholesale Sales	
Sales	Market penetration goals overall, by key account and product category.
	Sales activity planned by cycle — what's to be pushed during what period, how, wholesale and retail.
	Sales quotas and budget by district, territory, salesperson; by key account and product category, by program; month or selling cycle.
	Territory layout, staffing and compensation goals.
Distribution	Schedule of distributors or retailers to be added/dropped; quotas; dates; financial justification.
Promotion	Goals, plan for independent retailer, wholesaler promotions.
Sales Service	Service level goals.
Creative/Advertising	
Media	Creative objectives, strategies, roughs or mechanicals, flight schedule by media; cost, frequency, and reach-versus-target audience goals; production schedule.
Coop	Budget, spending plan for major customers, residual customers by month or selling cycle. Creative approach, roughs and mechanicals by cycle. Production schedule.
Collateral	Goals, objectives, strategies, roughs or mechanicals, cost, production pricing/terms for segment; timetable by piece.
Displays	As in collateral.
Retail Advertising	As in media, except for captive retail.
Design	
New Product Design	Schedule from idea through to market, based on product management direction; cost goals per program.

Exhibit III-1   243

Exhibit III-1.   Continued

Department/ Function — Plan	Functional Plan Contents
Market Research	
Market Research	Research schedule and expense tied into new products, advertising/distribution tests.
Style Use Testing	As above for new products.
Retail Operations	
Cycle Planning	Products, displays, windows, promotions and advertising to be featured for each selling cycle. May vary by store, region. Quotas by cycle or month, by store and salesman. Inventory goal by store by month. Goals for specific promotions by region/store.
New Stores	Overall plan for year — number, location, financials, demographics, concepts, management structure, opening promotional package. Financial justification for each store as details completed.
*Finance**	
Sales Analysis	Documented reasons: new products, changed distribution, market growth/decline.
Financial Analysis	Reasons/sound estimates for above planned changes.
*Human Resources**	
Organization	Staff changes, additions, deletions, reorganizations required.

*Usually departments reporting to the General Manager or CEO.

Exhibit III-2.   Tying Plan to Budget; Sources of Change Analysis*

Sources of Change

Contents

Table 1 summarizes the dollar and % changes forecast for 1986 versus estimated 1985 performance for major sales manufacturing, expense and asset categories.

Table 2 details anticipated financial changes from 1985 to 1986, giving reasons for "normal" changes and extraordinary changes.

Overview

We have been able to hold our pretax return on assets at 32 percent, even though a new line being launched significantly dilutes profits and wages will inflate from five–eight percent, other items by seven percent.

Gains will come from

Increased sales of basic line;
Decreased materials inventories and interest charges;
Decreased manufacturing cost due to lower materials prices, automated parts manufacture, and increased efficiency on the part of piecework employees.

* Based on a consumer products company marketing products such as tailored apparel and accessories.

Table 1.   Summary of Financial Changes 1986/1985 ($'000)

Categories	1985	1986	Δ%
Sales	31,150	38,250	+23
Price (unit)	$44.50	$48.73	+ 9.5
Manufacturing Cost			
Labor	5,005	6,080	+21
Materials	8,670	9,965	+15
Variable Overhead	1,170	1,485	+27

Exhibit III-2   245

Product Development	450	380	− 16
Fixed Overhead	1,835	2,115	+ 15
Total	17,130	20,025	+ 17
Unit Cost	$24.47	$25.51	+ 5
SG&A Expenses			
Selling	3,100	3,660	+ 18
Product Management	1,200	1,360	+ 13
Advertising	1,800	2,680	+ 48
Market Research	300	320	+ 7
Design	300	460	+ 53
Shipping/Service	825	765	− 7
Interest on Assets	1,190	1,485	+ 25
Corporate and Division Overhead	1,450	1,550	+ 7
Total	10,165	12,280	+ 21
Profit			
Profit Before Tax	3,855	5,945	+ 54
% Sales	12%	16%	
Assets			
Receivables	5,600	7,045	+ 25
Inventory	7,890	10,160	+ 29
Fixed	3,250	3,625	+ 12
Liabilities	(1,870)	(2,295)	+ 23
Total	14,870	18,535	+ 25
ROA	32%	32%	

Exhibit III-2. Continued

Table 2. Detailed Sources of Change Analyses, 1986/1985

Category (1)	Year End Estimate (2)	Normal Changes (3)	Reason (4)	Project/ Major Changes (5)	Reason/Key (6)	Next Year's Estimated Budget 2 + 3 + 5 (7)
Sales						
Units	700,000	35,000	Market growth, expanded distribution (5%)	50,000	New line introduction, pipeline fill, plus sales (1)	785,000
Average Price ($)	44.50	47.62	Justified 7% price increase	65.00	New line higher priced (1)	48.73
$ ('000)	31,150	3,850	Higher price, higher unit volume	3,250	New line sales, first year	38,250
Manufacturing Cost ($'000)						
Labor	5,005	670	Normal volume increase plus 8% base wage increase effective 1/1	755	New product line standard cost plus start-up variances (1)	6,080
				(200)	Labor reduction via automatic parts manufacturing equipment (2)	
				(150)	Increased efficiency for piece workers. 5% impact (3)	
Materials	8,670	435	Volume increase	960	New product cost	9,965
				(100)	Lower purchase price index 95 → 94 (4)	

Exhibit III-2   247

Variable Overhead	1,170	155	Volume increase plus 8% labor increase	160	New product cost plus start-up variances	1,485
Product Development	450	(250)	Expenses of new line nonrecurring	180	Development new line for 1987 (5)	380
Fixed Overhead	1,835	130	10% wage inflation, 7% other inflation	150	Additional IE and process engineering staff (6) Depreciation of new equipment, tooling	2,115
Total Cost $	17,130	1,140		1,755		20,025
(Per Unit)	24.47					25.51
Gross Margin $ ('000)	14,020	2,710		1,495		18,225
Gross Margin %	45	70		46		48
SG&A Expenses						
Selling	3,100	290	Increased commission on sales increases; salaried employee increase impact 5%	270	Addition new district manager, three salespeople guaranteed commissions (7)	3,660
Product Management	1,200	60	Salary inflation	100	New women's line brand manager, plus assistant	1,360
Advertising	1,800	180	Rate inflation 10%	400	Launch advertising, promo programs new line (1)	2,680
Market Research	300	20	Salary inflation	300	Increase brand awareness (8)	320

Exhibit III-2.   Continued

Category (1)	Year End Estimate (2)	Normal Changes (3)	Reason (4)	Project/Major Changes (5)	Reason/Key (6)	Next Year's Estimated Budget 2+3+5 (7)
Design	300	100	Reduction of staff by 2	60	Outside consultant for new women's line	460
Shipping/Service	825	60	Salary inflation, additional people for volume	(120)	Reduction of 4 due to new direct order entry on line 1/1	765
Interest on Assets (8%)	1,190	90	Interest on changed assets as result of sales growth, equipment write down	205	Increase due to sales growth, new equipment for automatic parts manufacturing, decrease on RM inventories (9)	1,485
Corporate Overhead Division Overhead Other	1,450	900	Normal inflation	—	—	1,550
Total	10,165	900		1,215		12,280
Profit						
Net Profit Before Tax	3,855	1,810		280		5,945
% Sales	12%	47%		9%		16%
Assets						
Accounts Receivable	5,600	695	Same ratio to sales (0.18) on normal sales increase	750	New line carries longer terms. Ratio = 0.23 to sales (1)	7,045

Exhibit III-2   249

Inventory	7,890	960	Normal ratio (0.25) increase	810	Increase for new product	10,160
Liabilities	(1,870)	(230)	Increase due to sales increase ratio = 0.06	500	Decrease due to reduction RM inventories (9)	(2,295)
Fixed Assets (net)	3,250	(325)	Depreciation reduction	700	Increase due to automated parts manufacturing	3,625
Net Assets	14,870	1,100		2,565		18,535
Return on Assets	32%					32%

Financial Notes

1. New women's line introduced last fall to hit high price point. Contribution (incremental) margin very low — 24 percent due to start-up promo, advertising, manufacturing costs, inventory build.
2. Automated parts manufacture. 80 percent of metal and plastic parts will be automatically fed, processed at high rates. Equipment debugged. Phase-in completed by 9/1. Get ⅓ year impact.
3. Changes in standards, plus longer training period, better training and ABC scheduling will reduce turnover, raise efficiency of piecework 5 percent. IE studies and trials have documented.
4. Though materials inflation will be eight–ten percent, average prices will go down by one percent. Result of reduction SKUs, consolidation of buys to place large orders, contracts with new sources.
5. Long-range plans call for expanding men's line into European styling; development, investigation of "American" casual line for mass merchandisers.
6. Needed for standards revision, Phase II of cost reduction engineering. Plan being prepared.
7. Redistricting due to study of penetration showing we're not covered in department stores, under-penetrated in SE, West Coast, can gain significant share next three years. First-year salespeople's commissions must be guaranteed.
8. Second step in increasing awareness now at 38 percent. Increase should produce 45 percent.
9. RM inventories reduced by ⅓ by writing off slow movers, combining materials, lowering inventories from $1,500,000 → $1,000,000. Complete.

Automatic parts manufacturing equipment increases assets by $700,000. 1/1.

Appendix IV

Exhibit IV-1. Summary of New Product Development Problems and Fixes

Problem	Fixes
A. Product Line Not Competitive	
1. *Line outmoded* — products don't meet consumer needs, competitive offerings	Reposition the line versus competition (see Chapter 4)
	Re-evaluate product marketing strategy versus competition
	Determine changes necessary to execute strategy
2. *Line churned* — high percentage replaced annually in an attempt to bolster sales	Reposition as in (1) above to insure right product marketed
	Market test to insure product is correct
	Establish goals permitting only a specified percentage of one line be replaced each year based on the market's need for product/style changes
3. *No or too few products,* resulting in decreasing market share	Establish new product goals: number to be produced annually, percentage of "new" products at any point
	Use trade research to insure goals appropriate to category, target market and distribution channel need

251

Exhibit IV-1. Continued

Problem	Fixes

B. New Products Fail

    1. They don't sell or have limited appeal

        Use trade and user testing to make sure that: product style/function are right; superior to competition; niche available in the market and distribution channels

        Trade research to make sure introductory pricing/terms/promotion right

C. Stale Product Design

    1. Not innovative or even competitive

        Hire new designers with fresh ideas, technical knowledge

        Use outside design firms to supplant or supplement inside people

        Use consulting designers for opinions, assistance

        Contract with freelance designers on a program-by-program basis

D. High Costs/Poor Profits

    1. High or uncontrolled marketing costs; cost overruns

        Careful budgeting, by program, for new products

        Institute financial controls and budget reviews by new product program, not just by functional department

        Require senior-level signatures on high impact items, large expenditures

    2. Substantial returns of poor sellers, diluting profits

        Trade and user testing to minimize chances of releasing a loser

        Develop channels such as outlet and discount stores, overseas outlets, where returned product can be discreetly dumped to recover costs

    3. Estimated product costs wrong, usually low

        Require detailed manufacturing process cost estimates. Detail labor, material, and overhead costs and probability of achieving goal, process-step-by-process-step

Exhibit IV-1   253

Exhibit IV-1.   Continued

Problem	Fixes
	Use pilot production to estimate real costs
	Make manufacturing absorb any cost variances resulting from missing cost goals
4. Sawtooth resource loading of new product development departments yielding inefficient use of people, facilities	A planning system forecasting new product load, by department, sufficiently in advance to allow level loading and slack time to address urgent problems

E. Poor Execution

1. Inadequate management and/or professional skills. No management process for new products	Hire, replace or train as dictated by current problems and technical needs, future directions
	Install a management system for planning, developing, and reviewing progress of new products, focusing on:
	Integration of all functions (marketing, manufacturing, etc.)
	Fostering identification, communication, and solution of bottlenecks and problems
	Detailed scheduling and review of projects and critical tasks
	Delegation of decision-making

F. Inadequate Distribution

1. Aren't in the right channels	Market research during development to establish correct channels and introductory package needed to gain distribution
2. Inadequate penetration of new channels	Research similar product introductions to determine a realistic penetration rate for a new product channel
	Set up realistic sales targets by customer by sales cycle and establish hit ratios agreed upon and frequently reviewed with the sales department (see Chapter 10)

Exhibit IV-1. Continued

Problem	Fixes

G. Poor Service

    1. In-line and new product service suffers during new product introduction

Establish a system for adequately forecasting the level and mix of new product shipments (a) in advance of release and (b) daily and weekly as mix shifts during early sell-through

Establish adequate buffer inventories of new products until demand pattern is clear

Insure that production planning system works well and can incorporate in-line products and anticipated new products so that both stay in service. If not, get a new system

Insure materials planning system works so that critical materials are identified, tracked, and available when needed; shortages don't hurt production. Replace or use manual tracking if it's inadequate.

H. Product or Technical Failures

    1. Products don't work, fail in the field, or aren't up to specified or competitive performance levels

Use laboratory and consumer use, durability, environmental, and safety testing prior to product release

Hire product designers with up-to-date materials and construction skills

Establish a pilot line to test, debug new processes, try new methods

Hire engineering people with up-to-date process skills to enable effective execution of designs

I. Poor Analytical Tools

    1. Inadequate analytical tools for key new product decisions

In-house or outside training of key managers and staff deficient in analytical skills such as product line positioning, market research techniques, critical path analysis, financial analysis

Exhibit IV-1   255

Exhibit IV-1. Continued

Problem	Fixes
J. Management	
1. Lack of marketing orientation	Train and/or replace key managers to get up-to-date skills and thinking
2. Goals or plan not established	Use team planning to establish them
3. Basic business not put to bed, running poorly, sapping management time, energy	Fix it before tackling any major new product projects or revising the new product development process

Exhibit IV-2.   Expected Recommendations from New Product Team

Area	Reports On	Offers Recommendations On
Organization Probe (Human Resources)	Critical barriers to success, means of overcoming	Organization (staffing/personnel changes)
	Organization, management, and personnel barriers to success	Skills/training to be obtained; cross-functional linkages (manufacturing, marketing, etc.)
	Skills lackings	Changes in attitude, atmosphere, decision-making methods, delegation, etc., to facilitate development
Outside Probe (Marketing)	How well we have, haven't done, and why	How to fix problems with outsiders — the trade and the consumer
		Our innovation rate, our position versus competitors'
		Magnitude of new product opportunity, potential payoff for us
		How outsiders should be involved in the new product process
		Sales role in product introductions
Financial (Finance)	What has our cost/return been?	What could/should our return be?
	How have we controlled new products?	What controls should be used for the new, recommended process?
		What can we expect in the future in spending and return, when, and from which recommended new product goals?
		What will happen to the business if we don't carry through with the recommended programs?

Exhibit IV-2   257

Bottom Line (Marketing)	Steps in new product process now — who makes decisions, how?	Recommended goals, criteria for selecting new products, pace
	Where have we blown it? Why?	Recommended process — why?
	Opportunities	Testing
		Recommended controls
		Pace/timing of any changes in process/people
		Cost/benefit. How much money can we make by changing?
		Specific new opportunities
Technology (Manufacturing/Engineering)	Technical barriers to cost-effective new product development	Engineering, tooling skills needed
	Cost/scheduling problems	New processes/equipment, technical staff required
		New product cost goals — how to set, meet
		Scheduling new products along with old, meeting time commitments
Design	Ability to get market defined, job done	Clarity of direction, time allowed, linkage with marketing, marketplace
	Creativity	Extent allowed to create product independent of marketing-imposed goals

Appendix V

Exhibit V-1. Concept Summary: Professional Women's Shoes

Season:	Fall 1982
Target Market:	Career formal and informal professional, age 25–45, individual income $20,000 + . Two years of education beyond high school — most college graduates or higher. Shops medium–high grade department, women's specialty and shoe stores. Shops twice a year for major purchases, rest on impulse.
Key Needs:	Fit/comfort, style, suitability for work and work clothes, quality, durability/life, price, ability to wear socially, wide range of sizes.
Price-Point:	$110–$140
Category:	Formal professional

	Description	Information Source
Work Environment:	Works in formal office, often as lawyer, business manager, sales manager, accountant, administrator, high-level secretarial.	Focus groups, prior style research
Clothing:	Wears tailored clothing, suits, skirt–jacket combo, dresses.	
Clothing Trends:	Less tailored clothing, softer suits, more feminine dresses. Skirt length from just below knee to 3" below.	Focus groups, '81 European collections, Spring '82 collections, fashion services

Exhibit V-1.   Continued

	Description	Information Source
Colors:	Rich darks, cool neutrals, earth tones with plaids and tweeds; traditional blue/grey, tan suitings; spike colors in lavender, purples, rusts, mustard, rose, teak.	'81 European collections, leather, fabric suppliers, fashion services
Textures/Detailing:	Lots of textures, multicolors in tweeds. Dresses silky, feminine with detailing in stitching, appliques, color contrasts. Blouses with ties, ruffles, and detailing.	Tailored clothing suppliers, dress designers, fashion services and magazines.
Probable Shoe Colors:	Black, navy, new burgundy, new taupe. Spike color will be mustard.	Leather suppliers, own interpretation of what fits with coming clothing, focus groups.
Shoe Detailing:	More detailing in stitching, subtle metal ornamentation, gathered leather patterns, contrasting leather textures and color, perforation, piping, underlays, crocodile material highlighting.	Early detailing in Europe by leading designers. Men's clothing trend supports conclusions. Consistent with similar historical clothing trends.
General Trends:	Heel heights lowering slightly, more sculptured heels, toes, more skin will show — vamp and ankle — for sexier look.	Style research, focus groups, fashion sources.
Styles Required:	Slings, walking shoes, pumps, open-toe pumps.	Focus groups, closet inventories.
Line Concept:	10–14 styles, carefully tested against target audience. Superior comfort/quality to existing imported shoes, carefully *coordinated as a collection* to go with career professionals' clothing, in wide range of always-in-stock sizes for superior fit. Spill-over sales to nonworking women significant.	
Competitive Advantage:	Brand name, market access, ability to advertise, display, promote as a collection targeted exclusively to career women. No other competitor is positioned as "the career woman's" brand. They don't style test. Concept tested well with target audience.	
Potential:	Market size, potential share, competitors, our potential competitive position detailed separately in business plan.	

Appendix VI

Exhibit VI-1.   Analyses to Diagnose Pricing Problems

Analysis	Purpose	Data Required	Source	Output
A. Key Product Trend Analysis	Determine for each product category or key product within the category whether prices *generally* are	Three-year history *Units Sold*		Categories you should consider: *Price increase* whether driven by high cost, lower than market price or volume increases out-stripping the market
	Keeping up with retail price inflation;	Your product sales	Company records	
	Keeping up with cost inflation;	Category sales in market for all competitors	Purchase panel Sample surveys	*Price decrease* whether based on low cost, higher than market price or disappointing volume versus expectations of market
	In line with category market price levels and increases.		If not available can index most readily available government or trade statistics on your category or broader section of your market or a similar category to show trend.	
	Determine how volume is tracking your price, market price, market volume.	Percentage share of category	Calculate	*Cost reduction* programs where category costs high, construction, manufacturing methods similar.
	Establish whether price-volume trends are out of line with the market (you may *want* them to be).	*Average Price* Your average price Average market price for your category	Company records As in units above	
		Consumer Price Index	Government statistics. Pick the index closest to your category	

Exhibit VI-1   263

B. PMV (Price–Margin–Volume) Analysis	*Materials Price Index*	
Determine for each category, individual product and line-item, if necessary, whether	Three-year history by category and product of	Candidates for
It meets target margins	Units sold	Pruning (low volume, low margin)
Margin trend is good	Average price	Price increases (low margin or high volume trend)
Price increase is necessary to enhance margins or decrease to enhance volume	Average cost	Price decreases (poor volume trend, high margin)
Volume is above breakeven or target	Gross margin	
Volume trend is acceptable	Unit volume	
	Your internal purchase price index if calculated	
	If not, use closest government commodity or wholesale price index	

} Company records

Exhibit VI-1. Continued

Analysis	Purpose	Data Required	Source	Output
C. Competitive Price Positioning	Determine how your price for each product stacks up to your top three competitors, if out of line	Current retail price (realized, not suggested) for each product (style, for example) within a category for		Candidates for price increases or decreases based solely on competition
		Your product	Company records	
		Your top three competitors	Competitive price sheets, verbal information from retailers, wholesalers, other customers	
			Store checks	
		Probable changes in future competitors' pricing with and without action on your part	Interviews with trade to determine competitors' plans, probable reaction to your changes	

Exhibit VI-1   265

D. Price-Value Index (*Note:* Adds more information to competitive price positioning)

Determine what each of your products is *worth* versus competition's, taking into account any pluses or minuses in tangibles such as function, construction, style, and intangibles such as image, prestige, distribution, awareness

Define key dimensions that mean value to target audience for each product *category*.

Quantify your value index versus your top competitor and other competitors

Put a percentage price difference or $ difference on index points

Own knowledge
Trade interviews
Consumer interviews — focus groups
Your subjective judgment
Customer ratings, trade ratings

Your subjective judgment, based upon consumer and trade inputs and what's actually happening in your and similar categories

Candidates for price increases or decreases based on value versus competition, your volume objectives and your market strategy

Appendix VII

Exhibit VII-1. Commonly Used Marketing Reports, Content, Users, Frequency

Report	Content	Level									Frequency
		I			II				III		
		VPM	GPM	DNP	CD	DS	FSM	PM	APM	S	
A. Overall											
P&L	Complete P&L statement for the business, each major product category, product line and new product	X	X	X		X		X			M
Expense	Broken down by (a) functional department and detailed category; (b) category and product line	X	X					X			M
Assets	Inventories in total by category, product line Receivables in total, aged	X	X					X			M
Individuals	Summary of qualitative and quantitative goals, results for each direct report	X	X	X	X	X	X	X			M
Marketing Calendar (6–12 months)	Cycle plan with major events including strategic plan, budgets, new line selection, choice of advertising strategies, "start sell" for next season; who does what, when	X	X	X	X	X		X	X		M

Exhibit VII-1   269

B. Sales/Orders

Overall	Total, broken down by product category, product line, distribution channel	X	X	X	X				M/W
Field	By sales region, district, salesperson, often by channel and product category	X		X	X		X		M/W
	By salesperson, by account, often by product category, product line, item	X			X		X		M/W
Top Accounts	Top 30–50 national customers; sometimes by product category	X	X	X					M
	Top 30 new account prospects	X	X	X					
	Top 10 accounts by salespeople	X		X	X		X		
	Top 10 prospects by salespeople	X		X	X		X		
Individual Salespeople	Results of special promotion programs, sell-in of new products versus goal, hit ratio for major accounts by salespeople, overall	X	X	X	X	X	X	X	W/M

Exhibit VII-1.   Continued

| | | Level | | | | | | | | |
| | I | | | II | | | | III | | |
Report / Content	VPM	GPM	DNP	CD	DS	FSM	PM	APM	S	Frequency
Programs										
Special promotions/new products, other special program results including customer hit ratios by										as needed
program	X	X		X	X	X	X			
sales region and district, top target accounts				X	X	X	X			
salesperson and account					X	X	X		X	
C. Product Management										
Sales-Profit										
Sales, orders, price, margin, unit cost by										M
category, product line, channel		X					X	X		
item									X	
Exception report on products/items not meeting sales/margin/price/cost goals		X					X	X		M

Exhibit VII-1   271

Report line							Freq
Performance versus Forecast							
Sales, orders, prices, margins, inventories versus forecast by							W
category		X	X		X		
product line		X	X		X	X	
item					X	X	
channel		X	X		X		
Market Share							
Share by category, product, channel		X	X		X		Q
Production							
Manufacturing output versus forecast							W
overall/broadload by capacity group	X	X			X		
by product			X			X	
by item			X			X	
Scheduled plant input versus forecast							W
overall, by capacity group	X	X			X		
by product		X	X		X		
by item		X	X				
Exception report: manufacturing inputs behind schedule		X	X		X		D
Manufacturing cost variances by category, product		X	X		X		W

Exhibit VII-1. Continued

Report	Content	Level I VPM	Level I GPM	Level I DNP	Level II CD	Level II DS	Level II FSM	Level II PM	Level III APM	Level III S	Frequency
Cost Variances	Manufacturing cost variances from standard by product line, SKU, major process step including total variance, scrap, labor, overtime, yield, etc.	X	X					X	X		M
D. New Products											
Newly Launched	Sales, orders, price, margin, unit cost, plant input, work in process, output, inventories and mix versus forecast for each launch by										M
	product group/line	X	X	X		X		X	X		
	item								X		
	Hit ratio (% sold), major target customers		X	X		X	X				W
	P&L, assets for each launch	X	X	X				X			M

Exhibit VII-1   273

Item							Freq
Planned							
New product progress versus development schedule			X		X	X	M
Exception report — off-schedule new products		X	X		X	X	W
Expenses versus plan							
overall			X		X		M
each program			X		X		
E. Creative							
Programs							
Creative/production progress versus goal by program			X	X			M
Exception report — off-schedule programs			X	X			W
Expenses							
Expenses by category, product line, and program versus budget		X	X				M
Committed and forecast expenses by category product line and program versus budget		X	X				M
Funds budgeted but uncommitted by category, product line and program		X	X				M
Exception report — over commitments or spending	X	X	X				M

Exhibit VII-1. Continued

Report	Content	I			II				III		Frequency
		VPM	GPM	DNP	CD	DS	FSM	PM	APM	S	
F. Quality	Average, by category and product line, percentage of major/minor defects versus AQLs rejected inhouse; shipped (final inspection)	X	X					X	X		W
	$ scrap, rework by category, product line manufacturing department	X	X					X			M
	Defective returns/reasons							X	X		M
G. Service											
Levels	Service level (% orders, SKUs shipped on time) overall, by category, by product line, by channel	X	X				X	X	X		W
	Number, percentage of SKUs backordered, out of service (below planned stocks), out of stock		X			X		X	X		
	Number of units backordered by SKU, when they will be delivered, in service		X			X		X	X		

Level

Exhibit VII-1   275

					Freq.
Problems					
Exception list of stock-outs, out-of-service items, promised shipment and "in-service" dates		X	X		D
Stockouts as a percentage of shipments,					W
by product		X	X		
by item			X		
H. Inventories					
Inventory units, $, turns, versus goal overall, by category, by product line and item	X	X	X		M
Exception report — products, items significantly over/under level or turn goal		X			W
Level obsolete/soon to be discontinued products	X	X			M
I. Receivables/Terms					
Overall performance (days sales outstanding)	X			X	M
Top problem account list					M
overall	X			X	
by sales territory				X	
Accounts receiving special terms/pricing	X		X	X	M

Exhibit VII-1. Continued

Report	Content		I			II			III		Frequency
		VPM	GPM	DNP	CD	DS	FSM	PM	APM	S	
J. Human Resources	Actual and forecast headcount versus budget for all functions, types of personnel	X									M
	Unabsorbed salespeoples' draw					X	X				M
K. Expenses	By appropriate category										M
L. Forecast (Next Quarter, Full Year, Versus History)	Sales, orders, production, expenses, P&L and inventories:										
	overall	X	X		X	X					
	by category, product line	X	X	X				X			
	Sales, production, inventories by item								X		M
	Spending										M

Key:
Titles mean different things in different organizations. The following definitions apply here:

VPM = Vice-president of marketing, to whom all marketing functions report

GPM = Group product manager, to whom product managers responsible for separate categories or lines report

Exhibit VII-1   277

DNP = Director new products, who manages technical development of new products

CD = Creative director, who handles advertising and promotion

DS = Director of sales, who handles field sales. inside sales, customer service

FSM = Field sales managers, regional or district; they manage the salesforce

PM = Product manager, who handles an individual product line or category

APM = Assistant product manager, who handles lower-level functions for the product managers

S = Sales representatives

Frequency of Reports:

M = monthly

W = weekly

D = daily

Index